SHADOW STATE

Luke Harding is a journalist, writer, and award-winning corre-spondent with the *Guardian*. He has reported from Delhi, Berlin, and Moscow, and covered wars in Afghanistan, Iraq, Libya, and Syria. Between 2007 and 2011, he was the *Guardian*'s Moscow bureau chief. The Kremlin deported him from the country in the first case of its kind since the Cold War. In 2014 he won the pres-tigious James Cameron prize.

He is the author of several books, most recently the number-one *New York Times* best-seller *Collusion: Secret Meetings, Dirty Money, and How Russia Helped Donald Trump Win*. Other titles include *A Very Expensive Poison: The Assassination of Alexander Litvinenko and Putin's War with the West*; *The Snowden Files: The Inside Story of the World's Most Wanted Man*; and *Mafia State: How One Reporter Became an Enemy of the Brutal New Russia*.

His books have been translated into thirty languages. Two have been made into Hollywood movies. Dreamworks' *The Fifth Estate*, based on *WikiLeaks*, written with David Leigh, was released in 2013. Director Oliver Stone's biopic *Snowden*, adapted from *The Snowden Files*, appeared in 2016. A stage version of *A Very Expensive Poison* premiered in 2019 at the Old Vic theatre in London. Written by Lucy Prebble, it won the Critics' Circle award for best new play.

SHADOW STATE

Murder, Mayhem, and
Russia's Remaking of the West

LUKE HARDING

First published by Guardian Faber in 2020
Guardian Faber is an imprint of Faber & Faber Limited,
Bloomsbury House, 74–77 Great Russell Street,
London WC1B 3DA

Guardian is a registered trade mark of
Guardian News & Media Ltd,
Kings Place, 90 York Way, London N1 9GU

Printed and bound by CPI Group (UK) Ltd, Croydon, CR0 4YY

A CIP record for this book
is available from the British Library

ISBN 978–1–783–35205–0

2 4 6 8 10 9 7 5 3 1

For John and Felicity

CONTENTS

PREFACE

The Russian players in the story of Vladimir Putin and the West are typically seen as little more than names. And confusing ones at that. Petrov and Boshirov, Aslanov and Morenets, Prigozhin and Udod . . . we get lost amid unfamiliar surnames and patronymics. They feature in indictments. But who they are remains a mystery.

In fact, the men who took part in the Kremlin's mission to upend US democracy, and to wipe out traitors in the United Kingdom, are real individuals. Complex ones, with ambitions of their own, childhoods, backstories. Some are true believers; others, cynics. They are shaped by common experiences: the collapse of the Soviet Union; the resurgence of national pride under Putin; and the rise of what you might call a shadow state—a regime of spies operating in the darkness.

These individuals have multiple identities. They roam across Europe and beyond. Russia has used them to wage an increasingly bold war, an asymmetric one featuring fake news, cyber intrusions, and the poisoning of our politics through dirty money. The tide of disinformation has been effective. Conspiracy theories have flourished not just in former communist territories but inside the White House. Meanwhile, Russia's kleptocratic model has gained ground. The same traits of corruption and dissembling are visible in Washington. Shadow actors have bent foreign policy to their advantage.

If the West is to push back against Moscow's aggression, it needs to understand its adversaries better, lest recent history repeat itself. They are assassins and fathers; soldiers and husbands; hackers and lonely hearts.

This is their untold story.

SHADOW STATE

CHAPTER 1
VISITORS FROM MOSCOW

Moscow–London–Salisbury–Washington, DC
MARCH 2018

A wolf circling sheep.
CHRISTOPHER STEELE ON VLADIMIR PUTIN

The two men who got on a flight from Moscow to London didn't look like assassins. They were dressed inconspicuously, in jeans and fleece jackets. Their names were Alexander Petrov and Ruslan Boshirov. At least that is what their Russian passports said. Both were about forty. Neither seemed suspicious. Businessmen? Or tourists maybe?

The plane trundled down the icy runway. In Moscow the temperature was cold and raw. It had fallen below –10°C, not unusual for early March. In Britain it had been snowing. The pair had brought woolly hats. And a couple of satchels. One of them contained a bottle of what looked like French perfume. In the event that they were stopped at UK customs, the Nina Ricci fragrance might be explained away as a gift—a gallant one, with "made in France" on the box.

Aeroflot flight SU2588 touched down at Gatwick Airport. It was Friday, March 2, 2018, and mid-afternoon. The two Russians made their way to passport control. Boshirov had dark hair and a goatee; Petrov was clean-shaven, his hairline thinning as middle age set in. We can only guess their mood. If they were nervous, no official noticed.

The British security service has a database of persons of interest—terrorists, criminals, fraudsters. Apparently Petrov and Boshirov weren't on it. At immigration their passports and visas were checked and they were nodded through. What the UK border force didn't know was that the visitors from Moscow were actually spies—ones working for a hostile foreign power.

They were career officers with Russian military intelligence. Colonels, even. Their real names were Anatoliy Chepiga (Boshirov) and Alexander Mishkin (Petrov). Their service had created a fake identity and helpfully, in the best traditions of Cold War spycraft, supplied them with real passports that supported their fictitious cover.

Chepiga and Mishkin had come to London on a secret mission. They were there to murder someone.

Probably this wasn't their first such assignment, known by the KGB as *mokroye delo*, or "wet work." Naturally, details of such activities are hard to come by, but travel records show a number of trips to Europe. This "work" had taken them to Amsterdam, Frankfurt, Paris, Geneva. Their employer back in Moscow was the GRU, or Glavnoye Razvedyvatelnoye Upravleniye. Full title: the Main Intelligence Directorate of the General Staff of the Armed Forces of the Russian Federation.

The GRU is the most powerful and secretive of Russia's three spy agencies. It's military, under the command of the Defence Ministry and the General Staff. Back in the USSR, the army-led GRU and the spy-led KGB were often in conflict. Some of this rivalry spilled into the post-communist era of Boris Yeltsin and Putin. The GRU was in competition with the FSB, the KGB's domestic successor, which Putin headed before becoming prime minister in 1999, and then president; and with the SVR, Moscow's foreign intelligence agency, the former KGB's first directorate, operating under diplomatic cover.

The FSB handled security at home. It sniffed out and quashed opposition to the Kremlin, arresting students and political activists, locking up bloggers and protesters, and maintaining order. From time to time it carried out foreign operations. Most took place in the "near abroad"—within neighbouring former Soviet republics, which Moscow continued to view as parts of its imperium.

The GRU, by contrast, was global. It dealt with external threats. Its mandate was everywhere. The organization's activities ranged from traditional military deployments, in war zones such as Syria, to coups and invasions. Its officers saw themselves as part of a glorious tradition, stretching back to Russia's battles against Napoleon and Crimea, through to World War I and II—the latter the Great Patriotic War, as Russians call it—and the Soviet conflict in Afghanistan.

Murder was something of a throwback to the GRU's twentieth-century heyday. The revolutionary state of Vladimir Lenin and its various successors had plenty of experience in political killings. Lenin, Stalin, even the ostensibly reformist regime of Khrushchev had all sent agents to snuff out "traitors." These deaths were seen as necessary to protect a noble and progressive state besieged by capitalist enemies. And by nationalist ones. Moscow hunted down Ukrainian leaders abroad, including Stepan Bandera, killed in Munich in 1959 by a KGB assassin using a cyanide spray pistol hidden in a newspaper.

In the late 1980s Mikhail Gorbachev ended such killings. It was a new age, in which Russia and the West were friends. The next Russian leader, Boris Yeltsin, confirmed and expanded this collaboration. Under Putin, however, murders stealthily resumed. Journalists, political critics, an ex-deputy prime minister turned irritant . . . all died in opaque ways. A former KGB officer himself, Putin had a particular loathing for those who betrayed the Fatherland. These people were scum. Traitors got what was coming to them, he said.

ARRIVING AT GATWICK, Chepiga and Mishkin picked up their travel suitcases. They strolled through a green corridor that said, "Nothing to declare." An automatic camera captured them exiting through parallel lanes. They headed into the capital. No one came after them.

So far, so easy. Britain—it appeared—was soft and weak. Despite a string of London–Moscow spy scandals, a country described unflatteringly on Russian television as "foggy Albion" was unprepared and sleepy. True, British spooks had picked up an unusual level of activity at the Russian embassy in Kensington. But this hadn't been connected to the two travellers with backpacks, riding the tube like anybody else.

The pair emerged into the daylight and went to the City Stay Hotel in Bow, east London. They were staying for two nights. The place was anonymous and a little shabby: Asian receptionist, a worn swivel chair behind a desk, ordinary rooms, white-painted walls. Next door is a Barclays bank. When I stopped by, a woman in a headscarf was in a queue at an ATM. Buses, cars, and taxis trundled past. There was a perpetual rumble of traffic.

The neighbourhood has a light railway station, a car rental company, and a Bangladeshi corner shop selling fruit, vegetables, and halal chicken. A statue of the Victorian prime minister William Gladstone adorns the local church.

Close to the spies' accommodation is a police station and a magistrates' court. The Edwardian-era outpost of the Metropolitan Police is no longer open to the public. On the wall is a plaque commemorating the district's Roman heritage. And a community noticeboard, which in the light of events looks faintly ridiculous.

One message reads, "Don't let a pickpocket spoil your day." Another shows a group of watchful meerkats peering out among urban tower blocks. The board says nothing about visiting assassins, or how you might spot one.

The next day, Saturday, March 3, the two GRU officers went to London's Waterloo Station and got on a train. Their destination was the west of England and Salisbury, home of the man they had been sent to kill. Police believe that their trip that Saturday was reconnaissance. Chepiga took a pair of black gloves. They spent a couple of hours there and went back to the hotel.

The person meant to die was called Sergei Skripal.

Skripal was living quietly in Salisbury, a place where nothing much happened. His personal story was almost incredible. He arrived in Britain in 2010 via a US-brokered spy swap. Skripal was the least well known of a small group of double agents and defectors now living in the UK and America.

The most famous, Oleg Gordievsky, betrayed the KGB for ideological reasons and did enormous damage to the Soviet espionage machine. He lived in Surrey. If a list existed of "traitors" the Kremlin might wish to kill, Gordievsky's name was surely at the top. It was closely followed by that of Oleg Kalugin, the long-time head of KGB operations in the US and a prominent critic of his old agency and of Putin. Kalugin was based in the state of Maryland, not far from Washington, DC.

Skripal was a lesser figure. He had begun his career as a Soviet paratrooper, taking part in daring clandestine missions in China and Afghanistan. In 1979 the GRU recruited him. In the 1980s Skripal worked for the GRU on the island of Malta, attached to the Soviet embassy there under diplomatic cover. By the time he got his next foreign posting—to Madrid, in Spain—the USSR had collapsed.

As Skripal saw it, the Soviet state's demise invalidated his obligations to it. Everyone was trying to survive in the new free-market economy. Skripal sought to invest in a Malaga hotel. Then something better came up: an approach from a pleasant businessman who charmed Skripal's wife, Liudmila, and bought presents for their kids. One day the businessman let it be known he had "friends" in the British government.

Skripal agreed to work for MI6.

The arrangement lasted eight years. So far as we know, Skripal was the US's and Britain's only GRU mole. He knew little about operational matters, but willingly handed over details of the GRU's hierarchy and structure—what MI6 teaches its new joiners to call ORBAT, or order of battle. There were meetings with his British handlers in Spain, Portugal, Malta, Italy, and Turkey. Recalled to Moscow, Skripal continued to communicate with London. He wrote in invisible ink in the margins of a Russian novel. His wife delivered it to MI6 during a vacation in Spain.

This was risky stuff, done for a few thousand pounds per meeting from Her Majesty's budget-minded government. Skripal appears to have been an un-Gordievsky: he did it for the cash. In 2004 the FSB got a tip-off from Spain and arrested him. He was convicted and imprisoned. Six years later he was picked up from his penal colony, flown by special plane to Austria, and swapped on the tarmac of Vienna International Airport for a group of Russian "sleeper agents" caught red-handed by the FBI. A throwback to the Cold War or a sign of things to come? Skripal left his homeland with a presidential pardon.

After so long in exile, Skripal might have been forgiven for thinking himself safe. Who would remember him? The colleagues he had betrayed—if you could call it that—were mostly retired or dead. The world had moved on. Perhaps his British minders who from time to time took him to a pub assured him that all was well.

The GRU, however, is an unforgiving entity. It has its own code of honour and brotherhood. And a good memory.

That Saturday, Skripal collected his daughter Yulia from Heathrow Airport. A friend and ex-neighbour, Ross Cassidy, drove him there. Yulia was visiting from Moscow. On the ride home Skripal and Yulia talked intently. At some point it became obvious that a black BMW was shadowing their car. Inside the vehicle was a woman with bleached blonde hair and a man in his forties, Cassidy said.

The next morning, on Sunday, March 4, Chepiga and Mishkin repeated their journey—leaving early from their hotel in Bow and catching the 8:05 a.m. train back to Salisbury. This was not reconnaissance. This time it was murder. According to police, the pair were carrying the French perfume bottle. It contained an unusual and terrible poison.

FOR A BRIEF period after the fall of the Soviet Union the Chekists were out. (The name comes from the Cheka, Lenin's first secret police, the All-Russian Extraordinary Commission.) The elderly KGB plotters who carried out a coup in summer 1991 against Gorbachev found themselves under arrest. Democracy in the shape of Yeltsin seemed ascendant. After decades of totalitarian rule, Russians were free—albeit with their savings wiped out in the new economy.

All Soviet institutions were demoralized and in a shambles, but the spies were intent on plotting a way back and were uniquely placed to do so. One of those who felt the loss of the USSR acutely was Putin, who had missed *perestroika* and instead spent communism's twilight years in Dresden and East Germany as a first directorate officer. Returning in early 1990 to his home city of Leningrad (soon to be St. Petersburg), Putin reinvented himself as an aide to its new democratic mayor, Anatoliy Sobchak. Putin's career took a sharp upward turn.

Power may have changed in Russia, but the system and its bureaucrats remained implacably Soviet in their thinking. Intelligence officers in London who had spent the Cold War fighting against what one called the "Dark Tower of the Soviet Union" believed that Moscow's intentions were still bad. The difference was that in the early 1990s the cash-strapped Kremlin lacked the resources to do anything about it.

By the time Putin became president in 2000, this was no longer the case. Oil prices rose. The state budget grew. Funds flowed into Putin's spy agencies, including the GRU, which in 2006 moved into a new headquarters building, known as the Aquarium, in downtown Moscow. Much of this happened while the West was preoccupied with other things—wars in Afghanistan and Iraq, and the spectre of Islamist terrorism. Putin offered Russian citizens a social contract of sorts: greater prosperity in exchange for fewer rights.

At this point the US and its allies viewed Russia as a regional power that bullied its neighbours and engaged in domestic repression. It did not see Moscow as a rival, a superpower, or as a source of strategic concern. Washington was late to appreciate that Putin had his own vision of Russia's place in the twenty-first century. A bigger and a darker one.

In 2007 Putin made his revisionist intentions known in a speech at a Munich security conference in Germany. He spoke shortly before standing down from the presidency, temporarily, in favour of his protégé Dmitry Medvedev. Putin attacked the US's domination of global affairs and reeled off a series of grudges: NATO expansion; Western "meddling" in Russia's elections; nuclear treaty violations. Russia, he said, would no longer accept a "unipolar" world.

What that meant became clear. In Russia's backyard the tanks started to roll—into Georgia, and into Ukraine, whose peninsular territory, Crimea, Moscow effortlessly stole in 2014. Across Europe—from Rome to Berlin and Prague—Putin rebooted old KGB ways of influence and political subversion. Secret military cells began to operate in Western Europe, the land of the enemy.

Historically, the Politburo had funded foreign communist parties. In nations such as France and Italy, the post-war communists were a significant force. Under Putin this support for the hard left continued. Western anti-imperialists opposed to American aggression often cheered Putin's stance.

Increasingly, though, the Kremlin's preferred international partners came from the populist far right—Viktor Orbán in Hungary, Heinz-Christian Strache in Austria, Marine Le Pen in France. They shared similar ideas: nationalism, sovereignty, power politics, and hostility towards immigrants. Moscow loaned assistance and sometimes cash to candidates who might disrupt the status quo, and discredit democracy and the European Union along the way. A new far-right internationale began to coalesce.

Putin wasn't a master of influence or an all-knowing villain sitting behind a console with flashing buttons. He was an opportunist. He was ruthless and well practised. His attempts to play God in other people's elections often didn't come off. Moscow's practical support for favoured external politicians fell into the category of let's try it and see. And if Russia got caught in the act, so what? That played to Moscow's advantage too. It showed strength to the enemy and instilled pride among those at home.

The Russian president's meddling reached an apogee in the 2016 US presidential election. Putin's candidate was Donald Trump. Moscow assiduously aided and encouraged his long-shot campaign to take the White House. If Trump was surprised by his improbable victory, so was the Kremlin. Moscow's expectations had been more modest: to undermine Hillary Clinton's future presidency and to fuel American turmoil.

The idea that Russia had helped Trump win was endlessly contested and disputed, not least by the president himself and by his Republican allies and base.

Trump dismissed any suggestion of collusion. He portrayed himself as a victim of a witch-hunt and "deep state" plotting by his own scoundrel-led intelligence agencies. Still, the notion that Trump had solicited assistance from a foreign power to get one over on a hated political opponent didn't go away. Indeed, it led directly to impeachment when the president did something similar again—not with Russia this time, but with its embattled neighbour Ukraine. And to acquittal by Republican senators after a perfunctory non-trial.

Across Trump's misbegotten presidency, the thesis that there was something odd about his relationship with Moscow failed to go away. Rather, it grew. The theme consumed national politics, network television, investigative journalism, and public life. Between 2017 and 2019 it was the subject of a special investigation by former FBI director Robert Mueller—rather a disappointing and hamstrung one, as it turned out.

US intelligence agencies were all of one voice: Russia had sought to influence the 2016 vote. Quite possibly, the Kremlin's operation had cost Clinton the election—a view Clinton shares. Inside the Kremlin and Russia's Duma, or parliament, Trump's victory was celebrated as a wondrous achievement. Was this the greatest espionage operation ever? The success of 2016 meant Russia was sure to return in 2020.

As in Soviet times, the Kremlin's ambitions were international. They grew, as the US's got smaller. From central Africa to leftist Latin America and Venezuela, through Syria and the Middle East, and across Ukraine and Europe, Moscow was building up a network of clients and military allies. It spread into a vacuum left by the Trump administration, as it retreated from the US's traditional post-war power role and Pax Americana.

After twenty years in office, Putin was reshaping the world to his advantage. He was using the same plucky tactics favoured by Yuri Andropov, the KGB's chairman turned general secretary. They included trickery, deceit, law-breaking, withholding and concealing the truth, as well as large-scale disinformation, rolled out at home and abroad. As Lenin, quoted by Kalugin, put it, "There are no morals in politics. There is only expedience."

There was a short-term objective: to get the US and the EU to drop economic sanctions against Russia. And a longer one: to create chaos and division within the West, not by starting from nowhere but through exploiting already existing tensions and cleavages. The ultimate goal was to smash apart Western institutions and democracies. And to push other countries from the non-corrupt to the corrupt side of the ledger.

Under Putin and Trump Russia and America began to resemble each other.

The two countries were very different, of course: one a kleptocracy run by a feudal-style KGB clique, the other a democracy still and the world's indispensable power.

But there were worrisome similarities. Both presidents attacked journalists and "fake news," lied without shame, propagated disinformation, and used the postmodern shtick that the truth was impossible to know. Moscow came up with false narratives that Trump and his Republican defenders willingly repeated, such as the idea that Ukraine rather than Russia meddled in the 2016 election.

The two men put their own personal and political interests before those of the nations they were meant to serve. Friends and relatives were more important than institutions or the law; the boundary between statecraft and moneymaking opportunities became increasingly fuzzy. It was hard to look at Trump's dealings with certain countries—Saudi Arabia and Turkey spring to mind—and not conclude that US foreign policy was somehow for sale.

Trump would exploit the might of the White House and the Justice Department to wage a political smear campaign against a rival, the former US vice president Joe Biden, and against other perceived "enemies." Putin enriched KGB cronies via lucrative state contracts and used state poison laboratories and secret soldiers to wipe out "traitors" living abroad. These were rogue deeds. They took place under the cover of foreign and security policy.

Shadow states, if you like, where the machinery of government was used for private benefit and personal enrichment.

THE ASSASSINS WHO arrived in London in the spring of 2018 were not the first hit men sent by Moscow. Or even by Putin. History was repeating itself. Eleven years earlier two different killers had flown in on a similar route. They had met with a troublesome dissident and former FSB officer, Alexander Litvinenko. And then poisoned him with a cup of radioactive green tea.

This operation had taken place in a Mayfair hotel, the Millennium, practically under the nose of the then US embassy in Grosvenor Square, London. It was an FSB plot. Litvinenko's killers—Dmitry Kovtun and Andrei Lugovoi—had brought with them from Moscow something portable and lethal. Litvinenko was dosed with polonium-210, an invisible, deadly isotope. He died three weeks later, in hospital.

Putin evidently was not fond of Britain. In the 2000s the UK refused to extradite leading critics of his regime who had fled their homeland and sought asylum in London. From Moscow's perspective, successive prime ministers from Tony Blair onwards had rolled out the red carpet for troublemakers and crooks intent on upsetting constitutional order.

London's response to the Litvinenko outrage was modest: four Russian diplomats were slung out of the country, and many words of indignation were offered. None of this would have troubled Putin. His method was to wait for a reaction—and to carry on emboldened if it failed to materialize. A public inquiry found in 2016 that Putin had "probably" approved the murder, together with his FSB spy chief. The KGB had a euphemism for this kind of hit: *fizicheskoye ustraneniye*, or "physical removal."

Chepiga and Mishkin had turned up with a different but equally nasty toxin. Traces were later found in their hotel room. The modified "perfume bottle" smuggled through UK customs contained a powerful nerve agent. Its generic name was *novichok*, a Russian word derived from *novy*, or "new," best translated as "newcomer." Novichok was a chemical weapon.

In the 1980s a group of Soviet scientists created a new class of chemical agents, more deadly than any previously known. They worked at a closed laboratory near Volgograd. There they synthesized organophosphates. One agent—known as A-234—stood out. Its effects on humans were ruinous. They included convulsions, paralysis, respiratory and heart failure, continuous vomiting, and diarrhoea. Death was pretty certain.

Novichok was now being deployed as a weapon. By coincidence or not, the UK government's chemical and biological research facility, Porton Down, was six miles down the road from Salisbury. The city was close to several military bases and home to various ex-service personnel. It was conservative, provincial, not especially affluent, and surrounded by sheep and green countryside.

The Salisbury that Chepiga and Mishkin came back to was hardly in a state of high alert. Two months previously the local Wiltshire council had turned on a new CCTV surveillance system. Thus far it had caught nothing more dastardly than a pair of teenage idiots stealing lights from a bike left at the local market.

After arriving back at Salisbury railway station, the GRU colonels headed left. They started walking down Wilton Road. At

11:58 a.m. they passed a petrol station, where they were recorded on CCTV: two grim and solitary figures carrying a backpack, walking side by side, and framed by the slate grey of road and pavement. The day was dull and damp.

Finding Skripal did not require the ingenuity of Sherlock Holmes. In 2011 Skripal had bought a house in his own name. He was a man of regular habits: he drank in pubs; bought scratch cards from a Turkish-owned corner shop; and visited the cemetery where his wife and son were both buried.

According to police, the assassins headed towards Skripal's home: redbrick, 1970s-built, semi-detached. The most likely route would have taken them through a covered and densely tree-lined footpath and into a suburban avenue. Skripal's house was around the corner, up an incline to the right. There were roses in his front garden; behind, a meadow of brambles and hawthorn. From the upper floor you could see Salisbury Cathedral and its spire.

The house had a porch. One or both of the killers headed towards it, detectives say, stealing up the driveway. The killers applied novichok to the front door handle. Mission done, they left—apparently unobserved. CCTV recorded them again at 1:05 p.m. on Fisherton Street, heading towards the train station. Their body language was different: they seemed relaxed, insouciant, Mishkin grinning and making a joke. By this point they were behaving like the day-outers they would later claim to be.

Soon afterwards Skripal and his daughter left their house at 47 Christie Miller Road. They shut the front door and got into Skripal's BMW 3 series. From there they drove into the city centre. Skripal parked next to a Sainsbury's. They had lunch in an Italian restaurant, Zizzi's, and shared some garlic bread. It was Sunday afternoon. Everything was normal.

And then it wasn't. The pair began to feel violently unwell.

They made it as far as the Maltings, a redbrick shopping centre with a grassy area and children's play park. Next to it was the Avon River. Normally you could see trout, but the melting snow had made the shallow waters turbid. A few people were milling around. This was the modern end of a medieval city. There were shops, a wishing well and a wooden bench.

It was here that passers-by first noticed something odd: a grey-haired man in his sixties cradling a younger woman. She was slumped and unresponsive. The man looked out of it.

Skripal was sitting on the bench bolt upright, rocking back and forth, eyes closed. He appeared to be talking to himself, as if in prayer, witnesses said. One of the pair had been sick. Drugs, perhaps, or an overdose? And yet something didn't fit with that: the man and the younger woman looked prosperous. At 4:15 p.m. the police arrived and summoned back-up. A helicopter took Yulia Skripal to Salisbury District Hospital, her father following by ambulance.

For a little longer, the case seemed routine. Officers in regular clothes sealed off the spot and began collecting evidence. The first reporters arrived from the *Salisbury Journal*. Rain fell. It grew dark. Meanwhile, the assassins were heading home. They arrived at Waterloo Station at 4:45 p.m. Three hours later they were at Heathrow. By 10:30 p.m. they had left London on an Aeroflot flight bound for Moscow's Sheremetyevo International Airport, never to return. The GRU's latest brazen hit was a textbook success. Or so it appeared.

IT TOOK ABOUT twenty-four hours before the British state began to grasp the scale of the crisis. Something terrible had happened to the Skripals. But what? The victims were in no position to explain. They were in a critical condition, unconscious, heavily sedated, and pumped full of atropine by two duty doctors recently trained in nerve agent cases.

Skripal's backstory and his links with MI6 were clearly sources of worry. So too was the news coming from officers and paramedics who had gone to the bench and to Skripal's home. They were reporting troubling symptoms: itchy eyes and breathing difficulties. The loss of muscle function in the victims suggested a nerve agent of some kind.

Biomedical samples were sent to Porton Down, where scientists carried out tests using spectroscopy and chromatography equipment. The result, when it came that Monday, was alarming. A rare nerve agent had poisoned the Skripals. It had been developed in the Soviet Union. It was 100 per cent pure, military-grade—meaning manufactured in a special lab.

It was not difficult to guess which country had the motive, means, and swagger to carry out another assassination on British soil. For SIS or, as it's more commonly known, MI6, this was a full-blown emergency that encompassed some difficult issues. Should the agency have done more to protect Skripal? Could his poisoning have been anticipated?

Meanwhile, urgent steps had to be taken, such as increasing security for the other Russian defectors living in the UK. British spies who normally took their weekends off found themselves working around the clock. The police—first the local force, then Scotland Yard's counter-terrorism branch—launched an investigation into the attempted murders. A complex search began for the killers and possible accomplices.

Hanging over all this were two questions. First, why had Moscow targeted Skripal? Second, why now? This was eight years after he arrived, and on the eve of Russia's presidential election and a summer World Cup. Nobody was in any doubt that Putin would win the poll. Nonetheless, his election victory would now be staged against the background of international confrontation.

It was hard to be definitive about Moscow's motive. Since Skripal had arrived in Britain, he had travelled to the US, the Baltics, and the Czech Republic. He had given lectures to friendly Western intelligence agencies, who were curious to learn about the GRU from the inside. Other former spies who had swapped sides did the same. This occasional work wasn't sufficient in itself to provoke Moscow's wrath. So was Skripal up to something else?

In exile Skripal had kept a low profile—in contrast to Litvinenko, who accused Putin in public and in print of lurid crimes. Indeed, Skripal appeared to approve of Putin and Russia's recent foreign adventures.

In summer 2017 the BBC's Mark Urban called at Skripal's home. He noted a stack of jigsaw puzzles, an Airfix model of HMS *Victory,* and a mini-version of an English country cottage on a bookshelf. This was a gift from the MI6 officer who two decades earlier had recruited him in Spain.

Skripal spent much of the day watching Perviy Kanal—Russia's foremost state propaganda channel—and backed Moscow's annexation of Crimea. Skripal was an "unashamed Russian nationalist," Urban concluded.

Whatever Moscow's motive, murder was a Kremlin speciality. In the pre-Litvinenko past its agents had used poisons, bullets, and bombs hidden in cakes—not to mention the ice pick that did for Leon Trotsky, or the ingenious ricin pellet used to fell Georgi Markov, the Bulgarian dissident and writer poisoned in 1978 on London Bridge. In that operation, the KGB provided technical assistance following a request from their Bulgarian comrades.

These killings sat on a spectrum. Some were invisible. Victims were silenced by injection under the guise of hospital treatment, according to Stalin's former special operations chief, Pavel Sudoplatov. The file would say "heart attack." Others were showy, and deliberately terrifying. All the better if the dying man had a few final moments to realize what was happening, the last face before him that of Comrade Stalin.

The attack on Skripal was in the second category. There was nothing subtle or delicate about using a nerve agent in a crowded civilian area. It was an act of stunning recklessness. The effect, as the GRU must have known, was to inculcate terror in the local population, and more widely among the Brits and their European and American allies. The choice of novichok was deliberate, a ghoulish calling card.

Officially the Kremlin would deny involvement. Clearly, though, the trail led to Moscow. As one former MI6 officer reasoned, "You can't conceal this. It was intended to be known."

The message of the Skripal affair, then, was directed at the British government and its spy chiefs. It could be boiled down to two words: "Fuck you." A former special adviser to a US president told me, "They really want to fuck the UK and fuck with British minds. They don't care about being discovered. It sends a signal that we have no respect for you."

But the message of Salisbury was also bound up with events in America and the election of Trump. A large number of people knew something of the Kremlin's secret operation to help Trump win. Senior Russian bureaucrats, high-ranking GRU and FSB officers, technical guys, diplomats and ambassadors working abroad, oligarchs who played the role of intermediary . . . it was a substantial list. Only Putin and a few around him knew everything. But many people knew something.

The gruesome attack on Skripal was a timely reminder of the penalties involved in treachery. The ultimate audience for this deed was the Russian elite, and any Russian in the GRU or elsewhere thinking of cooperating with special prosecutor Mueller, the CIA, or Western intelligence generally. Decoded, Skripal was poisoned to pre-empt further treason.

A new life in Virginia or Florida under an assumed identity might seem beguiling. Yes, you'd get a pool, a barbecue, and a condo! A better existence in America! But, the message said, the GRU was patient and all-seeing. It knew what your kids were up to. It would come for you at a time of its own choosing. And as you looked away it would deliver a mighty blow.

OVER THE COMING days Downing Street briefed allied capitals over the affair. It concluded that it was "highly likely" Russia was behind the Salisbury attack—a message the then prime minister, Theresa May, took to the House of Commons. Any response would be more effective if it were coordinated with the European Union and with NATO. The UK's most important allies were the United States and President Trump.

On March 9, 2018, British officials gave confidential details to their American counterparts. A senior British intelligence officer flew to Washington and—with May patched in—spoke at length with his US colleagues. "We received persuasive information from the UK that the Russian government had used novichok against the Skripals," a senior US State Department official told me. "Our experts concurred with the UK conclusion."

The British said only Moscow had the technical means, operational experience, and motive. Over the past decade Russia had produced and stockpiled small quantities of novichok. Putin was closely involved in this chemical weapons programme. Special units were trained in the use of these weapons, carrying out tests on how to deliver them. One method was to apply the poison to door handles, Washington told the UK, citing confidential intelligence.

It appeared, too, that the GRU had been tracking the Skripals for some time. Since 2013 the agency's specialists had been hacking Yulia Skripal's email. This would have yielded useful real-time information—about Yulia's movements and those of her father.

Putin's personal role in Salisbury was harder to prove. The

president's critics had a habit of dying in murky circumstances—inside Russia and abroad. In Soviet times, when the Politburo authorized state-sponsored assassinations there was no paper trail, with orders given orally. According to Sudoplatov, Stalin talked in indirect terms, in the case of Trotsky, merely asking if the political importance of the mission was understood.

There were few facts about how Putin interacted with his own modern spy agencies, and in particular with the GRU's bullet-headed director, Igor Korobov. Did the president concern himself with individual cases? Or merely set broad policy parameters?

As with Litvinenko, few thought it likely that a risky operation could be carried out in a foreign territory without Putin's direct approval. In Soviet culture, spies deferred to the boss. Nobody would take the risk of unsanctioned action. Moreover, Putin was responsible for the overall political climate, in which his security organs could carry out their repressive deeds without hindrance.

IN POWER, TRUMP governed as he campaigned. His presidency was defined by rancour, mean-spiritedness, and partisanship. Living through it was a psychologically exhausting and bruising experience. Political opponents were mocked, belittled, insulted. The president's style was confrontational and bombastic; his method of administration chaotic and dysfunctional. Under his errant and transgressive leadership, the country's divisions grew.

Meanwhile, the White House was a carousel where staff came and went. Defence secretary, secretary of state, attorney general, chief of staff, national security adviser . . . senior figures in Trump's administration headed for the door once their personal limits had been reached, or when Trump decided to fire them. James Mattis, Rex Tillerson, Jeff Sessions, John Kelly, John Bolton—all were in and then out.

There were few constants in Trump's world, where the president's whims, imparted via Twitter or uttered against the backdrop of a whirring helicopter, defined the media cycle. Except perhaps one. Since swearing an oath to defend the US Constitution at his inauguration, Trump had avoided criticizing foreign autocrats—one in particular. No matter what Moscow did, Trump could not, or would not, call out Putin.

This tendency had been on show long before Mueller hired some of the best legal minds in America and began his investigation into collusion. For nearly two years what was happening behind the doors of Mueller's office was a mystery. There were no leaks. Mueller's silence stood in contrast to a daily Trumpian cacophony. Mueller was simultaneously Washington's most present personality, the subject of myriad speculation—and a ghost.

Every so often the special prosecutor's indictments would appear without fanfare, as if dropped tablet-like from the heavens. They were written in cool, logical prose. Each told a story. The alleged crime was laid out. You learned something new: the substantial scale of Moscow's hacking and dumping operation, the use of anonymous cryptocurrency. There were often redactions, tantalizing deletions that encouraged flights of fancy, and at the end a right-slanting signature in black above the words "Robert S. Mueller III, Special Counsel, US Department of Justice."

What could one say about this? Well, Mueller seemed to be following the evidence, moving in a determined and thorough way towards an ending. Legal analysts said that he was proceeding in the manner of a vintage prosecutor seeking to take down a crime family step by step. This, we learned later, was wishful thinking. Nevertheless, Mueller's sober and professional approach seemed a rebuke to Trump's casual and disingenuous modus operandi, shaped by compulsive mendacity.

Over time, the indictments set out proof of how Russia had meddled in US politics, to Trump's benefit. They were convincing.

The details were vivid and often astonishing. Our understanding of the US's greatest scandal since Watergate grew as new facts were pushed out.

At the heart of Mueller's inquiry was intent.

Was Trump an unwitting beneficiary of Putin's effort to put him in the White House? Or did the candidate and his Republican campaign team know what was going on, and encourage and co-steer these efforts, coordinating with Moscow at crucial moments?

At the time of the Skripal hit, Mueller had yet to deliver his much-anticipated report. We were missing what one former White House adviser called a "unified field theory." (The reference was to Einstein's theory of how the moving parts of the universe fitted together.) The report would confirm that the Russian government had interfered in the 2016 election in sweeping and systematic fashion and identify numerous links between the Russians and the Trump campaign. The campaign expected to benefit from Moscow's help. This didn't—Mueller ultimately concluded—amount to the crime of conspiracy.

Mueller left much unanswered, not least the question of whether Trump had obstructed justice following his sacking in May 2017 of FBI director James Comey. It didn't explore money laundering, potential violations of electoral finance laws, and Trump's possible abuse of his own charitable foundation. Nor did it delve fully into Trump's financial ties with Moscow. Or the issue of collusion, which Mueller said wasn't a legal term.

On collusion, there was plenty of evidence in plain sight. From his early months as candidate in mid-2015, Trump had upended the Republican Party's view of Putin. In TV interviews Trump flattered a person previously seen as a KGB thug with sugary compliments—"Wouldn't it be great if we could get along with Russia," "Putin says I'm a genius," etc.

In office, Trump did nothing to banish the impression that he was under Putin's sway. There was still no criticism of Vladimir by Donald. No sign either that this was being offered during their private discussions. These were so alarming that White House aides hid the Putin chats behind a code-word classified system, reserved for the most sensitive intelligence—with Trump obsequious and rambling, according to the *Washington Post*. Putin's view of Trump was unknown. But the relationship appeared to be based on a model the Russian president knew from his old career as a spy in East Germany: that of KGB case officer and asset.

The Skripal case, therefore, was a telling moment. Two Russian assassins had turned up in a sleepy corner of England, seeking to murder a naturalized British citizen using a chemical weapon. No terrorist group had done as much. Locals found themselves in a horror movie. Mothers turning up with their babies at Salisbury library could see rescue workers on the other side of the window, tottering around in yellow hazmat suits. The intelligence shared with Washington implicated not just Moscow but also Putin personally.

Eleven days after receiving the UK's briefing, President Trump was put through on a secure line to the Kremlin. That weekend Putin had "won" Russia's decorative election. Ahead of the call White House aides had prepared briefing notes. The words "DO NOT CONGRATULATE" had been written in upper-case letters. A further note told Trump to condemn the murder attempt on Skripal.

Salisbury was a long way from middle America and the concerns of most Trump voters. Nevertheless, the incident had played big on cable television. Trump's favourite channel, Fox News, called it a "story of international intrigue," and pointed out that Skripal had been exchanged for the glamorous Russian agent Anna Chapman, a woman who appeared to have fallen from the pages of an Ian Fleming novel.

In short, a major ally had been attacked. The unanimous view inside NATO and the intelligence community was that Putin was responsible. Surely this was the moment when Trump would express his anger and frustration with Putin, or at the very least condemn him as a really bad guy?

Not exactly. Trump began by congratulating Putin on his election victory over a field of handpicked non-opponents. Then Trump proposed that he and Putin meet for a summit—in Washington or elsewhere. Skripal, still alive but only just, went unmentioned. Later that summer Trump told Prime Minister May he was sceptical that Moscow had tried to silence its ex-spy. May retorted that this was highly likely. Trump spent ten minutes insisting it wasn't.

It was unclear if Trump's uncritical support for the Kremlin was born of statesmanship or fear. The latter looked more likely. What exactly did Moscow have on Trump? Generally speaking, Russians murdered Russians. But in a post-rules age, who could be sure? While these questions went unanswered, the GRU continued its mission of murder and mayhem.

CHAPTER 2

BASHNYA

Moscow–Washington, DC
2016–2020

A most promising type of weapon.
RUSSIA'S CHIEF OF GENERAL STAFF VALERY GERASIMOV
ON "INFORMATION" OPERATIONS AS A FORM OF WAR

It looked like a regular business centre. Glass tower, twenty-one storeys high, in Moscow's northwestern suburbs.

The tower overlooked a slice of green forest and the Moscow Canal. In summer cruise boats went past, full of revellers tipsy on *shampanskoe*. They were on their way to the Bukhta Radosti, the Bay of Joy, a sandy beach with pine trees where you could swim or rent a yellow pedalo. The water network stretched all the way to St. Petersburg.

In winter the canal's waters froze. It was possible to walk or sleigh across. In one direction lay the thunderous MKAD ring road; in the other, Tolstoy Park, with birches, wooden dinosaurs, and the Kosmos bowling alley; nearby were wooden dachas and blocks of apartment buildings.

The glass tower at 22 Kirov Street wasn't quite what it seemed. A high fence with cameras ran around it. There was no access from an embankment footpath. When football fans turned up one day, hoping to get a glimpse from the upper floor of a sold-out game in the Khimki sports arena opposite, security staff shooed them off.

The complex had a parking lot for those allowed in and a comma-shaped annex. Its denizens worked regular office hours: 9:00 a.m. to 6:00 p.m., Monday to Friday.

The tower was protected for a reason. In February 2016 the man who built it—Denis Sablin—sold it to the property wing of Russia's Ministry of Defence. Sablin was a wealthy developer and a Duma deputy for Putin's ruling United Russia Party. He was also the organizer of patriotic Kremlin initiatives. One was a veterans' organization, Combat Brotherhood. Another was "anti-Maidan," a Russian riposte to the street rebellion in next-door Ukraine that had driven the country's president from power.

Putin often complained about the pro-Western "colour revolutions" in former Soviet territories such as Georgia (in 2003) and Ukraine (2004, 2014). These were national uprisings against government corruption and impunity. The last one in Ukraine's capital, Kyiv, saw President Viktor Yanukovych flee to Moscow.

In Putin's view, these revolutions were nothing more than CIA-instigated coups. At anti-Maidan rallies protesters bussed in by the authorities expressed support for the breakaway pseudo-statelets of Donetsk and Luhansk, carved from Ukraine by Moscow's brute hand.

The Kremlin liked to imagine Russia as a besieged fortress surrounded by enemies plotting to invade. This KGB mindset was unchanged since Cold War times. The *glavny protivnik* ("main adversary") was still America. Paranoia, xenophobia, a zero-sum approach to international relations, and a sense of Russia's victimhood and exceptionalism coloured official thinking and the propaganda put out by state TV anchors on the nightly news.

So how should Russia respond to these elemental threats, real or knowingly exaggerated?

In the past its generals had conceptualized conflict as taking place on land, air, and sea. For decades Soviet forces stationed in Warsaw Pact nations faced off against NATO and its tanks. Recently, though, the military's chief of staff, Valery Gerasimov, could be heard talking about a new wonder weapon.

It wasn't the Topol intercontinental ballistic missile wheeled out each May at the Victory Day parade in Red Square, trundling solemnly over the cobbles—a spectacle I saw for myself, and which one British analyst described to me as "willy-waving."

Something more powerful than that. A weapon that could slip past national borders and defences, cunning and undetected. A weapon that might wreak havoc from *inside* the enemy.

The weapon was information.

The "hidden realm" of the "informational sphere" offered interesting possibilities, Gerasimov told Moscow's Academy of Military Sciences in 2019, articulating an idea that the cyber world gave new force and potency. Russia could use information, released at the right time, to damage and disrupt its foes. Done properly, an asymmetric attack might be brutally effective. It was easy to carry out, deniable. And—relative to building a long-range nuclear weapon—cheap.

You could strike without warning, and remotely. The target might be a power grid or an enemy's banking system. Of course, such pre-emptive actions might be justified as a response to a possible future Western attack and to what Moscow viewed as continuous US meddling in its own affairs.

The mysterious glass building next to the canal belonged to the GRU. It was a secret sub-office, referred to colloquially within the agency as *bashnya* ("tower"). In spring 2016 a group of intelligence officers moved in. Their boss was Colonel Aleksandr Osadchuk. There are no images, but it's clear the spies brought computers, data storage stacks, and cables. Their unit, 74455, was the outreach department and publishing wing of Russian military intelligence—and a palace of invention and myth.

This GRU colony worked with another GRU team based in central Moscow, at 20 Komsomolsky Prospekt. Unit 26165 operated from a yellow-painted neoclassical building, designed in nineteenth-century imperial style by a Swiss architect active in St. Petersburg, Luigi Rusca from Lugano. The building was originally a barracks. A stroll away is the Moscow River, and on the other bank Gorky Park.

Unit 26165 was once part of a vast GRU and KGB signals intelligence empire. By the 1970s the USSR had established a network of secret listening stations. These ranged from large GRU facilities in Lourdes, Cuba—used for spying on US Navy communications and other high-frequency transmissions—to Ventspils, Latvia—designed to snoop on NATO and transatlantic signals—to smaller bases in Vietnam, South Yemen, and Mongolia. And in Kushka, the southernmost part of the Soviet Union, Vorkuta in the Arctic Circle, and Vladivostok. Historically the unit specialized in cryptography and military codes. It was part of the GRU's sixth directorate and known as the 85th Main Centre.

The unit's commander, Victor Borisovich Netyshko, was a talented mathematician and a Moscow University lecturer who had published a doctoral thesis on Boolean equations. From time to time members of his team—all of them men—took part in public conferences. Most of their work was in the shadows. Sometimes they put a boot into the light.

Journalists from Radio Svoboda found Netyshko's swooping signature on a series of cooperation agreements with local math schools. These schools agreed to refer promising students to the FSB Academy and its cryptography institute. As Minister of Defence Sergei Shoigu made clear, Russia was on a "big hunt" for a new generation of programmers who might work on the latest digital front line.

The GRU was spearheading this innovative battle. In March 2016 the two GRU units, together with others, were told to carry out a special mission. The plan was ambitious and wholly in the spirit of Gerasimov's doctrine of unseen influence. Netyshko's order was simple: to hack the forthcoming US presidential election. Such an order, as everyone inside the GRU perfectly understood, could only have come from the top.

The Kremlin's purpose here was to help Trump and to damage and derail the Clinton campaign. Putin loathed Clinton and the Obama administration. He held her responsible as US secretary of state for a series of anti-government protests in 2011–12 that greeted his decision to run for the presidency a third time, replacing Dmitry Medvedev. These demonstrations, in Moscow and elsewhere, were quashed. They fed the Russian elite's primal fear: losing power.

How the GRU went about fulfilling this secret order became apparent in summer 2018, when Mueller published a twenty-nine-page document identifying Netyshko and eleven other GRU staff officers.

The outgoing Obama White House published its own findings. It concluded that two Moscow hacking teams working independently—one GRU, one FSB—had compromised the servers of the Democratic Party and stolen data from individuals, including Clinton's campaign chairman, John Podesta.

Mueller's court docket set out this conspiracy in full. It was a stunning piece of work. It was almost as if the special counsel had been in the room when these deeds took place, sitting in the corner and making notes. It raised intriguing questions as to whether the US and the other allies had a mole or moles inside the GRU—supplying information on the GRU's faceless operators.

Sitting at their desks in Komsomolsky Prospekt, four officers—Major Boris Antonov, Dmitry Badin, Ivan Yermakov, and Aleksey

Lukashev—targeted the Democratic Party. Their way in was a tested method: spear-phishing. An email arrived in your in-box that looked like a security warning from Google. It told you to change your password. And offered a link. If you followed the instructions—entering a new password—you were caught. The new phrase went not to Google but to the GRU. The Russian hackers thereby gained access to all of your data.

On March 19, 2016, Lukashev sent a spear-phishing email to Podesta, from an account, "john356gh," modified to look like a Google alert. Podesta went to the link and changed his password. Using this new log-in, Lukashev accessed Podesta's in-box, taking fifty thousand messages. Bingo! Similar links were sent to Hillary staffers, including campaign manager Robby Mook and foreign policy adviser Jake Sullivan.

Next, the Russians set up a fake email account that purported to belong to a real Clinton campaign employee. (The address was one letter off from the actual spelling.) On April 6, the GRU used this account to email another thirty members of Clinton's team. It came with a promising link, "hillary-clinton-favorable-rating.xlsx. Those who clicked connected to a GRU-made website.

These spear-phishing raids continued throughout the summer of 2016. They were remarkably successful, allowing the GRU to harvest tens of thousands of emails and hundreds of thousands of documents.

Unit 26165 hacked into the Democratic Congressional Campaign Committee (DCCC) and the Democratic National Committee (DNC), the formal governing body for the US Democratic Party. Staff working at the DNC's office at 430 South Capitol Street in Washington knew nothing of this. An invisible platoon of Russian ghosts broke in—and remotely hijacked the network.

According to Mueller, Yermakov spear-phished the identity of an unnamed DCCC worker. The Russian then installed multiple versions of a piece of GRU-designed malware, called X-Agent, onto the DCCC system. It infected at least ten other computers. Stolen information was then relayed back to Russia using a computer in Arizona leased by the GRU.

The GRU team thus followed the activities of the Clinton campaign in real time. It broke into the DNC from the DCCC, stealing credentials from IT supervisors and others. The spies were able to monitor individual employees' computer activity, take screen shots, log keystrokes, and steal bank details. This was espionage—and voyeurism. On April 22, according to the indictment, the spies spent eight hours tracking a female DCCC worker—reading her chats and "personal records."

The operation's evident purpose was to find material that might be beneficial to Trump. Using a hacked DCCC computer, the "conspirators"—as Mueller called them—searched terms such as "hillary," "cruz," and "trump." They copied a folder titled "Benghazi Investigations," stole opposition research, and exfiltrated papers on voter outreach.

As this volume of material piled up, the Moscow hackers faced technical issues. They compressed multiple documents using an open source tool. The files were moved back to Moscow with another piece of GRU malware, "X-Tunnel." The route went through a GRU-leased computer in Illinois.

How the officers felt about their clandestine activities on behalf of the state is unclear. For a period at least they were unstoppable, running amok behind enemy lines. Was it too early to think about promotion? Did they experience pride or was it just a job?

The GRU has a medal for its distinguished cyber warriors, at least according to one example offered for sale on a Russian website. It features a crystal crossed with a sword and lightning bolt against a globe. At the bottom is the number of the military unit. On the back are the words "For service to the Fatherland."

IT WAS EASTER 2016. Someone inside the Doughnut picked up something odd. The anomaly lay in the metadata, and metadata didn't lie.

The Doughnut is the nickname given to GCHQ, the UK government's communication headquarters in Cheltenham. The headquarters resembles a giant silver spaceship, circular and with a hole in the middle, dropped to Earth from the stars. It has a staff of six thousand, and its purpose is eavesdropping. As the 2013 leak of secret documents by Edward Snowden showed, GCHQ is able to scoop up huge volumes of electronic traffic as it circles the globe.

GCHQ works closely with its larger, more powerful US counterpart, the National Security Agency, or NSA, based at Fort Meade, outside Washington. The two organizations are part of a unique pooling arrangement dating back to World War II. They share their intelligence products with Canada, Australia, and New Zealand, a deal known as Five Eyes. The US is the dominant partner. It pays most of the bills—giving GCHQ £100 million between 2009 and 2012 to cover "mastering the internet" and to support NATO's mission in Afghanistan.

Back in the 2000s, when Trump was merely a property developer and reality TV star, the MI6 officer in charge of the Five Eyes relationship was Christopher Burrows. Burrows left Her Majesty's secret service and went into private business intelligence. He founded a company, Orbis, with an ex-MI6 colleague. The colleague's name was Christopher Steele.

Daily, GCHQ analysts track the activities of hostile states and terrorist groups—the North Koreans, the murderous regime of Bashar al-Assad in Syria, ISIS. And Putin's Russia.

The GRU, Moscow's pre-eminent outward-facing spy agency, was obviously on the grid. As the US election drew closer, with Trump the presumptive Republican nominee, a GCHQ team member noticed unusual electronic traffic between Moscow and the Democratic Party. This traffic wasn't a one-off. Something weird was going on.

"We saw it happen," Robert Hannigan, GCHQ's then director told me, when we met in London for coffee in 2018, in the same week that Mueller accused the GRU of conspiring against America, as well as computer fraud and money laundering.

"We saw very odd communications between the DNC and known Russian actors. It jumped out." According to Hannigan, GCHQ was the first Western agency to pick up on these cyber intrusions. "At the time no one was aware there was Russian manipulation," he said.

In line with standard procedure, Cheltenham informed Fort Meade. "We passed it to the NSA, who passed it to the FBI," Hannigan explained.

This was the first time the FBI learned that Moscow was engaging in espionage activity around the US election—a theme that would engulf the bureau and put it on a collision course with Trump. GCHQ continued to send regular written updates to NSA, Hannigan said, featuring "cyber metadata." None of this, he added, constituted GCHQ spying on Trump—a meritless claim made later by the president and his early press secretary Sean Spicer.

Hannigan's news coincided with a new phase for the GRU's hackers. By late spring they had accumulated filing cabinets' worth of sensitive information. In itself, the stealing of foreign material was standard intelligence procedure. The US, the UK, France, Germany, and Australia all hacked the emails of foreign opponents when they could. This, as former NSA and CIA director Mike Hayden told me, was little more than "honourable international espionage." Given the chance, he would steal from Russian servers too, he said.

The question was what the GRU would do with this pillaged DNC stuff. We don't know what conversations may have taken place between GRU director Korobov and Putin's presidential administration. By April, however, a play was agreed. A decision was made to shove this material into the public domain and to activate it against Clinton, all the while concealing Moscow's event-shaping role. The publication of the Panama Papers—which revealed widespread corruption inside the Russian elite and a $2 billion money trail leading to Putin's Leningrad friend Sergei Roldugin—may have been a catalyst.

First, the Komsomolsky Prospekt hackers sought to register a website, electionleaks.com. This didn't work, so they set up dcleaks.com, bought using bitcoin. A GRU account, dirbinsaabol@mail.com, leased a server in Malaysia that hosted the domain. (The same email was used in phishing expeditions, Mueller said.) On June 8, dcleaks.com went live.

The website was a success. It became a portal through which the GRU could feed leaks to reporters, candidates, and ordinary Americans. By the time it was closed in March 2017, the site had received more than a million page views. The GRU didn't take credit for its work, understandably. Instead it claimed a group of "American hacktivists" were responsible and that dcleaks.com was a purely domestic thing.

To bolster this fiction the GRU invented a small village of fake "Americans." They had more or less convincing identities: Carrie Feehan, Alice Donovan, Jason Scott, Richard Gingrey. "Carrie" registered and paid for the dcleaks.com domain from an address in New York. "Alice" set up a dcleaks.com Facebook page. "Jason" and "Richard" promoted it.

The Facebook accounts' actual mastermind was Aleksey Potemkin, a GRU supervisor and officer with unit 74455, working out of the Khimki Tower. According to Mueller, Potemkin handled infrastructure and social media. His surname, Potemkin, was a good fit for a career in fakery. An earlier Potemkin, Grigory, famously painted backdrops to cover up the squalor of Russian villages visited by Catherine the Great.

A website, a Facebook page . . . the GRU invented a Twitter handle too, @dcleaks. This was run out of a Russian computer used for other intrusion operations. The same machine ran the Twitter account @BaltimoreIsWhr, Mueller said. The account encouraged Americans to "join our flash mob" against Clinton and posted images with the hashtag #BlacksAgainstHillary. (The GRU is white and overwhelmingly Slavic.)

The GRU's American honeymoon lasted until May. That month the FBI told the Democrats they had been hacked, and the DNC brought in a security firm, CrowdStrike, to investigate. (Despite what Trump falsely claimed, CrowdStrike was co-founded by a Russian-born American, Dmitry Alperovitch. It had nothing to do with Ukraine.) The firm's technicians discovered that two "separate Russian intelligence-affiliated adversaries" had penetrated the DNC network. These were "sophisticated" actors, CrowdStrike wrote in a blogpost—and familiar ones.

CrowdStrike identified the first group of intruders as Cozy Bear, or APT29. This was the FSB. It broke into the DNC in summer 2015. Cozy Bear had already infiltrated unclassified systems belonging to the White House, State Department, and US Joint Chief of Staff, as well as other organizations, universities, and think tanks. Cozy Bear's scope was impressive. Victims had been observed in Western Europe as well as in Brazil, China, Japan, South Korea, New Zealand, and elsewhere.

The second group named by CrowdStrike was Fancy Bear, also known as APT28—the GRU units based in Kirov Street and Komsomolsky Prospekt. Fancy Bear had been engaged in cyber operations since the mid-2000s. Like its FSB rival, its activities were global. It had targeted defence ministries. It had hacked Germany's Bundestag and the French television station

TV5, among others. CrowdStrike respected its twin opponents in Moscow. They used "superb" tradecraft and "operational security second to none," it said.

This may have been true, but the Tower now faced something of a problem. The *Washington Post* had reported a possible link between the DNC breach and Moscow, and security specialists were busy evicting the GRU hackers from US servers. Meanwhile, Trump was trailing Clinton in the polls. The GRU responded with a classic disinformation ploy. It came up with a piece of make-believe. This story said the DNC raid had nothing to do with Moscow and was the work of a lone Romanian hacker.

But what to call him? The GRU team in Khimki considered a name that was mysterious and cabbalistic. For their creation to be plausible, this incognito person would need a voice and a personality. And passable English.

A little research was needed.

ON JUNE 15, 2016, the weather in Moscow was pleasant, in the low seventies Fahrenheit, with a cloudy sky and a few spots of rain. Over in Lille, Russia was playing Slovakia in the European football championships in France, and was soon to go a goal down. The headlines on *Yandex*—Russia's internet search engine—were the usual. The Foreign Ministry in Moscow was protesting against a NATO plan to rotate troops into Poland and the Baltic states.

One of the Tower spies logged onto a local server. He spent just over half an hour browsing suitable words and phrases. These included "some hundred sheets," "some hundreds of sheets," "dcleaks," "illuminati," "worldwide known," "think twice about," and "company's competence." Plus the Russian for "widely known translation." By the time he wrapped up, Russia had conceded a second goal.

Two hours later, at 7:02 p.m. Moscow time, the GRU's alleged Romanian hacker—Guccifer 2.0—made his debut. In an anonymous WordPress post, Guccifer 2.0 claimed credit for the DNC attack using the same phrases searched by the GRU.

The statement—with phrases in boldface by Mueller—said:

> **Worldwide known** cyber security company CrowdStrike announced that the Democratic National Committee (DNC) servers had been hacked by "sophisticated" hacker groups.
>
> I'm very pleased the company appreciated my skills so highly))) But in fact, it was easy, very easy. [. . .]
>
> Here are just a few docs from many thousands I extracted when hacking into DNC's network. [. . .]
>
> **Some hundred sheets**! This's a serious case, isn't it? [. . .]
>
> I guess CrowdStrike customers should **think twice about company's competence**.
>
> Fuck the **Illuminati** and their conspiracies!!!!!!!!! Fuck CrowdStrike !!!!!!!!!"

There was more than a whiff of Dan Brown here. The idea of dark forces and conspiracy was one that Trump would himself energetically promote. To a native English speaker, Guccifer's phrasing looked clunky. But perhaps this might be expected from a Romanian. Certainly the documents Guccifer provocatively posted were real. They included a DNC report on Trump and a list of Democratic Party donors.

Guccifer became the main fictional intermediary between the hacked trove of documents and flesh-and-blood people seeking to exploit them.

That summer Russian military intelligence followed events in America and considered new ways to disseminate its stolen cache. One obvious conduit was WikiLeaks, whose founder, Julian

Assange, had been holed up since 2012 at the Ecuadorian embassy in London. WikiLeaks would become the GRU's chief publication outlet, with Assange obfuscating the origin of the DNC material and denying Russian involvement.

On or around June 22 WikiLeaks messaged Guccifer. It was the first in a series of direct communications between WikiLeaks and the GRU. Mueller has not revealed all of these exchanges. His indictment and report give us a snapshot, with WikiLeaks referred to as "Organization 1."

The message asked Guccifer to forward WikiLeaks "any new material here for us to review" since "it will have a much higher impact than what you are doing."

On July 6 WikiLeaks got in touch again. Ahead of the Democratic Party's national convention, it appeared anxious to divide Hillary supporters from those who had backed her main rival, Vermont senator Bernie Sanders.

The messages read:

> WIKILEAKS: if you have anything hillary related we want it in the next tweo [*sic*] days prefable [*sic*] because the DNC is approaching and she will solidify bernie supporters behind here after.
> GRU: ok . . . I see.
> WIKILEAKS: we think trump has only a 25% chance of winning against hillary . . . so conflict between bernie and hillary is interesting.

The GRU understood. According to Mueller, it made unsuccessful attempts to transfer the material to WikiLeaks. On July 14 it tried again, sending an email with the subject "big archive." A message said "new attempt." There was an attachment titled "wk dnc link1.txt.gpg." And a set of encrypted instructions explaining how the archive should be accessed. Four days later, on July 18, Assange or one of his co-workers confirmed "the 1Gb or so archive had arrived." The GRU learned a release would take place "this week."

We don't know if the Kremlin's spy teams had televisions in their offices tuned to CNN, MSNBC, and Fox News. One imagines they did. What's clear is that they were intimately plugged into American life and politics, fluent or conversant in English, and tracking developments on the East Coast of America, ten time zones and some 4,700 miles away.

On July 22—a day after Trump formally accepted the nomination at the Republican national convention in Cleveland—WikiLeaks dumped out more than twenty thousand emails and documents. It said nothing about the role played by Russian intelligence. Instead Assange hinted in media interviews that his source might have been Seth Rich, a Democratic Party worker murdered in New York.

The release worked better than Moscow could have dreamed, and was surely proof that Gerasimov was right about the way in which information might confound the enemy. It swept over the Democrats in Philadelphia and incensed Bernie supporters, many of them already poorly disposed towards Hillary. DNC chair Debbie Wasserman Schultz resigned over accusations of pro-Clinton bias. Even better, Trump's ratings jumped him into the lead.

The GRU understood that not everyone had to be taken in by the Guccifer lone hacker fairy tale. Rather, the disinformation worked if it created serious doubts in some people's minds about who might have been behind the hack, a scepticism that Kremlin bots and trolls could encourage.

In this, Trump's own comments helped. They were a smorgasbord of equivocation and deflection, expressed in shoulder-shrugging riffs suggesting that anybody might have done it, including China or a four-hundred-pound guy sitting on his bed in New Jersey.

The most notorious episode came on July 27, in Florida, when, among other things, Trump said of the hacking, "Nobody knows if it's Russia." He also made his direct appeal to Moscow to carry out espionage against his opponent, calling on the Kremlin to locate the thirty-three thousand emails that Clinton had apparently deleted:

"Russia, if you're listening, I hope you're able to find the thirty thousand emails that are missing," he said. "I think you'll be rewarded mightily by our press. Let's see if that happens."

Moscow was listening.

The GRU was listening.

Unit 26165 was listening.

It's unclear if Antonov, Badin, Yermakov, and Lukashev were staying late anyway, or simply hurried back to the office in central Moscow's Frunzenskaya in the wake of Trump's appeal to action. Mueller says that working "after hours" that evening, the spies tried for the first time to hack Clinton's email. They fired off spear-phishing attacks to her personal office and to seventy-six related accounts. That they were seemingly unable to locate the thirty-three thousand emails wasn't for lack of effort.

At the time it was filed—July 2018—Mueller's carefully constructed charge sheet made it possible to reconstruct the events of two years earlier for the first time. It didn't answer the central puzzle of Trump's presidency: was there knowing coordination between Trump and people around him with Russian espionage players?

If you were willing to give Trump the benefit of the doubt, it was possible to believe Antonov and his associates learned everything they needed from US cable networks. If you were suspicious of Trump's denials of collusion, it seemed likely that Russia's energetic spies may have benefited from inside help. And that the Americans who interacted with the GRU and its online creatures knew—or suspected—exactly with whom they were dealing.

The docket lays bare how the GRU reached out to influential Republicans, with Moscow leaning heavily on the scales of US democracy. One of these Republicans was the president's now convicted friend and long-term political fixer Roger Stone. Stone—as Mueller indicates—was "in regular contact with senior members" of Trump's campaign. He features in Mueller's later report, though many details are redacted.

We have a fragment of conversation.

On August 15, the Russian spies posing as Guccifer messaged Stone directly:

"thank u for writing back . . . do u find anyt[h]ing interesting in the docs i posted?"

Two days later, the GRU followed up, writing:

"please tell me if i can help u anyhow . . . it would be a great pleasure to me."

Then, on September 9, Guccifer referred to stolen DCCC documents published online, asking Stone, "what do u think of the info on the turnout model for the democrats entire presidential campaign."

Stone seemed underwhelmed. He responded, "[p]retty standard."

Through summer and into October the GRU published hacked material via Guccifer's WordPress page and funnelled leaks to a small group of politically useful contacts.

The spies were happy to help. When a Republican candidate for Congress got in touch, Guccifer provided documents about the candidate's Democratic opponent. Some 2.5 gigabytes of stolen DCCC data went to a political news website, The Smoking Gun, with further documents about the Black Lives Matter movement given to a grateful reporter.

The GRU engaged in a late-phase project to steal US voter data and other election material. Seemingly, the goal was to discredit the election. Anatoliy Kovalev, a GRU officer, led a state-level sweep, looking for website vulnerabilities. Targets included state election boards and other election-related entities, as well as email addresses belonging to state political parties, including Republican ones.

That July Kovalev found a way into the Illinois State Board of Election. Using malicious code, he broke into the paperless online voter database and stole the IDs of millions of registered Illinois voters, including Social Security and driver's licence numbers.

In October he made a similar attempt to compromise Georgia, Iowa, and Florida. Florida was a special target. Days before the November vote, Kovalev dispatched more than 120 spear-phishing emails to "organization and personnel" involved in administering the election at a county level. The GRU got inside at least one Florida county government.

By this point, of course, the GRU had released the contents of Podesta's email account, which it had possessed since March. The dump was via WikiLeaks. Some fifty thousand emails were published over the course of a month, beginning on October 7. Most were inconsequential and routine—dull, even. Still, they did Clinton no favours.

MUELLER'S INDICTMENT AND report gave a thorough account of the GRU's furtive acts. But certain aspects were missing—not least the role played by the separate hacking team from the FSB, which is still largely unknown.

There was also a bigger question: how was it that a small group of hacker-spies sitting in a tower could subvert a US election, with a comparatively modest budget stretching into a few hundreds of thousands of pounds?

After all, the Kremlin had previously taken a dim view of the internet. Putin viewed the web with suspicion, in 2014 calling it "a special CIA project." He didn't use email. He preferred brief-ings from his intelligence chiefs. At home, Russia took a sovereign view of internet use. It sought to control servers, to spy on domestic users, and to lock up critical bloggers.

The US, by contrast, was the world's dominant internet power and the innovative home of Facebook, Google, Twitter, Instagram, and other universal platforms.

The short answer: Russia had caught up.

True, the GRU's tradecraft could be clumsy. In May, after the DNC hack was discovered, the Russians tried to delete traces of their presence on the DCCC network. (They used the computer program CCleaner.) When CrowdStrike disabled the "X-agent" hacking tool, the GRU spent seven hours trying to reinstall it.

Andrei Soldatov, the foremost expert on the Russian internet, was underwhelmed by the GRU's professionalism. "You try and find some logic and you are lost, to be honest. It's really so stupid," he told me. Soldatov acknowledged that the GRU officers were "no Ciceros" but said he had once thought them superior operators to the FSB, an opinion Mueller's charge sheet made him revise. "It's about ambition. It isn't about logic. They [the GRU] are still seen as newcomers. They feel the need to prove themselves, to be more active," he said.

Despite imperfect tradecraft Putin's modern spies had several advantages over previous generations. In the Cold War period most KGB officers had a reasonable understanding of the West and of capitalism and its functionaries. But they had to write their reports in ideology-speak, to conform with Soviet thinking. Accordingly, Moscow's propaganda in America could be crude.

Once communism was abandoned, ex-KGB men with Western experience were at last able to use their skills properly. A new gen-eration of Russian intelligence officers learned English. One of them wrote Guccifer's lines and batted away accusations he was a

Russian agent with the words "Total fail!!!!!" Very few American spies spoke Russian.

Russian society was, therefore, opaque to most outsiders, while America's was utterly transparent. Hollywood movies and popular culture added to this knowledge imbalance. As the *Financial Times* pointed out, in 2016 the US was "outsmarted by foreigners it didn't understand."

After the collapse of the Berlin Wall young Russians were educated abroad and studied in Western schools and colleges. They lived in New York, London, and Paris, or among the new democracies of ex-communist Eastern Europe. "They know our societies very well," said Mark Medish, special assistant to President Bill Clinton and a former National Security Council director for Russia, Ukraine, and Eurasia.

Medish told me Moscow's foreign operatives of today reminded him of their predecessors of the 1920s and '30s. This was arguably the high point of Soviet espionage, when multilingual undercover agents stole cipher codes, seduced foreigners, and passed themselves off as Nazis while secretly working for Red Moscow. Many were subsequently wiped out in Stalin's purges. The most celebrated, Richard Sorge, became the subject of a later KGB cult.

"They [the Russians] are doing what they did, with a nuance that was lacking in the Cold War," Medish said. "They learned intimately how our societies worked from the inside and penetrated each country on its own terms." The GRU's spectacular success in America was in part a "malign by-product of globalization and integration," he suggested.

The FBI, CIA, and NSA all believed Putin had ordered a major influence campaign in 2016 to "undermine the US-led liberal democratic order." Their joint 2017 report described this effort as "unprecedented," Moscow's "boldest yet," and a "significant escalation in directness, level of activity and scope of effort." The Russian government had a clear preference for Trump, the agencies said, and was seeking to denigrate his rival and harm her electability.

Mueller released his charges against the GRU in the summer of 2018, just as the president arrived in Europe for a tour and an important summit. Until his report was published, the special counsel was like a sphinx. Still, the timing of his docket looked mischievous. Trump was about to meet the man who sabotaged the US election and who almost certainly ordered the GRU hack.

Clearly, Trump would bawl this person out. To do anything else would raise suspicions that—just as the critics said—he was Putin's willing stooge.

CHAPTER 3

YOU AND I

Helsinki–London–Osaka
JUNE 2018

Rudyard Kipling gave spies the key to success with his immortal Jungle Book. *You simply say to the person you wish to recruit "You and I are one blood."*
VIKTOR SUVOROV, SOVIET MILITARY INTELLIGENCE

The view from Kalastajatorppa was Nordic. Pines, silver birches, a shimmering expanse of water. Less usual was the temperature. It was hot—eighty-two degrees Fahrenheit—with white sky and glaring sun. In summer 2018 a heatwave gripped Europe. In Finland, Norway, and Sweden there were wildfires and burning forests, drought and dying trees, landscapes turning yellow as far north as the Arctic Circle.

Evidence of climate crisis, you might think, and a world out of joint, in a region where you rarely had cause to put on your shorts.

The man waiting impatiently in Kalastajatorppa's modernist state guesthouse was a well-known climate change sceptic. He had described the phenomenon as a hoax invented by the Chinese. After all, he said in TV interviews, how could it be real when the planet still suffered from freezing winter storms? When his own government put out a report on economic activity and its effects on climate, he promptly downplayed it.

The guest—President Trump—was in Finland for a bilateral meeting. It was July 16, 2018, and a little before 1:00 p.m. Trump was due to set off in his armoured convoy and drive to the presidential palace in downtown Helsinki, a seven-minute ride away. There he would meet Putin. It was their first official summit. What Trump wanted from the meeting was utterly unclear.

But where was he? Putin was late. Actually, Putin was always late—a mind game and form of one-upmanship that the Russian president liked to use when meeting fellow leaders. Merkel, Obama, even the Queen—all were made to hang around, often for hours. In an infamous encounter with Angela Merkel in the Black Sea resort of Sochi, Putin brought his pet Labrador Connie along and got it to sniff at the German chancellor's legs—knowing that Merkel hated canines.

Putin did at least have an excuse. The previous evening he had hosted the World Cup final at Luzhniki Stadium in Moscow, where France had beaten Croatia 4–2.

Trump, meanwhile, had arrived in Finland after a wrecking ball tour of Europe. In Brussels, he had berated NATO leaders for freeloading off the US over defence and for failing to pay their dues. He had attacked Germany, the Continent's leading power, for letting in too many migrants—a "big mistake." Oh, and he had called the EU a "foe."

Trump's visit to the US's loyal friend the UK was similarly contentious. In an interview with the *Sun*, the president disparaged Prime Minister Theresa May and suggested that her Conservative Party rival and future successor Boris Johnson would do a better job. Protesters had flown an inflatable blimp depicting Trump as an orange man-baby in the London sky. Almost certainly Trump didn't notice as he hopped around the English countryside by chopper and flew off to Scotland to play golf.

Was there a method, an ideology at work in Trump's abrasive

dealings with the US's allies? Certainly the president was no fan of "globalism." Trump and his aides used the term negatively to describe supranational institutions that "encroached" on the sovereignty of national governments.

The EU was a "globalist" project par excellence. And therefore, according to Trump world, an adversary. Within that camp, countries run by cultural conservatives—Hungary, Poland, Italy—were regarded as friends.

Still, it was hard to give a coherent summary of Trump's foreign policy. You might call it Hobbesian—with each nation out for itself, in imitation of selfish human behaviour. But it seemed unlikely that Trump had heard of the seventeenth-century English philosopher Thomas Hobbes or had devoted much thought to political theory.

Different factions in the White House were therefore able to interpret foreign policy in different ways. Some—such as the then secretary of defence, Jim Mattis—still believed in America's leading role and the use of US might abroad. This contradiction appalled former senior officials. "They are still using words. To call them ideas is an exaggeration. They are impulses masquerading as a philosophy," a former member of the National Security Council told me.

Other US administrations had come into office with a clear set of international objectives. Trump's was characterized by an absence, a vacuum. His early decisions—to withdraw from the Iran nuclear deal or the Paris climate change accord—signalled a strategic US retreat and a new, aggressive unilateralism. A bungled retreat, his critics said, citing Trump's disastrous exit from Syria—more America alone than America first.

Along the way, one dismal tendency was clear: Trump preferred the company of despots and authoritarians to that of elected politicians. For Kim Jong-un of North Korea, China's Xi Jinping, and Mohammad bin Salman, the crown prince of Saudi Arabia, there were warm words of affection and encouragement. Never mind the gulags or the murder of dissidents such as Saudi journalist and *Washington Post* contributor Jamal Khashoggi, chopped up at the Saudi consulate in Istanbul. For the Europeans, and for Merkel in particular, there was chastisement and obloquy.

There seemed to be consistency in one area only: Russia. While Trump was happy to bash the Germans (over migration, NATO, or car exports), he never had a bad thing to say about Putin. Indeed, Trump had a habit of parroting Russian talking points on Ukraine, Syria, and Venezuela. He even defended the Soviet Union's 1979 invasion of Afghanistan, saying that Moscow was "right" to go there because of "terrorists"—a bizarre and historically inaccurate view.

Hanging over the Helsinki summit, therefore, were questions. How would Trump behave with Putin? Which of the two would come out on top?

And—most significantly—would Trump at last condemn Russia's election intrusions, something he had previously been distinctly unwilling to do, apparently fearing this would diminish his great victory? Thus far Trump had equivocated, hedged, and whiffle-waffled. In Poland in 2017, for example, Trump had declared, "I think it was Russia," but had then added, "Nobody really knows," and "It was probably other people or countries."

Mueller's most recent indictment made this argument ridiculous. Seventy-four hours earlier, as the president inspected a guard of honour with the Queen at Windsor Castle, acting US attorney general Rod Rosenstein had given details of the GRU's hacking operation. The evidence of Moscow's meddling in 2016 was there for all to see. Trump could hardly ignore it, though it was clear he would try; when asked whether he would call on Putin to extradite the twelve GRU officers, Trump said he hadn't thought about it.

Putin's plane landed soon after 1:00 p.m. On the drive to

Helsinki's centre the Russian president went past billboards rented by *Helsingin Sanomat,* Finland's biggest daily paper. One said, in English and Russian, "Mr. President, welcome to the land of the free press." *Helsingin Sanomat* had taken out three hundred ads and plastered them on the three possible routes into town. "It was a great campaign. We got worldwide attention," the paper's features editor, Anssi Miettinen, told me.

It was hard to argue with the pro-free press sentiment. In Russia investigative journalism was a perilous calling. Reporters fell to their deaths out of windows. Or were ambushed outside their apartment blocks and beaten with metal bars. Some were murdered. Victims included the *Novaya Gazeta* journalist Anna Politkovskaya, gunned down in 2006 in Moscow, not far from the *Guardian* office where I arrived as bureau chief the following year. Others were little-known provincial writers who made the mistake of offending local power. The masterminds were rarely caught.

In the US the situation was better: Trump might be bad for America but he was good for the news industry, with subscriptions and revenues up.

Still, Trump's grinding daily attacks on the *New York Times,* CNN, and the "fake news" media had a debasing effect. At political rallies Trump directed his supporters to jeer at the press—an ugly ritual that saw TV crews abused and sometimes roughed up. When talking about the fourth estate, Trump used a phrase beloved by Lenin and Stalin: "enemy of the people," or *vrag naroda,* in the original Russian.

Curious Finns watched as Putin and then Trump pulled up outside Helsinki's harbourside market square and the modest presidential palace. There was a logic to using Finland as a summit spot. During the Cold War, the country was a neutral zone, an in-between place. It was neither NATO nor Warsaw Pact. Its common border with the USSR made it an area of Kremlin interest and espionage. Post-war Finnish leaders tiptoed around the Soviets, avoiding giving offence, a cowardly if pragmatic strategy. (It came with its own noun, Finlandization.) Latterly, Finland was steadfast in its support for the EU.

In 1975 US president Gerald Ford and Soviet leader Leonid Brezhnev met in Helsinki, together with the heads of Eastern Europe, Western Europe, and Canada. Their agreement—the Helsinki accords—ushered in a period of détente between the two superpowers and the communist and capitalist worlds.

One participant was Ford's secretary of state, Henry Kissinger. History was in a loop: Kissinger, now in his nineties, was advising Trump on global affairs. He was a frequent visitor to Russia and guest of Putin. In 2017 Kissinger popped up in the White House when Trump met with Russia's foreign minister, Sergei Lavrov, and its then ambassador to Washington, Sergei Kislyak. This was the day after Trump fired FBI director Comey for failing to make "the Russia thing" go away. The 1975 signing ceremony took place in Finlandia Hall; in 2018 the same building was used as an overflow press room.

Trump and Putin met for a photocall. There were pleasantries from Trump: praise for Russia's soccer World Cup ("beautifully done, so congratulations on that") and a wish for better ties ("getting on with Russia is a good thing, not a bad thing"). In a tweet that morning Trump had blamed the poor state of relations not on Moscow or its hyper-aggressive spies but on "US foolishness and stupidity." He meant the Mueller investigation, or the "rigged witch-hunt," as he put it. Russia's Foreign Ministry retweeted Trump with the line "We agree."

The two principals disappeared.

No cabinet officials were allowed to be present. Fiona Hill, the president's top Russia adviser, who would go on to play a starring role in the impeachment hearings, was shut out.

There would be no notes.

The meeting was to be secret.

AS EVERY SENTIENT human being was aware, Trump denied collusion with Russia. And yet his behaviour with Putin seemed, well, *furtive*. There was no other word for it.

Trump's preferred mode when talking to Putin was to ensure that nobody else was listening in. At their talks in 2017 at the G20 summit in Hamburg, Trump met Putin with Trump's then secretary of state, Rex Tillerson, and without aides. The arrangement looked odd. Tillerson later told the House Foreign Affairs Committee that there had been a "discrepancy in preparation" between the two leaders, with Putin able to "push what he wanted." At the dinner afterwards Trump ditched his interpreter and went to chat with Putin, using the Russian translator, and to the astonishment of the other politicians who were there and watching. Not that they could hear anything. What was said was a mystery.

The lack of an official record wasn't proof of anything, of course.

But it was, to say the least, unusual for the media to be denied even a list of topics that had been discussed; nothing like this had occurred under Khrushchev or Brezhnev, far less under Gorbachev or Yeltsin. It fed speculation that Trump had something he didn't want others to know about, even including, and perhaps especially, Hill and his national security team. One fanciful version: Putin used these private tête-à-têtes to threaten or even to blackmail Trump.

More likely is that the Russian leader used time-honoured KGB methods when dealing with the inexperienced US president. Back in Leningrad spy school Putin would have been instructed to establish a bond of personal friendship when seeking to recruit or to develop a target, a KGB objective. This process took time. It might feature lunches, social contact, gifts. It was, in its way, a form of seduction.

The most important tool was flattery, especially in cases where there was no obvious ideological sympathy from the subject towards communism. Flattery was an essential KGB skill. Those who rose to the top of the organization, occupying positions as department heads, were often superlative flatterers. Gennadi Titov, head of the Third Department of the KGB's First Directorate, was one such person, so the rumour went—using compliments to run the important Norwegian agent Arne Treholt, a diplomat and Norwegian Labour Party politician who was later jailed for spying.

According to White House aides quoted in the *Washington Post*, Putin did the same as Titov. In his meetings with Trump, and in their private phone conversations, Putin played to Trump's ego and took advantage of his need for praise. The Russian leader promised to stand loyally by Trump—like a rock—at a time when the president was beset at home by—as he saw it—opprobrious forces.

Putin would whisper conspiratorially into Trump's ear, US officials told the *Post*, saying, "It's not us. We get it. It's the subordinates fighting against our friendship." Putin would fan Trump's sense of victimhood and blame difficulties on a scheming cabal within America's own intelligence agencies. This, of course, fitted precisely with Trump's view of the FBI: as a hostile entity seeking to drag him from office. Thus Russian disinformation entered the Republican mediasphere.

Putin, then, was prepared for the Helsinki summit, with a playbook honed during Cold War espionage operations. As well as his background in "the organs," as Russians termed the KGB, Putin had nearly two decades of experience of top-level international politics. Other, democratic leaders were ephemeral creatures: they came and went. Unbothered by competition, Putin remained.

Trump, by comparison, was woefully unready. A former senior CIA agent I spoke to was sceptical that Trump had colluded with the Russians but acknowledged that in his encounters with Putin Trump was horribly outmatched: "Over the years Trump has been successful at speaking out from his ass. He's got accustomed to getting away with it," the ex-agent said. Of Putin, the agent added, "He's the smartest leader in the world right now. He's taken Russia from the trash heap and moved it right up."

Trump and Putin's conversation went on for more than two hours.

In the presidential palace, the journalists wondered what was going on. The *Guardian*'s David Smith had been assigned a spot in the balcony. He slipped downstairs and grabbed a seat in the front rows reserved for the White House press corps. Laura Saarikoski, *Helsingin Sanomat*'s DC correspondent, who had covered Trump and written a book about him, sneaked forward too. Saarikoski and her Finnish colleagues agreed on a question they would ask at the press conference, should one of them get picked.

In Saarikoski's view, Trump's lack of interest in Europe was the culmination of a trend. The last US president who was genuinely passionate about Europe, and had deep personal ties to it, was George H. W. Bush, she thought. In 2003 George W. Bush fell out with the French and Germans when he invaded Iraq. Obama's focus was elsewhere, as his administration tilted towards Asia. Now, in the era of Trump, EU–US relations were at a post-war low. "This didn't start with Trump," Saarikoski observed.

Finally the two men emerged and stood at adjoining rostrums. They were an incongruous pair. Putin was smaller—strikingly so—self-assured, optimistic, and cheerful, his pale, passionless features at times breaking into what looked to the press gallery like a winner's smirk.

Trump was bigger and more imposing. He seemed lacking in energy, downbeat, and almost bewildered, his jacket flapping open, and he often gazed listlessly at the floor—the lesser person in the room.

"It was as if Putin had employed a judo move to use his opponent's weight against him," Smith—sitting just feet away—observed.

Watching on TV in America, the ex-CIA agent was blunt. "I looked at the body language and thought, *Okay, Trump's fucked*," the agent said.

In his opening remarks, Putin denied that Russia was guilty of "so-called interference." Russia's leader had long since perfected the art of lying. He lied about big matters (the presence of Russian troops in Crimea during Russia's 2014 military takeover; the GRU's hit on the Skripals) and small. When he dissembled, Putin did it in a business-like manner. There were diplomatic phrases, such as "our American partners." European leaders had got used to Putin's lying, a habit that Boris Nemtsov—the Russian opposition leader murdered in 2015, just outside the Kremlin—described as deeply "pathological."

Standing with Trump, Putin declared that the Russian state never interfered in America's internal affairs, including elections. And never would. Any complaints might be examined by a joint US–Russian cyber forum, a proposal Putin had floated back in Hamburg—and akin to the robber going back to the bank he had just held up with a sawn-off shotgun to discuss security issues with the teller. Putin declared the Cold War "a thing of the past." The era of ideological confrontation was over, he said.

As for the twelve GRU officers . . . Putin said he didn't know much about this and would look into it. He then revealed his big idea, delivered to Trump during their private conversation. Mueller's team could visit Moscow and make inquiries there, aided by Russian investigators who would grill the alleged suspects. A generous offer! Meanwhile, and as a reciprocal gesture, Russian officials could travel to the US to interrogate American intelligence and law enforcement personnel involved in "illegal actions" against Russia.

Leaving aside the false equivalence here, it was obvious to everyone—except perhaps to the president—that Putin's offer was phony. Putin had made a similar offer of assistance to London following Litvinenko's 2006 polonium murder. A group of Scotland Yard police officers flew to Moscow. They found themselves in a ghastly PR pantomime. The detectives weren't allowed to question the two killers directly. Their efforts were thwarted at every turn. A key interview tape disappeared.

Invited to condemn Russian meddling, Trump went on a ramble about his favourite subject: why the Democrats lost an election they really should have won. Relations with Moscow were bad because of the Mueller probe, Trump said, adding, "The main thing—and we discussed this—is zero collusion."

Reuters asked Putin if he had wanted Trump to win and had directed his officials "to help" Trump do so. It was unclear if Putin heard the second part of the question. Nevertheless, his answer was illuminating. Putin said, "Yes, I did. Yes, I did. Because he talked about bringing the US–Russia relationship back to normal."

Russia's preference for Trump was hardly unknown. In the time immediately preceding the election, pro-Kremlin media channels had enthusiastically portrayed him as a friend and statesman, while depicting Clinton as an enemy and a warmonger. After Trump's victory, deputies in the Duma broke into applause and gave a standing ovation, while state TV hosts talked of a bright new era in relations. Even so, Putin's statement was a bold confirmation of official support.

The press conference was going badly for Trump. It was about to get a lot worse. Jonathan Lemire, of the Associated Press, asked two questions that the president had dodged:

"Just now President Putin denied having anything to do with the election interference in 2016. Every US intelligence agency concluded that Russia did.

"My first question for you, sir, is who do you believe? My second question is would you now, with the whole world watching, tell President Putin—would you denounce what happened in 2016 and would you warn him to never do it again?"

It was at this point that Trump might have condemned the GRU's intrusion—something every previous American president would surely have done. Trump could have expressed his intense displeasure and promised that any future attempt to do the same again—in the forthcoming 2018 mid-terms or the 2020 campaign—would lead to a thunderous US response. This might include further sanctions on Russia, travel bans slapped on senior Kremlin figures, even a shutout of Moscow from the Swift payment system. Instead Trump embarked on another incomprehensible riff. He talked about the "server" and Clinton's missing emails, a theme that would recur in his subsequent ill-fated attempts to browbeat the Ukrainians.

Trump said:

"I have President Putin. He just said it's not Russia. I will say this: I don't see any reason why it would be."

He continued:

"What happened to Hillary Clinton's emails? Thirty-three thousand emails—just gone. I think in Russia they wouldn't be gone so easily. I think it's a disgrace we can't get Hillary Clinton's thirty-three thousand emails. So I have great confidence in my intelligence people, but I will tell you that President Putin was extremely strong and powerful in his denial today. And what he did was an incredible offer. He offered to have the people working on the case come and work with their investigators, in respect to the twelve people."

For a few seconds, the press corps carried on typing. And then the magnitude of what Trump had said sank in: the commander in chief had sided with the president of Russia—no friend of America's—over the unanimous advice of his own agencies, all of which had concluded that the Kremlin had attacked America and its democracy in a warlike deed.

Seemingly, Trump viewed Putin as a more reliable source of information than his own intelligence community. To say that this was an error would be an understatement. It looked—at least to Trump's critics—like treason, or something akin to it.

In Finlandia Hall, reporters gawped at the video relay, unable to process what they had just seen. "Our jaws dropped. We were like, 'What did he just say?'" Finnish journalist Iida Simes recalled. Russian correspondents standing next to her were "really happy with everything," she said.

Moments earlier, the *Guardian* journalist Smith had watched as Putin gave a souvenir World Cup football to Trump, telling him the "ball is now in your court." Trump threw it to Melania, sitting in the front row. Smith said he almost caught the ball. He was dumbfounded by Trump's comments; the hall buzzed with furious clicking. "We wrote away, trying to get the story out," he said.

Lemire had a further killer question. He asked Putin if he or the Russian government had compromising material on Trump. Putin's answer: nope. Nobody, he said, had told him about Trump's 2013 visit to Moscow for the Miss Universe beauty contest. (Putin appeared to have forgotten about the lacquered box he gave to Trump as a gift at the time—shades of KGB training here—or the fact that a meeting with Trump had been in his diary and was cancelled at the last minute.)

Some five hundred American businessmen had visited St. Petersburg for Russia's annual economic forum, Putin said. He then asked, "Do you think that we try to collect compromising material on each and every single one of them?" The idea that Russia sought *kompromat* on foreign guests—well, that was "utter nonsense," Putin said. "Please disregard these issues and don't think about this any more again," he added with an eye roll.

For Putin, Helsinki was a triumph. For Trump, it was an unmitigated failure. In the harsh forum of a live press conference it showcased Trump's inadequacies.

The summit was notable too for what wasn't mentioned. Trump didn't bring up the novichok attack on the Skripals—a plot the UK government believed Putin must have personally authorized, in the same way he did with Litvinenko. No mention either of the shooting down in 2014 by Russian troops of the MH-17 passenger plane over eastern Ukraine, in which 298 people died. Or reference to Russia's murderous air campaign in Syria.

In sum, Putin got a free pass. And a prestigious platform where he could show himself as a pre-eminent global statesman. No wonder he was pleased.

TRUMP'S ABJECT PERFORMANCE in Helsinki prompted dismay at home, not just from the president's usual naysayers but also from his loyal friends. On the way back to Washington aboard *Air Force One*, Trump's mood grew foul as he became aware of the torrent of criticism directed against him, the *New York Times* reported.

The question of collusion was eclipsed, at least for a bit, by an even graver accusation: that Trump had betrayed America and Americans. His obeisance to Putin had been on show before. But in Helsinki, even those inclined to give Trump the benefit of the doubt had to admit that his behaviour was so craven and spineless, it was hard not to be suspicious.

John Brennan—the former director of the CIA under Obama, and a persistent Trump critic—wrote that Trump had exceeded the threshold of "high crimes & misdemeanors." In other words, his behaviour was outrageous enough to meet the constitutional standard for removal from office after impeachment. "It was nothing short of treasonous. Not only were Trump's comments imbecilic, he is wholly in the pocket of Putin. Republican Patriots: Where are you??" Brennan tweeted.

Nancy Pelosi—the next Democratic Speaker of the House—echoed this. "What does Putin have on Trump that he's so afraid?" she wondered. It was Pelosi who would later push the button on impeachment over the president's abuses towards Ukraine.

Republicans were damning too. Newt Gingrich, the former Republican Speaker, called Helsinki the "most serious mistake" of Trump's presidency and asked him to clarify his remarks about US intelligence. Gingrich's colleague Paul Ryan said Trump "must appreciate that Russia is not our ally." Senator John McCain called it "one of the most disgraceful performances by an American president in memory."

Even media outlets favourable to the president were unimpressed. The *Wall Street Journal* said it was a "national embarrassment." The *New York Daily News* ran the headline "Open Treason." Beneath was a cartoon of Trump shooting Uncle Sam in the head on Fifth Avenue while holding the hand of a topless Putin.

The idea that Trump was treason-like, or treasony, or treasonish, or a treason weasel seeped into popular culture, gifting comedians and late-night hosts some easy gags. It prompted spikes on Google. According to the *New York Times*, citing Dictionary.com, searches for "treason" went up by 2,943 per cent. In the immediate aftermath of Helsinki, the word "traitor" appeared on Twitter 800,000 times, while "treason" clocked in at 1.2 million mentions.

Some forty-eight hours later, and back in the White House, Trump rowed back on his remarks, sort of. Reading from a prepared script, he claimed that at the crucial moment he "misspoke." He had meant to say, "I don't see why I wouldn't . . ." or "I don't see why it wouldn't be Russia," he explained, saying that he accepted "our intelligence community's conclusion."

Trump delivered this mini-speech with the sincerity of a hostage victim forced by his kidnappers at gunpoint to read a list of demands in front of a wobbly camera, the stubbly guy with the Kalashnikov just out of shot. It was clear that he didn't really mean what he said. As soon as the statement was finished, Trump reverted to his previous ambiguous superposition, in which the question of Russia's culpability was vague and cosmically unknowable.

He observed, "It could be other people also. There are a lot of people out there."

What conclusions might we draw? Trump's behaviour in Helsinki was part of a pattern. His next encounter with Putin took place almost a year later, in Osaka, Japan, on the sidelines of the G20 summit. With journalists looking on, the pair smiled and swapped jokes about "fake news media." Asked if he would warn Putin not to interfere again in America's elections, Trump said, "Yes, of course I will." He grinned, raised a finger, and—in playful mock rebuke—told Vladimir: "Don't meddle in our election."

This ingratiating little show contrasted with Theresa May's awkward meeting with Putin at the same summit—a glum affair, in which the British prime minister refused to smile. According to Downing Street, she demanded that Putin hand over the two Skripal poisoners for trial and complained of Russia's malign activity around the world—disinformation, cyber attacks, state murder. All subjects not mentioned by the US president.

Way back, the Russians had psychoanalyzed Trump and identified him as having no limits. Trump wasn't a traitor in the conventional sense, it seemed. Nor did he hate America. Rather, he was someone with no moral compass, Moscow concluded. If treason, then it was of the pedestrian kind. Trump was driven by rank amorality and self-advancement, as shown by the way he had done business in a long career of screwing banks, contractors, the IRS, and practically everybody else.

Now everything seemed to be for sale, if the transaction bene-fited Trump personally, including American foreign policy. These were weaknesses that Russia could exploit. Meanwhile, Putin played a role laid out by Rudyard Kipling in the *Jungle Book*—that of "you and I," the eternal secret friend or blood brother.

One person sitting in London followed Helsinki and Osaka keenly. His name was Christopher Steele. His dossier on Trump's relationship with Russia—a controversial document, to say the least—still offered the most persuasive explanation of Trump's cowed behaviour with Putin and the anxious shadow that crossed Trump's face whenever the two men met.

CHAPTER 4

FOUR PILLARS

London
JULY 2018

It doesn't matter how often Trump says it's fake and fraudulent. That doesn't make it so.
CHRISTOPHER STEELE ON HIS TRUMP–RUSSIA DOSSIER

A month after Helsinki I made my way by foot and Tube to London's Victoria Station. The district is home to Buckingham Palace—an ugly, outsize slab of a building, to my mind—as well as to tourists, cafés, and pubs.

If Trump and his most fervent supporters were to be believed, this was also the birthplace of a "deep state" coup against the president of the United States. London was ground zero in a perfidious scheme to bring down a great man. It was the place where bad Brits—or foreign agents, as Trump liked to call them—had done some spying.

Not far from the station is Victoria Square. It's an oasis of quiet, set back from the traffic streaming past the Queen's busy front door. There is a small garden, fenced off with traditional black railings and lanterns, with a statue of Queen Victoria and an Indian bean tree. A group of cream-coloured mansions look over it. Ian Fleming lived in an elegant corner house. Fleming worked in British naval intelligence before becoming a thriller writer and thinking up his most popular and enduring creation, James Bond.

In 1963 Fleming threw a party after the film premiere of his novel *From Russia with Love*. The movie, starring Sean Connery, includes a scene where the Soviets secretly film Bond—agent 007—making love with a glamorous Russian cipher clerk, Tatiana Romanova, in an Istanbul hotel room. After vanquishing the villains of SMERSH, Bond retrieves the sex tape. He drops it from a gondola into Venice's Grand Canal.

The plot wasn't Fleming's invention. It was espionage reality. Throughout the Cold War Moscow sought to entrap, compromise, blackmail, and recruit Western visitors. One method was to use "swallows" run by the KGB's Second Chief Directorate. Swallows were female agents sent to sleep with a target. Victims included ambassadors (a British one and a French one); a CIA station chief; a lonesome US Marine guard; and visiting American businessmen. Swallows were even sent to seduce Her Majesty's diplomats travelling on the Trans-Siberian Railway.

Putin's secret police carried on this KGB tradition, taping foreigners during intimate moments, and Russian critics as well. As FSB chief, in 1999 Putin had filmed Prosecutor General Yuri Skuratov frolicking in the early hours with two prostitutes. (Skuratov's error was to investigate President Yeltsin, Putin's then boss. The prosecutor was forced to resign after steamy highlights were shown on TV.)

As every diplomat in Russia knew, the FSB had a specialist break-in and bugging department. It installed devices in private apartments, including my own in Moscow, where I spent four years as the *Guardian* correspondent between 2007 and 2011. Quite often the FSB broke into the family home, where I lived with my wife, Phoebe, and our two small children. On one occasion Putin's goons left behind a sex and relationships manual next to the marital bed, bookmarked to a page on orgasms. This was crude and darkly amusing. The message: we are watching you.

Might something similar have happened to Trump?

One of Fleming's real-life neighbours had claimed as much. Cut north from Fleming's mansion and you reach Grosvenor Gardens. The office of Orbis Business Intelligence is at numbers 9–11. You go through a classical pillared entrance and take a lift or stairs up to the second floor and an L-shaped suite of rooms, the bigger one decked out with desks, computers, and a *National Geographic* map of the world. There is a smaller boardroom used for client meetings, with a glass-fronted bookshelf containing works on espionage.

The office belongs to Steele and Christopher Burrows. Steele spent twenty-two years working for SIS—Britain's Secret Intelligence Service. Orbis was once known to a group of loyal clients, mostly blue-chip British companies. By the time of Trump's Finland meeting with Putin its profile had exploded. The Washington-based research firm that commissioned Steele's dossier, Fusion GPS, was equally well known. Or, as its founders Glenn Simpson and Peter Fritsch put it, it was in a "shitload of trouble." Legal suits, cyber attacks, endless hit pieces in the pro-Trump media . . . the two firms' activities had certainly made the president and his supporters mad.

As imagined by some in Washington, Orbis was the centre of a teeming and treasonous conspiracy.

The reality was rather different. Steele wasn't Bond, SIS's most famous fictional spy. His lifestyle was more regular. He journeyed to work from his home in Farnham, Surrey, in a crowded commuter train strewn with copies of the free sheet *Metro* and the Russian-owned *Evening Standard*. In appearance Steele was smart—jacket and tie—of medium height, black hair going grey as he entered his mid-fifties, good at eye contact, and with a sharp intelligence and an encyclopedic knowledge of Russian names and contacts.

Steele came from a less privileged background than many of his ex-colleagues from the British spy world. He had working-class roots. His grandfather was a Welsh miner; a great-uncle died in a pit accident; Dad was a weather forecaster for the Royal Air Force. Much of his childhood was spent on military bases—Aden, Cyprus, and the Shetland Islands. An unlikely backstory for the world's most high-profile ex-spy.

I MET STEELE on the concourse of Victoria Station. I was curious to learn what he made of Helsinki. And if he stood by his memos on Trump's links with Russia, written in 2016—the dossier as leaked by the former US assistant secretary of state David Kramer during a meeting in Foggy Bottom. (Kramer, an aide to Senator McCain, had given the dossier to *BuzzFeed* reporter Ken Bensinger. This was soon before Trump moved into the White House. The fallout from Kramer's well-meant gesture continued.)

It was mid-morning. I met Steele at the bottom of an escalator. We travelled upwards, walked through an upper-storey shopping centre, found an American diner, and sat down at a table with red banquette seats and shiny chrome fittings. Nobody else seemed to be around. We ordered breakfast—a couple of bacon and egg muffins, cappuccino for Steele, unlimited black coffee for me.

The events of Finland were fresh. And, we agreed, incredible.

What was remarkable, Steele said, was that Putin had openly admitted his support for Trump: "Most leaders would say, 'We want a good relationship with America. We don't get involved between candidates.' That's not what Putin said. We got it from his mouth."

He mused, "We are living in a strange world." And, "Why is Trump meeting in secret with Putin for two hours without any official present? You have to pinch yourself with some of this stuff."

The Helsinki press conference, I said, strengthened the idea that Trump was beholden to Moscow in some profound and intangible way. Might Trump be considered a Russian asset?

As Steele saw it, Kremlin assets fell into three broad categories. The first was a secret agent—a fully recruited operative who accepted direct instructions from Moscow. The second was an agent of influence. That was a person who willingly supplied a flow of intelligence to Moscow Centre, as the KGB and its successors were known, but who wasn't formally a spy. The KGB's aspiration was to promote an asset to full agent status.

Trump was too volatile and unpredictable for that, Steele argued. He was a better fit with a third, lesser category: confidential contact, or *doveritelnaya svyaz* in KGB language. This was a high-level source who might supply information to Russia, wittingly or unwittingly, and who was unlikely to develop into a full-blown secret operative or agent in the field.

Since the dossier came out Orbis and Fusion had been under fire. The attacks came from multiple directions. Steele's company was hit with more than eight thousand cyber raids, suspected Russian ones. From Trump there was a regular mauling. The president described him as "a failed British spy," a "foreign agent," "discredited," a "Trump hater," and a "lowlife," among other insults shared with his sixty million Twitter followers. Steele's professional work was "phony," "corrupt and fake," the dossier an outrageous slur.

How was he taking all this? Steele seemed sanguine about being vilified by the leader of the free world, though clearly this wasn't something he relished much. His confidence stemmed from a certainty that his dossier was—with a few caveats—fundamentally right. As he put it, "It doesn't matter how often Trump says it's fake and fraudulent. That doesn't make it so."

The dossier's central idea was that Russia had wanted Trump to win: something Putin had recently confirmed and that Mueller's report would later corroborate. It had supported, assisted, and cultivated Trump for at least five years, Steele's sources had reported.

Moscow's aim in backing Trump was to drive a wedge between America and its traditional allies. Putin wanted to return to a nineteenth-century model of great-power politics and to disrupt the ideals-based international order established after World War II, the sources said. These were long-standing KGB goals. With Trump, to some degree, this transatlantic rift had actually happened.

The dossier's most contentious aspect concerned Trump's sexual behaviour and the question of entrapment. Russian spies, Steele's sources said, had amassed compromising material on Trump, some of it collected during Trump's many trips to Moscow, going all the way back to July 1987, when he toured the Soviet capital and Leningrad with his Czechoslovak-born wife, Ivana. This *kompromat* could be exploited to blackmail him, the sources said.

In November 2013 the FSB had used hidden cameras and microphones to record Trump in the presidential suite of Moscow's Ritz-Carlton, it was claimed. Knowing his peccadilloes, it had "arranged" a golden shower show featuring two prostitutes. The hotel was "notorious for this kind of thing," Steele explained.

Okay, but might the Russians have made up the Ritz-Carlton episode to embarrass and hobble Trump? Or embellished a true story with additional invented detail?

Steele acknowledged that the existence of a covert FSB recording was "very difficult to prove."

But he said he firmly believed the incident happened. Seven separate sources and subsources had confirmed the hotel allegation, two of them from inside the Ritz itself. Trump's wish to defile Obama was "deep-seated." (The prostitutes allegedly urinated on the bed where the Obamas had slept.) The idea went back to the 2011 Washington press correspondents' dinner, when Obama had poked fun at Trump, who was sitting in the audience, mocking Trump's "birtherist" fantasies and his presidential ambitions—leaving Trump in a state of smouldering fury and humiliation.

"This is one of the reasons Trump is in politics," Steele suggested.

By way of response to these crushing allegations, the president and his allies had come up with an alternative version of reality. It was a mythical retelling of events—a counter-plot so sprawling and baroque that it became increasingly difficult to follow. It was a conspiracy theory. It exonerated Trump by flipping what had actually happened on its head. There was collusion . . . by the Democrats.

This Trump version said Russia and its spies were not to blame. Rather it was the "deep state"—Obama and his intelligence chiefs—who had done the real and damaging "spying." They had "spied" on Trump and his campaign. The Brits had assisted. This treasonous behaviour had been executed to prevent Trump from becoming president. When he won anyway, the "deep state" sought to remove him in an illegal coup or takedown.

Steele was a leading member of this conspiracy. Other guilty parties included Brennan; Hillary (who colluded with the Russians and the Ukrainians); Bruce Ohr, Steele's contact inside the Department of Justice; "angry Democrats" generally; Mueller; ex-FBI chief James Comey; and sacked FBI lovers Peter Stroyk and Lisa Page. Plus the fake news *New York Times*, CNN, et al., who were co-parties to the deception.

The myth made little sense. It included wildly contradictory elements. Plus a chronology so wonky and inconsistent it might have fallen from an episode of the popular time-travelling sci-fi TV show *Doctor Who*. It was hard to know if Trump genuinely believed in his "deep state" narrative, or simply saw his counter-version as a way of confusing the voters, and of shoring up his fact-indifferent Republican base.

Is any of this true? I wondered.

One claim was that Steele had written his dossier at the behest of the Kremlin. Well? "I'm more likely to go to the moon than work for the Russian government," he replied. Another was that

Russia's enemy Ukraine had fed disinformation into his memos. "Absolute bollocks," Steele said. A third, more plausible variation: the Russian tycoon Oleg Deripaska had passed dubious intelligence to Steele via his lawyers. "Untrue," Steele said. "No one in government had a role in the dossier. Nor did oligarchs."

As Steele saw it, these claims were outright inventions, lies, and innuendos. Right or not, they formed the basis of articles and TV interviews, of solemn press statements by leading Republican representatives, and of GOP talking points aired in Capitol Hill hearings screened live on the cable news channel C-SPAN. *The Trump-supporting US media is out to impugn my motives and damage my reputation*, Steele thought. Some of these complicit outlets were influential, such as Fox News or the *Wall Street Journal* and *The Hill*, which would go on to play a role in the Ukraine impeachment scandal. Others—the conservative *Daily Caller* or the *Gateway Pundit*—were pretty marginal.

This feeding frenzy was happening because the dossier was right, he believed. Otherwise, why bother? The attacks hadn't succeeded because they failed to engage with its substance. "They can't because it's true. I would say they have not landed a single punch," he said. Some of these hit pieces struck him as "desperate."

Steele was certain he'd got nothing "fundamentally wrong," a view that remained the same after Mueller's report emerged. The dossier was, in Steele's assessment, "80 to 90 per cent correct." It didn't purport to be wholly perfect but it did claim to be credible—a "crucial distinction," as Simpson put it. There were "a few minor mistakes" in the memos, as is the case with any raw intelligence product, Steele said. Some dates may have been "fuzzy." It was originally conceived as a jumping-off point for further investigation, something to be "briefed off orally" rather than meant for publication.

Overall the dossier offered the most plausible account of why Trump behaved so weirdly and meekly towards Putin. It laid out some of the multiple strands connecting Trump's team with the Russians. A proven network of sources and subsources underlay it. These were people with access to internal conversations in Moscow, taking place in the corridors of power, sources who—while human and therefore fallible—had previously got it right.

The dossier had "four pillars," Steele said:

Pillar one: Russia interfered in the 2016 US election, in an operation approved at the highest level.

Pillar two: Its goal was not just to denigrate Clinton and create chaos but also to get Trump elected as US president.

Pillar three: The Kremlin had been cultivating Trump over a sustained period, going back at least five years.

Pillar four: Trump and his circle had responded positively to Russia's overtures.

The special counsel and Steele had both been investigating Russia's influence operations around the 2016 US election. But, as Steele noted, their approaches were different. "I'm a counter-intelligence intelligence officer, not a prosecutor," he pointed out.

Mueller was trying to find legal evidence sufficient to prove—or disprove—a criminal conspiracy. This was a high standard. Steele was examining similar events from a counter-intelligence perspective. As he noted, his subsources were in Russia, not America. None of them would appear before a US grand jury. To do so would be a death wish. Orbis had been commissioned to produce HUMINT—human intelligence—gathered from Russian Foreign Ministry officials and former high-level intelligence officers still active in the Kremlin. As Burrows put it to me, "What you are doing is egressing commentary from people who may have only a partial picture of what's going on." Some of it was "unprovable." Or it might not be "wholly accurate," Burrows said.

Steele's work on the dossier was the result of three decades spent covering Russia, much of it as a government spy. He entered via a well-established route: a degree at Girton College, Cambridge, followed by an interview with MI6 and an intensive Russian-language course in London.

One of the first terms Steele learned as a junior intelligence officer was an acronym, ORBAT—order of battle. This referred to the hierarchy within the KGB and its residencies based in embassies abroad. There were the PR Line (political intelligence and active measures), the KR line (counter-intelligence and security), and Line X (scientific and technical). Plus Line N, which supported illegal undercover agents.

It was a thrilling time to be an MI6 spy. The Eastern Bloc was unravelling; the ideological plates that held the twentieth century together were shifting rapidly. Soon after the fall of the Berlin Wall, Steele was sent to the Soviet Union. From April 1990 to April 1993 he was based at the British embassy in Moscow, officially working as a "diplomat" and second secretary, and travelling across the country at a time of rapid change.

Steele watched close up as the Soviet Union fell apart. In August 1991 the KGB tried to seize power in a coup. Steele was in Moscow. He walked into the centre of the capital and saw Yeltsin denounce the plotters from a tank in front of the main government building, the "White House." Gorbachev survived and returned from house arrest in Crimea. Steele met him days later. Soon afterwards the UK's then prime minister John Major flew to Moscow. (Steele's father was visiting and went to Red Square, where Major bumped into him and mistook him for a local.)

By the time Steele exited Moscow the USSR was gone, replaced by the Russian Federation.

There were strong indications that despite the change of regime, the Soviet system was still intact. This was especially true of its secret enforcers, the KGB. During his Moscow tour KGB officers routinely tailed Steele. They broke into his apartment, as they did with my own office fifteen years later, which was next to Steele's in a Gruzinsky Pereulok block. The KGB disappeared for only a brief moment during the coup. In other East European revolutions, the secret police ran away, never to come back. In Russia they resumed surveillance three days later.

By the 2000s, after a spell at the British embassy in Paris, Steele was in charge of Russian operations in London. He was based at MI6's headquarters in Vauxhall Cross, overlooking the Thames River.

Steele tracked how Putin's Russia was acting with increasing boldness and aggression. The number of Russian spies in the UK surpassed Cold War levels. In 2006 Litvinenko was poisoned in London. The murder stunned British intelligence and coloured Steele's already gloomy view of Moscow. Steele was MI6's lead investigator. He quickly concluded that the Kremlin was behind the assassination. It was—as he saw it—a seminal event. It marked a paradigm change in Russian behaviour: the first use of a radio-active device by a state actor in the West. He briefed Tony Blair's government. Some ministers understood that Putin was now effec-tively at war with liberal democracy, seeking to destroy it. Others struggled to understand this ghoulish plot.

The UK's response to Litvinenko was low-key—a few Russian diplomats kicked out. London had trouble persuading its allies to act; George W. Bush was quite taken by Putin, it seemed. The poverty of the British response led to more rogue state episodes by Russia, in Steele's analysis: the military invasions of Georgia and Ukraine and Skripal's 2018 poisoning, a few months before we met—a reminder, if it were needed, that he had to protect his own sources at any cost. The West seemed to think restraint would lead to restored relations with Russia. It didn't.

Steele, then, was someone who had direct experience of the Kremlin's methods. He knew about political murder and poison; bugging, surveillance, and apartment-breaking; and how to recruit sources and use secret agents. He understood how to sift real from planted information. He wouldn't discuss precisely what tasks he had done for MI6. Such matters were officially secret.

But he could talk in general terms. With any source, you would use a critical box of tools. One question: has the information been falsified by third parties or falsely seeded by state operatives? There were questions about the reliability of a source. Is the source in a position to know this information? And what sort of reporting track record does he or she have?

Steele used these work skills on the dossier. He got his best material from Moscow at the beginning of his inquiry, he said, when nobody was asking questions about Trump–Russia and when Clinton's victory seemed inevitable. One "collector" in particular provided invaluable intelligence. The anonymous source was a "remarkable person with a remarkable story who deserves a medal for service to the West," Steele said.

This material on cultivation and *kompromat* appeared in Steele's first memo, written in June 2016. Subsequently it became harder to obtain intelligence from inside Russian power circles, he said, as the GRU's hacking operation was exposed and Trump's links with Moscow came to the fore.

Steele was confident he hadn't been fed disinformation. The Russians genuinely wanted Trump to win at a time when victory seemed beyond his grasp. It made no logical sense for them to damage him—especially at first, when he was behind in the polls. And what about his sources? None of them had vanished, an apparent sign that they hadn't been playing a double game or had duped him.

Steele believed the Russian espionage visible in 2016 was still going at full pace, in the US and elsewhere, and would continue in 2020 and beyond. "Despite all the decay and dysfunction the Russians remain, and probably always will be, very formidable adversaries. It is perilous to underestimate them," he said, according to Simpson. There were some signs that Moscow had shifted its attention to Europe. Orbis was tracking Russian interference in Western elections—in France, Germany, Italy, Spain, and the UK. The lack of pushback emboldened Putin.

THE WAITRESS FROM Ed's Easy Diner brought us a refill of coffee. The restaurant was still empty, somewhere in the dead zone between morning and the lunchtime rush.

The campaign against Steele went beyond hit pieces in the American right-wing media. Leading Republicans were actively seeking information on his links with the FBI. Two congressional staffers working for Devin Nunes, the then chair of the House Intelligence Committee, flew to London in an apparent attempt to ambush Steele. Soon after my meeting with Steele, Nunes made his own London trip. The attacks on Steele included congressional demands for information and FoI requests. They were explicitly political. The objective was to discredit the FBI's Russia counter-intelligence probe and to characterize it as illegal and anti-Trump. And to suggest that ideological or financial factors shaped Steele's work—an allegation he wholly rejected.

Trump seemed determined to go after his opponents and to use the Justice Department to do so. This was arguably an abuse of power and a manifestation of the same shadowy tendencies that would lead to his impeachment.

The president was reluctant to divulge material that cast him in a bad light, such as his tax returns. He had no scruples about selectively declassifying documents if they served his purpose and could be spun as evidence of "deep state" crime. Steele was key. If you could prove the dossier was false or improperly utilized, then its accusations of collusion dropped away. It could be dismissed as political trash, a view shared by some high-brow commentators from the left.

With time, this invented conspiracy took on a Frankenstein-like life. It gained new impetus in 2019, once William Barr became Trump's attorney general. The hunt for "evidence" would shift to Ukraine; Nunes would team up with Trump's personal lawyer Rudy Giuliani; the White House would sink into deeper scandal.

Steele said there was nothing improper about his links with the FBI, which went back almost a decade. His interactions with the bureau were fully authorized—by the Department of Justice and by the government in London.

His first private sector assignment was with the English Football Association. England was bidding to host the 2018 World Cup, and Russia was its chief rival. Steele's brief was to investigate Moscow's bid. His sources said Russia had initiated a major influence operation, ahead of a vote by the executive committee of FIFA, the sport's governing body, in Zurich. One target was Sepp Blatter, FIFA's president.

At first Putin was a reluctant backer of Russia's bid and only become actively involved in mid-2010, when it seemed that Russia might lose. Russia's victory, the sources said, came about through bribery. Putin instructed a group of oligarchs to sway the vote. One played a crucial role. Steele found a covert operation carried out by billionaire intermediaries—a deniable one, naturally, with nothing ever written down.

In 2011 Steele gave his findings to the FBI. No payment was involved. His information helped to kick-start a Stateside investigation into FIFA murk.

Federal prosecutors went on to indict fourteen individuals. The Kremlin believed that the US probe was a politically motivated attempt to strip Russia of the World Cup, Steele's source reported, adding that Blatter's resignation in 2015 as FIFA's president "saved" the tournament for Moscow.

In August 2013 the FBI put Steele on its payroll. The bureau formally contracted Orbis to supply intelligence. Steele wrote to his old employer MI6, clearing this new arrangement with the head of liaison. Despite what Republicans claimed, Steele was never an FBI "source." He was a subcontractor. His role was to pass information on Moscow's global espionage operations to Washington.

The FBI deemed Steele credible. This perception grew when he passed on 120 reports on Russia's war in Ukraine, written between early 2014 and early 2016. They were shared inside the US government. One government employee who read them said they featured sensitive information from the post-Soviet world and the Russian and Ukrainian leaderships.

This person told me, "The intelligence was excellent. It was good material. The sources were protected. It was well sourced, as far as I could tell, and matched other information the State Department had. None of it related to domestic US politics or partisan issues." Steele's summaries found their way up to Victoria Nuland, the then assistant secretary responsible for Europe.

Steele provided the FBI with memos on other themes. One note set out tasking instructions for Russia's spy agencies—orders telling the GRU, SVR, and FSB to gather intelligence on Western sanctions and the supply of lethal weapons to Ukraine. Another concerned the Kremlin's relations with the European far right and the National Front of France's Marine Le Pen. A third dealt with Russia's attempts to manipulate international sports and to discredit the world anti-doping agency.

These sources were the same sources that would go on to supply information on Trump.

THE TRUE STORY of the FBI and the dossier was straightforward. Steele left MI6 for private business with certain conditions attached. One was an obligation to report national security concerns to his former service. He began his Trump investigation after Simpson and Fritsch hired him to provide human intelligence. The former *Wall Street Journal* reporters had started their own open-source probe in August 2015 on behalf of a Republican client. By the time Steele joined in May 2016 the Democrats had taken over the contract. Steele discovered this later, after he had already asked his source network to find out about Trump's Russia ties.

As with his investigation into soccer corruption, Steele passed his subsequent "hair-raising" discoveries about Trump to the FBI. In June 2016 he flew with Burrows to Rome. There they met an FBI contact, Michael Gaeta—the former head of the bureau's Eurasia and Serious Crime Division, whom Steele knew from the FIFA probe. Gaeta was an authority on Russian organized crime. He was working at the US embassy in Rome, liaising with Italy's police and security services. In October 2016 a second meeting took place in London, between Steele and four FBI agents.

Soon afterwards Steele and the bureau fell out. The FBI was unhappy that Steele had given off-the-record briefings to journalists—to *Mother Jones*, Yahoo News, the *New York Times*, and others, at Fusion's initiative. Steele pointed out that the dossier belonged to a private client. It was up to the client what should be done with it. He asked the FBI why it had reopened its investigation into Clinton's emails—while sitting on explosive material concerning Russia and Trump. At this point the FBI "backed off," Steele said.

All of his interactions with the FBI were formally authorized, Steele said. So were his conversations with Bruce Ohr, the former head of the Justice Department's Organized Crime and Racketeering Division. Steele knew Ohr from his MI6 days. They had recently teamed up on a National Security Council project to recruit Russian oligarchs as intelligence assets. Ohr's wife, Nellie, a former CIA analyst, worked for Fusion GPS. Neither of the

Ohrs had anything to do with the dossier, Steele said, adding that Ohr was a "decent and upstanding" public servant who had been unfairly "crucified" by malicious smears.

In late October 2016 the FBI ended its contract with Orbis, but Steele's relationship with the bureau continued. Meanwhile, he raised the alarm in London. In November he briefed the UK's top security official, Charles Farr. Farr took Steele's reporting extremely seriously. An ex-MI6 officer himself, he wrote an executive summary and shared it with the cabinet and Andrew Parker, the head of MI5.

The British government and MI6 subsequently brokered a meeting with Mueller's office. In September 2017 two members of the special counsel's team flew to London and spent two days debriefing Steele in Victoria. He talked them through the dossier and his counter-intelligence findings. The agents—a man and a woman—flew home. By early 2018 Mueller had "caught up" and confirmed much of his reporting, Steele said.

Republican attacks on Ohr were part of a dark trend, Steele believed: the politicization of intelligence by an unscrupulous White House. Steele was told that confidential details from his FBI file were being "sprayed around" DC. There was an attempt by congressional Republicans to discover his sources—something that could endanger them. One of Steele's assignments at MI6 was to prepare top-level intelligence that went across the Atlantic by way of the president's "daily brief." British spies were now wary about sharing highly classified material with Trump, fearing it might reach the Russians or be used by family members to cut commercial deals in China or elsewhere.

As the Russian scandal roiled Washington, Steele was caught in a crossfire between Democrats and Republicans. In 2018 Trump declassified a four-page memo written by Nunes. It alleged that the FBI had used Steele's dossier to obtain a Foreign Intelligence

Surveillance Act (FISA) warrant to snoop on Trump's former foreign policy aide, Carter Page.

Steele told me he knew nothing about the FISA warrant on Page, a secret government process. The dossier only reached the relevant FBI team in mid-September 2016, several months after the FBI's Russia probe had already begun.

Trump's campaign against Steele might have been highly personal, but it was being enacted using full executive powers. The Justice Department appointed an inspector general, Michael Horowitz, to review the Page affair and comb through Steele's history with the FBI. Horowitz was engaged in this task as Steele and I ate our breakfast muffins.

Horowitz's report cleared the FBI of a "deep state" plot. At the same time, it was critical of the FBI's handling of the FISA application process. On the eve of publication, Barr declassified several pages of sensitive information concerning Steele's main "collector," known as the "primary subsource."

This was a calculated move by Barr. It was done to damage and discredit Steele, who was given no opportunity to respond. In the frenzied months after the dossier was published, the FBI's Washington office interviewed the "subsource" twice. He distanced himself from his own work and suggested that much of the intelligence passed to Steele was "word of mouth and hearsay," "conversations had over beers," and—concerning Trump's sexual behaviour—"jest." The tenor of Steele's reports was more "conclusive" than was justified, he said.

There were good reasons why the "primary subsource" would wish to downplay the dossier and his role in it. Its publication left him vulnerable, isolated, and terrified of Kremlin retribution—a fear that was entirely reasonable, given Skripal's fate. The "subsource" was angry with Orbis and worried. It had put him in danger, he felt.

In Machiavellian style Barr had consciously created a dilemma for Steele. He knew that Steele couldn't discuss his sources publicly. In truth, the "sub-source" had a long record of reporting. Over the years, his information had been of variable quality. None of it turned out to be embellished or the product of disinformation. Orbis had meticulously recorded its debriefings with him. It could point this out and put him at legal risk for misleading the FBI. Or it could take the hit. Source protection superseded everything in the business intelligence world. And so, out of necessity, Steele accepted damage to his reputation.

Horowitz's report revealed a tantalizing fact known only to a few of Steele's close colleagues. In 2007, while working for MI6, he met Ivanka Trump at a dinner in London. They kept in touch and developed a "personal" relationship. In 2010 Steele met Ivanka at Trump Tower in New York and discussed the possibility of Orbis working for the Trump Organization. He bought her a gift: a tartan scarf in the MacLeod colours, in honour of Trump's Scottish mother, purchased in Edinburgh. Steele told the FBI that the idea he was biased against Trump from the beginning was "ridiculous." If anything, he was "favourably disposed" towards the family and had chatted with Ivanka about her Scottish ancestry.

In 2019 Barr announced a second review into the FBI's Russia investigation, led by attorney John Durham. It would examine whether FBI officials were guilty of anti-Trump feeling. Durham's mandate included gathering information from foreign states. Where his criminal probe might go was unclear. It was inevitable that the UK would be sucked in, with a small outside chance that charges of some kind might be filed against Steele.

What would the UK government do if faced with a highly politicized request from the US for Steele's extradition? You would like to think that Britain would say no. London's mayor, Sadiq Khan, openly criticized Trump. Generally, though, British politicians seemed cowed by the president and anxious not to offend him, at a time when Downing Street was seeking a post-Brexit trade deal with the US.

Trump's animus towards the Brits grew with the leak of unflattering cables by the UK's ambassador in Washington, Sir Kim Darroch. Darroch described the Trump administration as "uniquely dysfunctional" and "inept." He wrote that Trump "radiates insecurity." And "Something could emerge that leads to [his] disgrace and downfall." Darroch's private remarks weren't unusual—practically all the ambassadors in Washington agreed. Darroch was forced to quit after Boris Johnson—soon to be prime minister—refused to defend him. Johnson probably wouldn't defend Steele either.

Overall Steele was pessimistic about American democracy. His view was that there would be no return to normal once Trump exited and that under him US institutions were being permanently degraded as his presidency shaded into "regime." Partisanship, a politically appointed judiciary, culture wars, a blatant disregard for truth and facts—all looked like trends that were there to stay. Trump's bombastic mode of rule had similarities with Mussolini's Italy, Steele reflected—but with the power of Germany underneath.

And what about his enemies in Moscow? Was he at risk? During the Cold War the KGB bugged, surveilled, and hounded foreign spies. It didn't kill them. It had nastier rules for Russians whom it judged to be traitors. Steele probably wasn't in physical danger. At the same time, it seemed likely that Russian intelligence would monitor him carefully. Later Steele would receive confirmation of this.

We left the American diner, Steele first, and headed off on separate paths. Steele's sources had reported that Trump's business dealings with Russia were extensive. And hidden. The president had insisted that they didn't exist.

Actually, during his election campaign Trump had secretly sought Kremlin help to make real one of his long-cherished ambitions: a skyscraper, no less, towering over the skyline of a foreign city and adorned with the name "Trump."

CHAPTER 5

THE SERVANTS

New York–Moscow
2015–2020

*My weakness can be characterized as a blind
loyalty to Donald Trump.*
MICHAEL COHEN, DECEMBER 2018

Moscow, January 2016. Elena Poliakova was scrolling through her office emails. Poliakova worked as personal assistant to one of the most powerful men in Russia. Her boss was Dmitry Peskov, Putin's press secretary and long-time deputy chief of staff.

In the soap opera of Kremlin politics Peskov appeared in most daily episodes. He could be seen on the TV news standing at the president's side or whispering in his ear at Putin's annual all-Russia press conferences—a tall, immediately recognizable figure with groomed features and a sandy moustache. Peskov grew up abroad, the son of a diplomat. He joined the Soviet Foreign Service, translated for Prime Minister Putin, and in 2000 joined him in the Kremlin as official spokesperson.

Typically Peskov's public email account was filled with junk. There were notes from Russian reporters seeking comment, requests from newly arrived foreign correspondents demanding exclusive interviews with Putin. Naive souls! These, almost always, went in the wastebasket. And other flotsam and jetsam: script proposals, circulars from luxury brands, and invitations to exclusive cocktail parties. As a VIP, Peskov got plenty of those.

Amid this electronic rubbish Poliakova spotted an email written in English. The sender was someone called Michael Cohen. Cohen had sent his message to Moscow several times, it emerged later. He had initially got the address for Peskov wrong, mistyping "gof.ru" instead of "gov.ru." He fired off a further two emails, two days apart. He was anxious to speak with Sergei Ivanov, Putin's chief of staff.

Cohen, Poliakov learned, was an American. And something of a supplicant. He wanted the Kremlin's help.

His January 14, 2016, email read:

Dear Mr. Peskov,

Over the past few months, I have been working with a company based in Russia regarding the development of a Trump Tower-Moscow project at Moscow City.

Without getting into lengthy specifics, the communication between our two sides has stalled. As this project is too important I am hereby requesting your assistance.

I respectfully request someone, preferably you; contact me so that I might discuss the specifics as well as arranging meetings with the appropriate individuals.

I thank you in advance for your assistance and look forward to hearing from you soon.

Random begging emails of this kind normally went unanswered. But the mention of "Trump" gave Cohen's note an entirely different—almost magical—quality. A quick Google search would have confirmed that Cohen was an executive vice president of the Trump Organization. And a lawyer. He had worked with Trump since 2007. He was special counsel to an American running for president—one who just happened to be the Kremlin's preferred Republican candidate.

Peskov, we can infer, must have told Poliakova to reply. On January 20 she wrote back to Cohen using her personal email account. She said she had been trying to reach him. She gave him her number. After finding her message, Cohen got up—it was 6:00 a.m. in New York—and dialled Moscow. They spent twenty minutes talking, lawyer and Kremlin aide. Poliakova asked detailed questions. She took notes.

The story of Trump Tower Moscow, as relayed by Cohen to the Russian government, was one of delay and frustration, as well as of vision, ambition, and soaring entrepreneurship.

Trump's dream of building a hotel in Moscow went all the way back to 1987, when the Soviet government invited him to the USSR to discuss potential business opportunities. The travel agency Intourist, its guides and officials KGB officers and informants, arranged the trip. Trump travelled to Moscow and Leningrad, met with Soviet officials, and on returning home mused about a possible presidential bid, even taking out newspaper ads in the *Washington Post* to share his foreign policy ideas. But the dream didn't lead anywhere. No hotel got built.

The dream came back when Trump revisited Moscow in 2013 for the Miss Universe beauty pageant. His host was Azeri Russian property tycoon Aras Agalarov. In the sugary aftermath of the event Trump and Agalarov talked about building a hotel on a site owned by Agalarov's Crocus Group. By 2014 negotiations had petered out. In summer 2015 the Trump Organization started dealing with another Moscow firm, the I. C. Expert Investment Company. A letter of intent was signed. Despite this, nothing was happening.

As Cohen correctly recognized, political support was necessary if Trump's plan were ever to become a reality. The Moscow property market was a swamp of corruption, even for those familiar with its devious ways; hence Cohen's email to Peskov. Cohen asked Poliakova if the Kremlin might help move the project along. Cohen's celebrity boss needed land. And money. Could the Russian government assist in locating a prime real-estate spot where the 150-room hotel, plus 250 top-end condominiums and a "Spa by Ivanka Trump," might be built? And, ideally, finance the project?

Poliakova was attentive and professional, Cohen said. She ended the conversation saying she would go away and consult with others in Russia. Cohen saved her contact information in his Microsoft Trump Organization file. It was 6:22 a.m.; New York was waking up.

By accident or design Cohen had got through to the right man. Peskov was the portal through which—with a bit of political luck—you might reach Putin, Russia's ultimate decision maker.

Peskov didn't normally deal with municipal issues. His function was to comment about the news of the day to the domestic and international media. He spoke perfect English (and Turkish and Arabic, serving twice in the 1990s at the Russian embassy in Ankara). His biography and immaculate language skills hinted at foreign intelligence training—something Peskov naturally denied. Spy or not, he was the main point of contact between the Kremlin and the Western world, a functionary who translated and ventriloquized his master's thoughts.

He was also someone who lied. So what?! It went with the territory. Peskov's day-to-day job involved large dollops of deceit, faking the appearance of democracy where none existed. His lies were officially sanctioned, delivered on behalf of a KGB-led regime that took a laid-back and instrumental view of falsehood. Like its Soviet predecessors, the Kremlin believed truth was subordinate to higher sovereign goals. Not Marxism these days, of course, but Putin's twenty-first-century quest to remake Russia as a great power.

Done fluently and well, lying might be useful tool. It disconcerted and confused the Europeans, for example—a naive, credulous, and weak bunch, as seen from Moscow. And, after all, Peskov might have reasoned, didn't so-called democrats dissemble too?

I FIRST MET Peskov in 2007, soon after taking up my post as the *Guardian*'s Moscow correspondent, having arrived via reporting jobs in New Delhi and Berlin. I dropped in to see him at his office in the Kremlin. This was a couple of rooms, not especially tidy, with a large desk and a fax machine in one corner. (The Kremlin demanded faxes long after the rest of the world moved over to email. The faxes may exist somewhere in a dusty, unread heap.) I perched on a sofa. Peskov gave me his business card.

My subject for a forthcoming article was Russian civil society and the harsh treatment of activists in St. Petersburg. They were being squeezed out of politics, arrested, and sometimes roughed up—phenomena taking place more than a decade later, in summer 2019, when Muscovites protested election fraud. Peskov told me it was sad that the country's anti-Putin opposition was weak. He said he wasn't a supporter of Putin's United Russia Party. That didn't mean he was a liberal, I discovered. He voted for Vladimir Zhirinovsky. Zhirinovsky was an ultra-right demagogue, famous for his clownish, brawling antics in the parliament and on TV talk shows.

Later the same year I was among a group of Western correspondents invited to meet Peskov at one of Moscow's Italian restaurants. Peskov had gathered us to give the Kremlin's side of the story of the Litvinenko affair. Litvinenko's murder had plunged relations between London and Moscow into crisis. The then British foreign secretary, David Miliband, had expelled four Russian diplomats in protest at

Russia's refusal to extradite the two suspects, Lugovoi and Kovtun.

Over a carpaccio starter, Peskov said he "strongly rejected" the idea that Moscow had been involved in the polonium plot. He called the recent expulsions "unfortunate." Where, he asked, was proof? Peskov reeled off a list of grievances. They included the UK's failure to send back fugitive oligarchs hiding in London. According to Peskov, Britain was going through the kind of "Russophobia" more commonly associated with Eastern Europe. "We weren't the initiators of this crisis," he said. He spoke in smooth tones that you might call Peskovian—a rational-sounding faux regret.

These restaurant sessions dried up as Moscow got used to its negative image abroad and relations with the subsequent Obama administration turned rotten. In the early years Peskov had been accessible to journalists. He chatted with them in Russian using the informal *ty* form. Over first one Putin decade, and then another, he became harder to reach.

And an awful lot richer.

Cohen and Peskov played similar roles. Both were fixers. Over time they used their connections to the rich to become wealthy themselves. Both married women born in Soviet Ukraine. And served their masters with loyalty and complete discretion, seemingly untroubled by conscience or ethics. "He's a one hundred per cent cynic," Sergei Pugachev—an exiled banker who fell out with Putin—said of Peskov, speaking to me from his villa in Nice.

Over time Peskov's lifestyle grew into that of a minor Russian oligarch, complete with yachts, sumptuous villas, and international travel.

There was a luxury house in Rublyovka, the wooded area west of Moscow where Putin and Medvedev live, bought from an aide to Russian billionaire Alisher Usmanov. And regular vacations to the Maldives and Dubai. Critics began to wonder how Putin's spokesman could afford this on a humble civil servant's salary.

Peskov's personal life offered one explanation. After his second marriage collapsed he began dating Tatiana Navka, a celebrity ice dancer who won gold for Russia in the 2008 Winter Olympics. Navka had sponsorship deals and a popular ice dance show on Russia's state-run Channel One. In summer 2015 the pair married in Sochi. Peskov wore a limited-edition Richard Mille watch with a skull on it. The watch was worth $670,000. A gift from his new bride, he said. Their honeymoon was spent on a €370,000-a-week yacht.

Meanwhile, Peskov carried out his government tasks with cynical brio. He belittled the opposition leader, Nemtsov, after he was gunned down and murdered in 2015 on a bridge outside the Kremlin. Nemtsov was "just a little bit more than an average citizen." He posed no threat to the "current Russian leadership," Peskov said. He dismissed a British public inquiry when it ruled that Putin had "probably" approved Litvinenko's London murder. "Subtle English humour," he told the press.

What did Peskov know of Trump?

The answer: plenty. For a start, Peskov's wife had personal experience of the brand and had owned one of Trump's New York condominiums. Navka lived for more than a decade in the US with her then husband and coach, Alexander Zhulin, training at an ice rink in New Jersey. In 2004 the couple bought a loft apartment in the "Trump Parc" complex beside Central Park in Manhattan. The following year they purchased a two-bedroom apartment in the Milan, a luxury block on Second Avenue.

Navka had something else in common with Trump, it seemed: an aversion to paying US taxes. She was a permanent US resident from at least 2006 until September 2015, when she notified the Department of Homeland Security that she had gone back to Moscow. During this period she and Zhulin paid $1,168 in taxes on a combined income—spanning wages, business profits, rental property revenue, and income from property sales—of $3.4 million. The couple took advantage of tax credits and generous write-offs legally available to landlords.

After she divorced Zhulin in 2010 Navka filed married tax returns for several more years, I discovered. She wrongly told the IRS that she and her then husband had sold a $1.2 million house in New Jersey at a loss. (It was repossessed and sold a decade later, in 2019.) Navka's fraught tax affairs led her to fire her New York accountant, Ilya Bykov, after he warned her that the IRS might seize her Manhattan apartment. Bykov's other celebrity clients included Trump's friend Agalarov.

Seemingly, the Russian elite knew each other, professionally and socially. Peskov and Navka made plans to live in a palace on Agalarov's luxury estate in the Moscow region. They commissioned a design from a US architect, Bob Zampolin, which Agalarov personally approved. American and Russian property tycoons, apartments in Moscow and Manhattan, glossy-magazine lifestyles . . . the worlds of the Trump Organization and Russia's ruling power couples were not so very different.

AT THE TIME of Cohen's speculative email, the Kremlin was intensely curious about Trump and those around him. A cultivation effort was under way.

According to Steele, Peskov was involved in this operation. He was a player in Russia's sweeping efforts to help Trump to become president. Peskov was the "main protagonist," according to two of Steele's sources. Peskov reportedly controlled a dossier of compromising material on Clinton. This had been compiled on Putin's "explicit instructions," the sources said, with Peskov part of a hawkish faction that favoured aggressive interference in US politics.

Such claims are challenging to prove. What is a matter of record is that the Russian government made multiple attempts to bring Trump, Cohen, and others in the candidate's entourage to Moscow, using the prospect of a Trump Tower deal as a point of enticement.

It failed ultimately to get Trump across. It succeeded with other, lesser figures, such as Trump's oddball foreign policy adviser Page. During his July 2016 Moscow trip Page met Russia's deputy prime minister, Arkady Dvorkovitch. Dvorkovitch expressed "strong support for Mr. Trump," Page reported, according to Mueller. Not true—Dvorkovitch told me. The five-minute chat wasn't about politics, he insisted.

For six months, until June 2016, Moscow engaged with the Trump Organization over the project. There were discussions between New York and Moscow. These conversations were private. And entirely unknown to US voters.

A day after his phone call to Peskov's office, Cohen was invited to Russia. The offer was made via Felix Sater, a New York real-estate adviser and one-time felon who served as the Trump Organization's informal Moscow agent. In late-2015 emails Sater sketched out to Cohen the "game changing" political dividends a hotel deal might bring—a trip to Moscow by Donald, a ribbon-cutting ceremony with Vladimir. The invitation envisaged a working trip by Cohen to inspect possible sites and a follow-up visit by Trump.

As these exchanges continued, Peskov found himself embroiled in a scandal of his own. A leak of offshore records from the Panamanian law firm Mossack Fonseca—the Panama Papers—revealed that Peskov's wife had three bank accounts in Zurich, with the Banque International à Luxembourg. As the wife of a senior Kremlin official, she was supposed to declare offshore accounts. She hadn't.

Meanwhile, one of Putin's oldest friends—the cellist Sergei Roldugin—was linked to a $2 billion trail of loans and offshore deals. Peskov dismissed the reports as "Putinphobia." The journalists behind the leak, myself included, were shadowy CIA and MI6 operatives, he said. He denied that his wife had an offshore company. I found copies of her passport, electricity bill, and emails, and also corporate records: once again Peskov appeared to be lying.

In late spring the Kremlin approached Cohen again and invited him to the St. Petersburg economic forum, to be held over three days that June. This was Russia's showpiece business event. Western moguls attended. So did Russian politicians. Peskov would be there. According to Sater, Peskov promised to introduce Cohen to Putin and/or Medvedev. They could discuss "anything," Sater told Cohen by text.

Separately, other senior figures in the Russian government were in touch with Trump. Deputy Prime Minister Sergei Prikhodko invited him twice to the same forum.

These subterranean negotiations—revealed fully only in 2019—went some way towards explaining Trump's flattering behaviour towards Putin. The Russians understood that Trump might easily be manipulated by the prospect of money. The Moscow City skyscraper represented a lucrative opportunity for the Trump Organization. It was worth $1 billion, Cohen told Donald Trump Jr. in spring 2016—one of several conversations Cohen said he had with Trump Jr. and Ivanka about the hotel deal. These talks were "not idle chitchat," Cohen said.

Trump too was fully briefed. Cohen said he talked to Trump in March and April about developments in Moscow, and again in May, when the possibility was discussed of Trump going to Russia to advance the project. There was a further conversation about St. Petersburg, Cohen said. Trump agreed to fly to Russia on the condition that Cohen could "lock and load" on an agreement. Three days before the forum was due to start, Cohen cancelled the trip. He told Sater in the lobby of Trump Tower that he was sceptical Russian officials actually wanted to meet with him.

Peskov would have been thrilled by what happened next. In the wake of the DNC email dump, Trump denied having anything to do with Russia. As for a possible hotel project, Trump claimed, "We decided not to do it." Cohen said he raised this with Trump after his denial-laden press conference that July and assorted tweets in which Trump asserted he had "zero investments" in Russia. Trump allegedly replied, "Why mention it if it's not a deal?"

Moscow knew Trump's claims to be wrong. Trump realized this too. The actual version of events was understood by only a few—Russia's leadership and spy agencies, Trump's family, and personal aides. The Kremlin could exploit this discrepancy—or not. It was leverage.

That November, as Trump celebrated his stunning election victory, Peskov flew into New York. This was a strange moment. Officially Peskov was there for the World Chess Championship in Manhattan. (Chess was an informal part of Peskov's portfolio; Russia ran world chess, a soft power tool.) Peskov was representing Kirsan Ilyumzhinov, the world chess president, who was banned from the US because of his sanctions-busting role in Syria.

Other senior Russians were also on their way to New York, including Kirill Dmitriev, the head of Russia's sovereign wealth fund. Their mood was jubilant. On election night Dmitriev received a text that said bluntly, "Putin has won." The FBI subsequently investigated rumours that Trump had stopped by at the chess championship, which the Russians had originally proposed could take place at Trump Tower. It concluded he didn't.

The saga of the hotel deal would be highly damaging to Trump if it were ever revealed. Once Trump became president, Cohen went down a path of cover-up. He decided to follow the "party line": to corroborate Trump's fictitious claim that he had no financial dealings with Russia. Cohen told the *New York Times* that discussions over Trump Tower ceased in January 2016. This date set up a fake timeline, with Trump exiting Russia well before the primaries and the Iowa caucus. Cohen fed a similar story to the *Washington Post*.

Misleading a bunch of reporters was one thing; lying to Congress was a bigger, graver matter. After receiving a request to testify, Cohen got in touch with the president's personal counsel, Jay Sekulow. A period of close, and intense, coordination followed. The messages he got back from the White House were encouraging: stick to the script, keep any statement minimal, investigations by Mueller and others would soon wrap up. Oh, and the president loves you and has your back, Cohen said later.

With the counsel's help Cohen set about drafting a statement to the Senate and House Intelligence Committees. The text ran to two pages. Cohen claimed he dropped the Moscow hotel idea in January 2016 and that his email to Peskov had gone unanswered— seemingly lost in the Kremlin's in-box. In the original text Cohen wrote, "The building project led me to make limited contact with Russian government officials." Sekulow examined the draft and sent it back. The line had gone.

By this point contacts between Moscow and Trump's campaign had become radioactive, a matter of political scandal. The question for the Russian government was: should it play along? Putin was in a position to sabotage and embarrass Trump if he so wished. Alternatively, the Russians could support the White House and be complicit in Trump's lie and cover-up. They could . . . well, collude.

The *Washington Post* published Cohen's original email to Peskov. Sitting in Moscow, Peskov put out a statement of his own to CNN. It backed up Cohen's fake version. It was a lie, told to help an American friend in trouble.

Peskov wrote:

And so, indeed, I can confirm, that among the total number of e-mails received, we received an email from Mr. Michael

Cohen. It really happened. This email said that a certain
Russian company together with certain individuals is building
a skyscraper in the Moscow city district, but things aren't
going well and they asked for some help with advice for
moving things forward. But, since, so I repeat again, we do not
react to such business topics—that is not our work—we left it
unanswered.

ANDREY KOSTIN'S LIFE was full of luck. He was fortunate in his
parents. His father, Leonid, was a high-ranking Communist Party
official. In the USSR of the 1970s the elder Kostin served on the
State Committee for Labour and Social Affairs. These *apparat* connections may have helped Andrey Kostin early in his career. In
1979, and straight out of college, Kostin joined the Soviet Foreign
Service. Not for him a backwater posting or a dull office job! At age
twenty-three and with a mere BA in economics, Kostin showed up
at Moscow's consulate in Sydney, Australia.

A series of coveted diplomatic posts followed. All were in
English-speaking capitalist countries, places that most Soviet citizens could only imagine. There was New York, three years back
in Moscow, and then another plum assignment, Britain. Kostin
arrived in London in late 1985, at a time of turmoil. The KGB's
designated London resident, Oleg Gordievsky, actually worked for
British intelligence. A double agent, Gordievsky betrayed all of the
embassy's espionage officers and the Brits kicked them out.

Kostin spent five years in the UK. He was responsible for bilateral relations, including parking fines. His time in London coincided with crisis at home and perestroika. In April 1989 Mikhail
Gorbachev flew in for talks with Margaret Thatcher. The general secretary called in at the Soviet embassy in Kensington Park
Gardens. He sat at the ambassador's desk—protected from bugging

by jamming equipment—and addressed about twenty staff members through a fog of cigarette smoke.

One of those in the audience was Kostin's friend and colleague Alexander Lebedev. Lebedev was a KGB lieutenant colonel, a bright and upwardly mobile fellow. Lebedev followed economic matters. He was pessimistic, as he later wrote in a memoir, about Moscow's ability to pay its debts, telling Gorbachev as much. Lebedev would become a person of influence in London and the owner of British newspapers, including the *Evening Standard*, run by his son Evgeny. The *Standard* was a supporter of Boris Johnson.

Was Kostin also KGB? Kostin says he wasn't. Russian bankers, Western investors in Russia, and intelligence sources on both sides of the Atlantic all think he was—a First Directorate officer, they say, focused on US and British Commonwealth targets. "Please. Everybody knows! It's so funny," Pugachev, the former banker who met Kostin in the 1990s, told me when I put Kostin's KGB denials to him.

Back in Moscow, Lebedev and Kostin embraced the new capitalism. They went into business together and founded the Russian Investment Finance Company. According to Lebedev, it did many things, including property, consultancy, and trade. It bought TVs (which didn't work) and a consignment of women's shoes (for the same foot). There were encounters with gangsters. And, finally, a successful bond deal that allowed them to buy a mini-bank.

In 1996 Kostin was again blessed with fortune. Despite having limited experience, he was named chairman of Vnesheconombank, VEB. This was a sensitive post. The bank was state-owned and answered to Yeltsin. One former CIA analyst described it to me as the Kremlin's "cookie jar." Kostin did the job until 2002, when Putin promoted him to be head of Vneshtorgbank, or VTB, Russia's number-two bank.

Kostin would become Russia's leading financier. And an entertaining and robust defender of Putin and his policies before Western audiences. Kostin stood up for the boss at Davos, in interviews with Bloomberg and the *Financial Times*, and during feisty meetings with US investors. A favourite word was "bullshit" (Putin's link to the Panama Papers, etc.). Some wondered whether Kostin's true vocation was the stage. At one VTB conference he came as Stalin; at another he did a take-off of *Star Wars* and dressed up as Obi-Wan Kenobi.

"I looked forward to my meetings with him because he was so bombastic and funny," Chris Barter, former head of Goldman Sachs Moscow, told me. "He's a crowd-pleaser, very witty. You ask him any question, and he would give some answer that was at least interesting. You would meet oligarchs who were full of themselves, touchy and angry if you say the wrong thing. Kostin, by comparison, is a very pleasant guy. He acts stupid. He's not."

And truthful? "You could never trust him with anything. He's a product of that system," Barter said.

Kostin's bank is no ordinary bank. According to Barter, it has multiple functions. One is to support external banking operations; if, say, Angola wants to buy Russian weapons, VTB will provide the finance. Another is to offer commercial banking services within Russia. That means loans to small and medium-size businesses and to large corporations and oligarchs. Plenty of scope here, I was told, for bribes.

The third alleged function is delicate: to do the president's bidding.

Kostin disputes the idea that Putin gives him orders. Yet that, more or less, is how the system works, sources in Moscow say, adding that the state uses VTB for deniable international operations. VTB facilitates transactions for top Kremlin insiders, the sources add. In 2005 VTB swallowed up two banks used in Soviet times for espionage and for moving currency to Western communist parties: the Narodny Bank, based in London, and Eurobank, in Paris.

According to Mueller, VTB got involved in the GRU-led project to shape American politics—specifically by lining up finance for Trump's elusive Moscow hotel. Not up front but via a smaller Russian bank, Genbank, run by an alleged criminal, Evgeny Dvoskin. The US deported Dvoskin in 2000 for stock fraud. By 2015 Genbank was under US sanctions: its lending was centred in Crimea.

In late 2015 Sater wrote several times to Cohen. His objective was to get Trump and Cohen over to Russia to advance the deal. VTB, Sater suggested, would play the role of intermediary. The obvious political dimension of a Trump–Putin meeting would be hidden under a cloak of business.

A December 19 email said:

> Please call me I have Evgeny [Dvoskin] on the other line. He needs a copy of your and Donald's passports they need a scan of every page of the passports. Invitations & Visas will be issued this week by VTB Bank to discuss financing for Trump Tower Moscow. Politically neither Putins office nor Ministry of Foreign Affairs cannot issue invite, so they are inviting commercially/ business. VTB is Russia's 2 biggest bank and VTB CEO Andrey Kostin, will be at all meetings with Putin so that it is a business meeting not political. We will be invited to Russian consulate this week to receive invite & have visa issued.

Trump's executive assistant Rona Graff took Trump's passport to Cohen's office. It's unclear if it ever reached Sater. Cohen sent an image of his own passport to Sater by text.

In Moscow the same week, Putin lauded Trump at his annual Kremlin press conference, calling him a "very colourful and talented man" and the "absolute leader of the presidential race."

On a public level, there was praise and mutual encouragement between Putin and Trump. Privately, Russia was offering its candidate secret incentives in the shape of potential finance worth hundreds of millions of dollars from a leading Moscow bank. Trump didn't mention this. Nor did Putin.

Putin added, "He [Trump] says that he wants to move to another level of relations, to a deeper level of relations with Russia. How can we not welcome that?"

IN PERSON, KOSTIN was as big and boisterous as I had been led to believe—a large, fun, lively figure in late middle age, wearing glasses, the boy still visible beneath a pudgy sixty-something chin. It was 2018. Kostin was on a charm offensive. By this point the US had sanctioned VTB and Kostin personally. The fear was that the European Union and the UK might soon follow suit. Kostin flew into London, his mission to flatter opinion formers and newspaper editors and to knock down some of their wrong ideas about Putin.

Kostin acknowledged that Trump had sought to build a tower in Moscow. But he said that VTB—that is, he—had never been "approached about this matter." As for Sater—well, he was a crook who had spent six years in prison and was now working for the FBI and American secret agencies. In short, a dubious person whose account to federal investigators of his interactions with Moscow couldn't be trusted.

The banker shrugged off claims that the Kremlin had hacked the US election or helped Trump get into power—the finding of every American intelligence agency and Mueller as well. Russia and America were morally not very different, he suggested. "You can never trust secret services on both sides. The Americans invent things! Russians also! We are used to the West always interfering in Russian affairs. I think it's a game on both sides," he said.

The opinion in Moscow was that Trump had won on his own merits—he was "more sincere" than his rival, Kostin said. Trump entered office with the intention of improving relations with Russia and removing sanctions. There had been a "good meeting" with Putin in Helsinki. Allegations of collusion were bunk. Russia knew little about Trump when he ran for office, Kostin said, saying, "I didn't [even] know Trump Tower belonged to Trump."

This last claim seemed a stretch. More plausible was Kostin's description of his friendly relations with Putin, which—he said—went back to 1998, when Putin was a little-known, mid-ranking government official. Since he became president Kostin said they chatted about "what I'm doing" rather than politics. "I know him very well," he said. Kostin said he was on good terms with other members of the elite. "I know everybody in Russia. It helps me, of course," he explained smoothly.

Kostin's superior understanding of the Russian political game appeared the key to his successful career. Power wasn't determined by your official position but by a set of fluid interpersonal relationships. The Kremlin was less like a government, more like an Ottoman court. Since the 2008 financial crisis VTB had received $18 billion in state cash. This was more than any other Russian bank—and a testament to Kostin's skill at avoiding falling into the shark pool, where less adroit officials might be devoured.

Kostin presented a positive picture of Russia, after two decades of the same leader in charge, and with little prospect of change. The country was "some kind of democracy." Russians were free to travel abroad, they could listen to the BBC, and unlike China there was no internet censorship, he said. He conceded that the state controlled all major TV stations and that space for opposition publications "is shrinking." Putin was genuinely popular, he suggested.

I was curious about VTB's relationship with Deutsche Bank, Germany's biggest lender. Deutsche's most famous client is Trump.

Deutsche loaned Trump large sums of money at a time when Wall Street was refusing to give him credit, following corporate bankruptcies in the 1990s. In total, Trump borrowed about $1 billion. Ivanka, Jared Kushner, and Kushner's mother, Seryl, are Deutsche clients.

The circumstances of these loans remain murky, despite repeated attempts by Congress to get hold of Deutsche's records.

In 2008 Trump defaulted on a $40 million repayment against a $640 million loan used to fund the construction of the Trump International Hotel & Tower in Chicago. Deutsche sued. Trump counter-sued, claiming the bank was co-responsible for the global economic crisis. Trump got out of this hole after he was loaned more money by the private wealth division of a major bank—Deutsche in New York. It was this story that in late 2015 had prompted me to seek out Steele. "Is this normal?" I asked one former Deutsche New York insider. "Are you fucking kidding me?" he replied.

At the same time, Deutsche's Moscow division began making remarkable profits of $500 million to $1 billion a year. A key figure in its success was Kostin's son Andrei, who in 2007 moved from Deutsche in London to Deutsche in Moscow. Deutsche and VTB worked closely together, issuing stocks and bonds, with VTB generating 50 to 80 percent of all revenue. (Kostin Jr. died in a 2011 snowmobile accident.)

Deutsche correctly regarded VTB as an invaluable partner. As a financial institution quasi-joined to the Kremlin, VTB was able to lend to and, most importantly, collect debts from pretty much anyone. Deutsche could therefore carry out profitable and complex transactions with Russian counterparts, while selling off the undesirable part of the business—the credit risk—to VTB.

KGB or not, Kostin had excellent contacts with Russian intelligence. Putin's FSB spy chief Nikolai Patrushev—and Patrushev's successor, Alexander Bortnikov—both sent their sons to work at VTB. Deutsche had a similar model of hiring clients' offspring.

VTB's deputy chief executive Vasily Titov chaired the FSB's public council. (Titov made no secret of his Chekist connections and once gave, as a gift in a glass case, a vintage pistol that had belonged to Felix Dzerzhinsky, Lenin's spy chief.)

Between 2011 and 2015 Deutsche Bank Moscow ran a money-laundering scheme in Moscow for a group of special clients. Some $10 billion was changed from roubles to dollars via "mirror trades." This wasn't an oversight by the bank. Rather, insiders meticulously arranged the scheme, allowing money laundering to go on for years—not undetected exactly, but ring-fenced so it was safe from exposure. A KGB alumnus was said to control these illicit flows—a *smotryaschi* in Russian—and was across operations without being outed by either side.

The New York State Department of Financial Services and British regulators subsequently fined Deutsche $475 million and £163 million respectively. Seemingly, the FSB had captured Deutsche's Moscow outpost and was running it for its own purposes.

The strange case of the German bank hung over Trump's presidency. Investigative journalists, Democrats in the House and Senate, and former bank insiders had sought answers to a few questions. The main one was whether Deutsche had sold any part of Trump's debt to VTB or other Russian state entities. It seemed plausible that Deutsche treated the Trump Organization in the same fashion as its high-risk Russian counterparts. In other words, wary of lending to a creditor who had defaulted in the past, Deutsche would be looking for ways to mitigate its credit exposure. One solution would be to buy credit protection from VTB.

Also, did the Trumps get special treatment?

Or had other favours been traded?

The answer to all these, according to Kostin, was no. The scenario—that VTB underwrote Trump's German loan, possibly telling him and passing on the Russian president's warm wishes—was entirely false, Kostin said.

"I know how we work with Deutsche Bank. We don't have any special agreement on that with Mr. Trump," he told me.

Kostin added, "I know what my bank was doing." His late son had worked for Deutsche for ten years; it had been a leading bank in Russia lending money to "many major Russian companies." VTB had worked closely with it.

The story of Russia and Trump was more made up than real, Kostin suggested, led by a pack of journalist sleuths intent on chasing down conspiracies and non-clues. Why would Moscow seek to meddle in America's affairs? Kostin pronounced himself baffled. "I'm an admirer of Agatha Christie. I can't find a motive," he told me. Kostin didn't expect to convince. What he did want, I reflected, was for you to admire the masterful way he played the game.

THE GROUP THAT came in from the street didn't look like the usual clientele. Too formal, too serious, too intent. It was April 2018, early morning, Manhattan.

Most of the well-heeled guests at the Loews Regency were upstairs and asleep. The hotel, at 540 Park Avenue, catered to a wealthy bunch: the transient rich. In the lobby, velvet sofas, coffee tables adorned with photography books of Parisian architecture, and an amaryllis plant. There was a bar (big man, large neck; young woman in a cocktail dress when I dropped by some months later) and a cigar terrace.

The new arrivals hadn't come for a society wedding or to gossip amid the art deco furniture. They were from the FBI. They were acting on a multi-page warrant from a federal court in the Southern District of New York, at this point secret. Their assignment was to

search a room on the seventeenth floor. And to take away potential evidence: paper, computers, electronic devices, recordings, and
phones.

After a discussion with a hotel employee, the federal agents realized they had the wrong room. The one they were looking for was
actually on the floor below: 1628. This was three rooms converted
into a suite and currently rented for several months. The guest had
moved in while his family apartment two blocks away was being
renovated.

The guest was Michael Cohen, personal attorney to the forty-
fifth president of the United States.

Unbeknownst to Cohen, since summer 2017 federal investigators had been carefully examining his affairs. Judges had permitted
them to scoop up Cohen's emails. And to sift through his financial dealings—a heap of invoices, shell companies, and mortgage
applications. These had been used, among other things, to pay hush
money during the campaign to two women with whom Trump had
allegedly been having affairs.

The agents rode the elevator to the sixteenth floor. At the same
moment other federal representatives were on the move. One unit
searched Cohen's mid-town work space, inside the law firm of
Squire Patton Boggs, on the twenty-third floor of 30 Rockefeller
Plaza. Another visited Cohen's apartment. A fourth went to a
branch of TD Bank. The target was a fifteen-by-ten-inch safety-
deposit box belonging to Cohen and his wife, Laura.

These raids marked the beginning of a journey—a path, as Cohen
told a judge later—that would lead him out of darkness and into the
light. It was a road that Cohen would dramatize as every bit as stony
and allegorical as the one trodden by Christian—the hero of John
Bunyan's *Pilgrim's Progress*. Christian moved through the Slough of
Despond and the Valley of Humiliation. This progress was akin to
the route Cohen was about to take as he broke with Trump.

The end point of Cohen's journey was less exalted than Christian's Celestial City: it was federal prison. Nonetheless, Cohen would style his moral awakening as an act of personal and spiritual liberation. Cohen was no longer in thrall! After losing his way Cohen had now returned to righteousness!

The question was: just how repentant was Cohen? Was he sincere or sincere-ish? Was he telling the whole truth or merely some of it?

It took a few months before Cohen's "emancipation" began. After the raids Trump called him and urged him to "hang in there" and "stay strong." In summer 2018, however, Cohen did the thing the president predicted wouldn't happen: he flipped. He pleaded guilty to two counts of campaign finance violations, based on payments he had made to the adult film star Stormy Daniels and the former *Playboy* model Karen McDougal—payments, Cohen said, that were done at Trump's explicit request. He admitted to Mueller's team that he'd lied to Congress over the Moscow Tower project. (Trump, by contrast, could recall little of these negotiations. In written answers submitted to the FBI, the president said he didn't have memorable conversations on the subject.) Cohen acknowledged cheating the IRS out of more than $1.3 million.

By the time of his sentencing in December 2018 Cohen cut a humble figure. He said he wanted to ensure that history didn't remember him as "the villain of the story," despite the president calling him a rat, a liar, and other hurtful names. As a lawyer, he should have known better, prosecutor Robert Khuzami said. The judge gave Cohen three years.

In February 2019 Cohen appeared once more before Congress, the body to which he had previously lied about events in Russia. It was a mesmerizing performance. He was rueful about his misdeeds and sardonic towards Trump's Republican allies, who gleefully rubbished Cohen as a real-life Pinocchio and all-round fraud.

Cohen's opening statement was a humdinger, a Brutus moment in which he stuck the knife into his erstwhile boss:

> I am ashamed of my weakness and loyalty—of the things I did for Mr. Trump in an effort to protect and to promote him.
>
> I am ashamed that I chose to take part in Mr. Trump's illicit acts rather than listening to my conscience.
>
> I am ashamed because I know what Mr. Trump is.
>
> He is a racist.
>
> He is a con man.
>
> He is a cheat.

There were newsworthy claims. Roger Stone called Trump after speaking with Julian Assange and told him that WikiLeaks was about to dump out DNC emails, Cohen testified. Trump deliberately inflated his assets in his dealings with Deutsche Bank. And negotiations over the Moscow Tower went on for months, across 2016. Trump hadn't instructed him to lie directly to Congress about Russia—"That's not how he operates," Cohen explained. Trump had duped the American people about his dealings with Moscow because he had never expected to win the primary, let alone the election, seeing his White House bid as nothing more than an audacious "infomercial" for the Trump brand.

The most significant exchange concerned Prague. The Steele dossier said that in August 2016 Cohen met secretly with Kremlin officials in a European country. Subject of discussion: how to conceal "Moscow's secret liaison with the Trump team." And how to co-pay "Romanian hackers" who stole DNC emails. Details of where these alleged meetings had taken place were sketchy. One possible venue was the office of the Russian cultural organization Rossotrudnichestvo, generally understood to be a spy front and situated close to the Russian embassy in central Prague.

Investigative reporters expended much time and shoe leather in trying to verify Steele's memo. I had been to Prague too, walking past the giant embassy building and scouring the Rossotrudnichestvo noticeboard for clues. Cohen's "trip" went to the heart of the Trump–Russia story. If it took place, this was proof of conspiracy. If it didn't, the dossier's other findings—of sexual compromise—looked in question. Steele's sources said that the meetings were originally scheduled for Moscow, at about the time when Peskov was actively trying to bring Cohen over to Russia, and later moved to a soft EU country. ("Soft" meant a zone where Russian intelligence might operate largely free from CIA surveillance.)

Asked by Republican Ralph Norman if he had ever been to Prague, Cohen said he hadn't. "I've never been to the Czech Republic," he said.

Cohen had initially denied the Prague story, at the same time as he insisted that negotiations with Moscow had ceased in early 2016—a lie. What could be said now? Cohen could be telling the truth. Or his statement might be literally true but misleading, with the "meeting" taking place outside Prague or somewhere else. The FBI looked closely at Cohen's travel movements. Mueller reported Cohen's version: no meeting. But the special counsel didn't say that the FBI had independently concluded there wasn't a Prague rendezvous. Steele's view, expressed to friends, was that a meeting of some kind had indeed happened.

Seemingly, this was the end of the Prague saga. There was one weird aspect to the affair, however, that gave one pause for thought. Sitting to Cohen's right, as he gave evidence to Congress, was a senior white-haired figure: Cohen's attorney, Lanny Davis. In summer 2018 Cohen hired Davis. Among Davis's other clients was a person with East European connections. His name was Dmitry Firtash, and he was a Ukrainian oligarch wanted by the US government for fraud.

For several decades Firtash was a major player in gas transit between Kyiv and Moscow, an exceptionally murky trade even by the standards of the region. Firtash was fighting US extradition attempts from exile in Vienna, Austria. Davis was his main US lobbyist. According to Department of Justice filings, Davis's law firm was earning $60,000 a month from Firtash. Meanwhile, Davis offered his services to Cohen pro bono. Davis's indirect connections with shadowy figures in the post-Soviet world—linked in turn to the Kremlin—were matters of public record. An unusual choice of lawyer for a person in Cohen's situation.

Regardless of his attorney, there were doubts about the credibility of Cohen's testimony. Was his forthcomingness real? Or was he still withholding some of what he knew? The bigger problem for investigators was that Russian spying remained opaque. Its practitioners lived in a tenebrous world. They suffered the same challenges as everyone else, however: bad days at work, unreasonable bosses, long hours.

And tricky personal issues such as how to get a date.

CHAPTER 6
CLOSE ACCESS

Moscow–The Hague–Western District of Pennsylvania
2018

Wanted: woman age 21–30 for friendship,
chatting, love, relationship, and sports.
DATING AD POSTED ON MYLOVE.RU BY ALEKSEI MORENETS

On paper Aleksei Morenets had everything. A glamorous career, excitement, adventure! Morenets's life was something from a modern espionage thriller. He worked for GRU intelligence. He was a Russian spy! Not just any old spy, but a spy engaged in sensitive, cutting-edge projects.

Morenets grew up in one of the most isolated parts of the world. He was born in Ostrovnoy, a closed administrative territory in the Murmansk region, on Russia's northern Kola Peninsula. Ostrovnoy was a city of desolate housing blocks overlooking the Barents Sea. It was home to the USSR's nuclear submarine fleet. It was bleak. And cut off—reachable by ships that tracked along the icy coast and often broke down.

A bright student, Morenets escaped this frozen outpost and went to study in St. Petersburg. He was a cadet at the Alexander Mozhaysky Military Space Academy. The academy is one of several higher education institutions used to train future GRU personnel. From there Morenets became a full-time military intelligence officer.

Morenets went from a Soviet naval colony visited by polar bears to a whirl of international travel. On any particular day he might be at his unit's headquarters in Moscow, at 20 Komsomolsky Prospekt, the yellow-painted building that belongs to the GRU. Or he could be off to an airport to catch a plane, his destination multiple time zones away. Morenets would swap the pewter sky of the Russian winter for the warmth and colour of Asia.

His diplomatic passport entitled him to skip the queue. (Printed on it was "Murmansk Oblast," his place of birth.) On the road Morenets stayed in a better class of hotel. His arrival was coordinated with Russia's diplomatic missions. And—as long as he kept a receipt—everything he spent could be billed back to the GRU's Finance Department.

Traditional GRU activities included assassinations, diversions, and sabotage. Morenets's speciality was different and more subtle. He was a hacker—an elite "onsite" cyber operator.

He and a colleague, Evgeny Serebriakov, were members of a shadowy group that had been on the radar of US intelligence for some years—since 2014 at least. They formed what was known as a "close access" team.

As a first step their GRU spying unit, 26165, would attempt to break into a target's computer server remotely, from Moscow. That involved classic GRU techniques: spear-phishing emails, custom-built malware, one-shot burner accounts . . . all of the tricks successfully deployed by the unit against the Democrats in spring and summer 2016.

Sometimes, though, this didn't work. And so Morenets and Serebriakov—the deputy head of directorate and section chief—were sent off to try more hands-on methods. They would fly to where a potential victim was located. This might be a regular workplace or a hotel used for conferences or a building belonging to an international organization.

The two Russians travelled with sophisticated hacking equipment. Their first task was to compromise a hotel's or office's wi-fi network. Colleagues in Moscow would offer support, breaking passwords using brute force programs.

Once inside a network, it was easy to sneak into a target's laptop—assuming he or she had logged on. Morenets and Serebriakov could download emails, install malware, and steal log-in credentials. Anything recovered was relayed back to Russia. A couple of GRU colleagues came along on these foreign operations to make sure nothing went awry.

Morenets and Serebriakov were professional hackers. Their employer was a secret or shadow state. They were also mop-up merchants—spies deployed to clean the mess left by Russia's erratic adventures abroad.

One example: for years, the Kremlin had run an undercover sports-doping programme. It had achieved extraordinary results—gold medals at the 2012 London Olympics, a Russian first-place medals finish at the 2014 Winter Olympics, hosted by Putin in Sochi.

A series of Russian whistleblowers revealed this scam. They included Grigory Rodchenkov, Russia's own anti-doping chief, who later fled to the US. At Sochi FSB officers swapped contaminated urine samples in the dead of night for clean ones, via a hole in the floor of the testing lab, Rodchenkov said. Russia was guilty of "fraud, lies, and falsifications of unspeakable proportions," he added.

This cheating emerged in 2014 and caused outrage among international sports bodies. The US anti-doping agency, USADA, based in Colorado Springs, led calls for Russian athletes to be excluded from the 2016 Rio Olympics and the following Paralympics.

Moscow might have admitted wrongdoing, apologized, and pledged to clean up its act. It didn't. In public Putin blamed the

West. He said his country was a victim of an "anti-Russia policy" and an attempt to defame the country's sportsmen and sportswomen.

In private, Putin let loose the GRU. The apparent order was to dig up information that might be used to discredit Russia's critics. The hacking of American democracy and moves by world sports to ban Russia were intimately connected. The former was payback for the latter, from Moscow's perspective. Putin regarded the punishment of Russian sports stars as a US-led affront to his authority.

In July 2016 Morenets was sent to Rio de Janeiro. This was soon before the Olympic Games began. The International Olympic Committee (IOC) allowed individual sports federations to rule on a ban on Russian competitors, to the dismay of US sports officials and others. Some Russian athletes were due in Brazil, but many—humiliatingly—were left at home.

That summer the GRU launched an attack on two fronts. One was Clinton's Democrats; the other, international sports bodies. Three of Morenets's colleagues—Ivan Yermakov, Artem Malyshev, and Dmitry Badin—hacked the DNC's servers. They also targeted USADA; the Canadian Centre for Ethics in Sport (CCES), based in Ottawa; and the World Anti-Doping Agency (WADA), head-quartered in Montreal. Yermakov began probing WADA's electronic defences.

In August, with the games under way, Morenets made a second trip to Rio. This time Serebriakov came too. According to US prosecutors, they stole the user name and password of an IOC official. This allowed Yermakov to plunder medical and anti-doping records from WADA's athlete database. These were sent back to Moscow and to the GRU's publication and outreach wing—unit 74455, based at the Khimki Tower.

By this point the tower had invented Guccifer. In analogous fashion, the GRU devised an entity that would release stolen sports data: the "Fancy Bears Hack Team." The team posed as a group of citizen "hacktivists." It had a Twitter account and a website, fancybears.net. The site was decorated with cartoon bears in police uniforms, some wearing "Anonymous" masks. There was a panda. And a friendly salutation: "Greetings citizens of the world. Allow us to introduce ourselves. . . . We are Fancy Bears' international hack team. We stand for fair play and clean sport."

This was untrue. As a US indictment put it, Fancy Bear was part of an influence and disinformation campaign cooked up by the Kremlin. Their task was to smear American and other Western athletes and to accuse them falsely of doping. The GRU hackers got hold of medical records and other data from about 250 athletes in nearly thirty countries. The information included details of therapeutic use exemptions, known as TUEs. Competitors with medical conditions were allowed to use otherwise prohibited substances— but only with agreement from WADA.

Fancy Bear published the private records of Simone Biles, Serena Williams, and the British cyclists Bradley Wiggins and Chris Froome, all of whom had taken TUEs. Files were shared with 180 media representatives. Stories appeared in the *New York Times* and *Der Spiegel* magazine (over the objections of some German reporters, I was told, uneasy at the Russian intelligence connection). The aim, as ever, was to distract from Russia's state-run doping system—which was illicit—and to label the West as hypocritical.

Unit 74455 set up the "Fancy Bears" domain using false accounts. It paid using Bitcoin. Meanwhile, Morenets and Serebriakov enjoyed Brazil. Serebriakov hung out with Russia's accredited Olympic delegation. A photo found on his laptop shows him with his arm around a young raven-haired woman wearing a *"Rossiya"* T-shirt. Serebriakov looks relaxed, smiling, his dark glasses tucked into a T-shirt.

The GRU pair were good at what they did. Mostly their victims had no clue that they were being stalked—first remotely and then by undercover operators circling around them like phantoms. In September the hackers set off again, flying to Lausanne in Switzerland. The quarry was a Canadian CCES official who was attending a WADA anti-doping conference. Serebriakov booked into the same hotel, the Alpha-Palmiers; Morenets checked into the Palace Hotel nearby. And then the usual play: hotel wi-fi, laptop, emails, malware.

On this occasion the operation was detected. The official glanced at his "sent" folder and saw something off: an email written to the chief medical officer of another international sports organization. It contained several typos and a rogue spelling of the official's regular email signature. The "g" had fallen out. It said: "Sent from my SamsunCopenhagen." The message had a malware link.

Perhaps the long hours on the road were taking their toll. Or maybe these clues were deliberate.

FROM OUTSIDE, ESPIONAGE looks like a thrilling affair. But the endless *kommandorovki*—business trips—were bad for one's personal life. Hard to strike up a relationship when you were unable to talk about your work or explain what you did for a living. Sure, international hotels had bars, but an attractive young woman sitting there alone enjoying a cocktail might be a Western spy. Serebriakov let off steam by playing football for an amateur Moscow team. It was mostly comprised of intelligence officers and called the "Radiks." According to one former team-mate, speaking to the *Moscow Times*, he was a "decent" defender. Morenets's world was dominated by men. GRU staff, travel companions, diplomatic contacts, fellow hackers, locker-room mates: all were just other guys. How to meet girls? In 2018 the Russian spy set up an online dating profile on the website Mylove.ru. It gave his age—forty-one—and star sign, Leo. Name, Aleksei. A photo. No surname.

It looks as if Morenets slipped out during his lunch break to pose for a profile picture. The photo was taken on the Frunzenskaya embankment, about two-fifths of a mile from his GRU office. A sunny day! In the background the Moscow River, the trees of Gorky Park, and a tall building with a Panasonic billboard—the National University of Science and Technology. Morenets is wearing a white shirt and tie. He looks a little formal.

The profile gives us some insight into Morenets's personality. He says he's looking for a Moscow woman aged twenty-one to thirty for "friendship, chatting, love, relationship, and sports"—in other words, a partner at least a decade younger than he is. About himself, Morenets admits, "I am calculating, rational, and cynical." He name-checks the Soviet mathematician Andrei Kolmogorov, who theorized that women reason emotionally rather than logically.

Morenets writes: "If Kolmogorov's rule of female logic applies to you we won't get along. If you don't understand what the above proposition is about—the same."

Morenets, then, comes across as chilly, intellectually superior, and with probable chauvinist tendencies. The reason for his disillusionment is not stated. An unhappy love affair? A tough childhood spent in a decaying Soviet backwater? Mother issues?

The spy appears to be moderately well off. He owns a car—at one point a metallic grey Lada, according to traffic police records—and rents his own apartment. He earns a normal salary. He mentions a carpet. And "I am a lark (I like to get up early)."

Maybe someone out there in cyberspace would notice him.

From Russia in search of love.

ON TUESDAY, APRIL 10, 2018, Morenets set off on his latest mission. It was another foreign expedition. The destination was a country of seventeen million people in Western Europe. The front of the GRU barracks was an area of activity. Young men in uniform and clutching briefcases came and went. Morenets left his office via the quieter back entrance of the building, slipping out past the security guard and into the street. Waiting for him was a car ordered through a regular Moscow firm, Be Taxi. The driver's name was Tsvetkov.

Tsvetkov drove down Nezvishkiy Pereulok and headed north. Some twenty miles later Morenets got out at terminal F of Moscow's Sheremetyevo Airport. The fare was 842 roubles. We don't know if the spy left a tip. Tsvetkov wrote out a receipt and then signed and stamped it. The officer added his name in blue pen and countersigned—proof of journey for the bean counters who dealt with GRU expenses.

Morenets was travelling with three colleagues. One was Serebriakov; the other two were older, beefy-looking operatives, Oleg Sotnikov and Alexey Minin, both forty-six years of age, whose roles were reconnaissance and support. The four GRU officers had been dispatched to deal with the fallout from another high-profile operation, which had misfired. Not state-sponsored doping on this occasion, but the Salisbury plot to kill Skripal.

The hit attempt carried out by their two GRU colleagues in Britain was—all things considered—a mess. Skripal had survived. London accused Russia. Moscow denied everything. The US and the international community were inclined to believe the UK. At the centre of this blame game was the question of novichok: where did it come from? Which state had been crazy and reckless enough to deploy it in a crowded city, in what was the first use of a chemical weapon on European soil since World War II?

The Organization for the Prohibition of Chemical Weapons, the OPCW, based in the Netherlands, was seeking to get to the bottom of this. It would be central to how this row played out and what diplomatic consequences the Kremlin might face, short- and long-term. Another interested body was the Spiez chemical laboratory in Switzerland, where the Brits had sent a sample of novichok for analysis.

According to the UK government, days after Salisbury the GRU launched a cyber offensive. It targeted the Foreign Office in London, headed by then Foreign Secretary Johnson, and the UK's Defence Science and Technology Laboratory. It hit the OPCW, based in The Hague.

None of the sallies was successful, hence the decision to activate the close-access specialists. Their apparent brief was to steal anything that might be exploited by Moscow to undermine Britain's case.

The OPCW was working independently to confirm the UK government's conclusions. It was also examining the most recent attack by Russian-backed Syrian government forces using chemical weapons against the city of Douma.

The Netherlands was familiar turf for GRU operatives. They had repeatedly tried to compromise the work of Dutch investigators. The country was leading an international probe into the shooting down in July 2014 of Malaysia Airlines passenger plane MH17 over eastern Ukraine. Some 298 people—nearly 200 of them Dutch—died. The trail went back to Moscow. A Buk anti-aircraft missile launcher had travelled from a Russian military base in the western city of Kursk into rebel-controlled Ukrainian territory. After the plane was downed it returned across the border.

The four Russians landed at Amsterdam's Schiphol Airport. This was the same airport from which MH17 had taken off on its doomed journey. Waiting at the terminal building was the attaché from the Russian embassy in The Hague, Anton Naumkin. He met the visitors at the gate and escorted them through customs, where they showed Russian diplomatic passports. The group headed to the exit, Sotnikov and Minin in front, looking like business travellers in jackets and open-necked shirts, with Serebriakov and Morenets bringing up the rear. Sotnikov appeared to be sharing a joke. Naumkin was smartly turned out in a camel coat and a tie.

Though they didn't know it, the men from Moscow were being watched.

The Dutch defence intelligence service—the Militaire Inlichtingen- en Veiligheidsdienst, or MIVD—knew who they were.

Over the next four days it would follow them.

FROM AMSTERDAM, the five Russians went directly to The Hague. The city is home to the International Criminal Court, the International Court of Justice, the Dutch parliament, Europol, and other multi-state agencies. It is the world capital of the rule of law—something distinctly lacking from Putin's politically susceptible justice system, where sentences are often decided before trial and told to a judge in a phone call.

The spies' first stop was the Russian embassy. Its villa, with a high roof, is at the end of a peaceful cobbled road named after Andries Bicker, a Renaissance mayor. It overlooks a small waterway. Swifts and gulls circle above; when I called late one sunny summer afternoon a Russian embassy family was arriving back at the compound on bikes. The US and other embassies are close by.

A gold sign in Russian and Dutch reads: "Embassy of the Russian Federation." Below it, in English: "Permanent mission of the Russian Federation to the Organization for the Prohibition of Chemical Weapons (OPCW)."

The embassy has a public side and a private side. On Russian national days the ambassador entertains guests in a wood-panelled room. Dutch politicians, ambassadors from allied countries, writers, and artists are invited to receptions with music and vodka.

In 2017 there were toasts to Dutch–Russian friendship. The then ambassador, Alexander Shulgin, cited Peter the Great—described by Putin as his favourite "world leader" in an interview with the *Financial Times*. Three centuries ago Peter the Great visited the Netherlands to study ship building. Dutch carpenters travelled back to Russia. This friendship continued. The Dutch king Wilhelm was a regular visitor to Moscow and in early 2014 had a beer with Putin in Sochi. Until the same year Putin's daughter Maria reportedly lived in Holland with her Dutch partner, in a penthouse near The Hague.

There was a darker, unpublicized side to the embassy's activities. Like all Russian missions it was home to two clandestine residencies. One belonged to the SVR foreign intelligence agency. The other was GRU.

According to Russian media reports, the four met inside the embassy with a fellow spy, Konstantin Bakhtin. Bakhtin was a thirty-nine-year-old GRU colonel based at the embassy's villa. Colonel Bakhtin's job was to coordinate the hacking mission. He had liaised with Moscow in advance. The OPCW—a large concrete building of semi-circular design—was a two-minute drive away.

Bakhtin had studied at the GRU's conservatory at the same time as Anatoliy Chepiga, now back in Russia from Salisbury. According to the veteran Russian investigative reporter Sergei Kanev, citing GRU sources, Chepiga and Bakhtin were friends. They went for walks together and celebrated birthdays and national holidays, Kanev—who has extensive police and crime contacts—told me.

They even shared a cover story. While attending GRU lectures they were registered as students at Moscow's civilian University for the Humanities. Registration was necessary for anyone moving to the capital: without it you couldn't send your kids to kindergarten or access municipal services. Officially both lived at a university student hostel at 25 Kirovogradskaya Street—Bakhtin in apartment 10, Chepiga in 28.

After graduation, the two friends went off in different directions. Bakhtin was assigned to the First Department, known as the "jackets": GRU officers who operated abroad under civilian cover. Chepiga was in the Third Department. This was a diversionary group. It specialized in cut-throat skills, including how to murder and poison. (The GRU's Second Department prepared military attachés working under diplomatic cover.)

Kanev's sources told him that Bakhtin was blamed for what happened next. Others, working for Dutch intelligence, suggest that Bakhtin's role may have been exaggerated to shuffle responsibility onto a single disposable officer.

The visiting Russians spent two days doing reconnaissance. Minin hired a black Citroën C3 car. The men travelled out of town—followed by the Dutch MIVD. One destination was Rotterdam and the headquarters of the investigation into MH17. Another was to the coastal town of Nordwijk, and the European Space Agency. (The beach is nearby but one imagines they didn't buy ice cream or dip in the North Sea.) These road trips may have been hacking expeditions that were unsuccessful because they couldn't get close enough to their targets. Or they may have been scoping exercises.

The spies stayed for two nights at The Hague's Marriott Hotel, which is directly next door to the OPCW building. Minin took surveillance photos. He and his colleagues were security-conscious. They followed what appeared to be GRU protocols. They collected their own rubbish—cans of Heineken, bottles of fruit juice—and stowed it in the boot of their hired vehicle. They paid for equipment using cash.

On the day of the planned hack they got as close to the target as they could. The front of the OPCW is busy: black diplomatic limousines come and go; staff arrive on bikes, walking up steps to an entrance where the OPCW's name is written in several languages, including—ironically—Russian.

The spies approached from another direction. They parked the Citroën in the Marriott's parking lot, reversing it up to the OPCW building, visible a few yards away on the other side of black railings. The spot faces a loading bay with blue recycling bins. Everything was prepared. The hackers had obtained the OPCW's wi-fi access codes. The next step was to creep inside the network—an incorporeal raid done on many previous occasions.

It was at this delicate point that officers from the MIVD ambushed the GRU team as they emerged from a hotel lift. The Russians seemed surprised. They claimed that they were tourists.

According to the MIVD, Morenets tried to smash his phone. The Dutch officers recovered several mobiles from the scene and a host of other devices. One of the phones had been switched on in Moscow the day before the trip. It had connected with a cell tower next to . . . the Komsomolsky Prospekt GRU office.

The Citroën had become a mobile hacking unit. In the back was a wi-fi antenna panel, hidden beneath a coat. There was a transformer, a bag with a twelve-volt battery, and a laptop. The laptop was connected to the antenna and a 4G smartphone. The spies were carrying $20,000 and €20,000 in cash. The officers recovered Minin's camera, Serebriakov's backpack containing his laptop, and Morenets's taxi receipt with his signature on it.

The haul offered an unusual insight into the GRU's working habits. Evidently the spies had not considered the possibility that they might be arrested. Stored on the laptop was a photo taken in Rio de Janeiro of Serebriakov with a young Russian woman.

There were other leads. The laptop's web browsing history revealed searches for the OPCW, as well as previous wi-fi connections. In December 2017 it was used to log onto the wi-fi of the Grand Millennium Hotel in Kuala Lumpur. According to British ministers, Serebriakov flew to Malaysia to steal information about the country's MH17 investigation. Using diplomatic cover, he had hacked into the office of Malaysia's attorney general and the local police force.

There was evidence of what was planned next. After The Hague, the GRU's target was the Spiez laboratory in Switzerland. The Dutch found a train ticket from Utrecht via Basel to the Swiss capital, Bern, booked for April 17. This was a further indication that the close access team coordinated its activities with the Kremlin's diplomats abroad. The GRU officers were carrying Google map printouts of Moscow's missions in Bern and Geneva.

The Russians were escorted out of the country. Morenets's life of international travel came to a stop, his cover blown. It was an ignominious end to what had looked like just another road trip. British intelligence worked closely with their Dutch colleagues. According to Kanev's sources, GCHQ may have eavesdropped on Bakhtin's phone conversations with the GRU in Moscow and passed this information to the MIVD.

For the moment, the arrests were secret. The GRU might have reckoned that the fiasco in The Hague would stay that way. Previously, Dutch intelligence was reluctant to say anything about its activities.

Behind the scenes, however, Washington was pressurizing its ally to take a more public stand. The FBI was already working closely with Holland's other main agency, the General Intelligence and Security Service, known as the AIVD. Back in summer 2014 an AIVD hacker had penetrated the computer network of a university building next to Red Square in Moscow. This, it turned out, was no ordinary network.

The building was being used by Cozy Bear, the notorious Russian hacking group associated with the FSB. It was Cozy Bear that broke into Democratic Party servers several months before Fancy

Bear and the GRU conducted their own parallel intrusion. The AIVD got access to a security camera perched above the entrance to the Moscow building, overlooking a curved hallway. The camera recorded everyone who visited.

The Dutch were able to identify a group of about ten regular hackers by comparing their pictures with a list of known spies. Details were shared with the US. In 2014 the Dutch tipped off the NSA about Cozy Bear attacks—against the US State Department and two years later against the Democrats. The American agencies were grateful. They sent their Dutch colleagues flowers and cake, *de Volkskrant* newspaper reported, citing its own intelligence sources.

The latest arrests in The Hague meant that the US intelligence community had a comprehensive view of the GRU and its international operations.

The agency was malign. And ubiquitous. Its activities in America were far more extensive than the DNC hack, and older too. Beginning in late 2014 one of the Moscow GRU hackers, Yermakov, broke into the Westinghouse Electric Company. The nuclear power developer is based near Pittsburgh. Westinghouse supplies energy to Ukraine—hence the hack. (It went on for two years and involved a spoof domain name, "westinqhousenuclear.com," with a "q" for a "g.")

Other doping-related attacks were made against the Court of Arbitration for Sport, in Lausanne; the International Association of Athletics Federation (IAAF), in Monaco; and FIFA, in Zurich. It was hard to think of a sports body the GRU hadn't tried to compromise. A month after the Hague arrests, GRU hackers sent another round of spear-phishing emails to OPCW staff, purporting to come from Swiss federal authorities.

The FBI drew up a forty-one-page indictment against the GRU hackers. It was filed in a federal district court in the western district of Pennsylvania, where the Westinghouse Electric Company has its headquarters. Morenets and six others were accused of conspiracy against the United States as well as wire fraud, identity theft, and money laundering.

The indictment might be read as a rebuke to President Trump, whose refusal to admit Russian hacking looked increasingly out of step with the facts. The phenomenon was so blatant and so universal it left few major countries untouched. Ukraine was its prime victim, with America not far behind.

In October 2018 the Dutch and the British gave details of the Hague operation. The bureau's indictment was unsealed later the same day—part of a push towards greater transparency concerning Russia's operations.

The GRU was restlessly ambitious. Its hackers roamed the world. But was it competent? Russian military intelligence was certainly suffering a large number of setbacks and embarrassing reversals. An agency known for its ruthlessness and professionalism during the Cold War now gave the impression that it was incompetent and bungling, a shambling golem, lethal and dopey. GRU director Korobov was having a bad spring.

Actually, the greatest threat to the GRU in its twenty-first-century incarnation came not from Western counter-intelligence agencies and old foes such as the CIA and MI6. It emerged from a new and unlikely direction: a group of geeks and glasses-wearing gamers sitting in a living room.

CHAPTER 7
EVERYTHING IS OPEN

Tripoli–London–Seattle–Dagestan
2011–2020

The spying breed of animal keeps itself to the depths. Muddy
waters and darkness are more to its liking than publicity.
VIKTOR SUVOROV, SOVIET MILITARY INTELLIGENCE

In 2011 a civil war gripped Libya. There was revolution, the Arab Spring. Rebels backed by the US, the UK, and France were advancing on the capital, Tripoli. I was in Libya reporting for the *Guardian*. The insurgents moved forward through bombed-out towns as Muammar Gaddafi's forces retreated. Coastal cities in the west and east, oil refineries, Roman ruins and temples . . . all fell, one by one, as the regime lost ground.

These were dangerous times. In the town of Zawiyah I found locals celebrating victory in the main square. They were shooting in the air and doing wheel skids with Nissan cars and Jeeps. Gaddafi's soldiers had left the previous night. They had fled down the road. I saw a small, tubby boy—eight, perhaps—stomping on a Gaddafi flag. "The city is ruined. No problem. We will rebuild it," one local, Tariq Sadiq, told me.

The signs of battle were everywhere. The square's four-star Zawiyah Jewel Hotel was a ruin. The lobby was filled with rubble. Mattresses where Gaddafi's soldiers had slept lay strewn amid crates containing mortar cases and empty plastic water bottles. The air crackled with jubilant gunfire and shouts of *"Allahu akbar!"* and "The blood of martyrs will be avenged!"

The celebrations turned out to be premature. From their new positions, and without warning, Gadaffi's army began shelling the square. I took shelter in a building. First one mortar, then six more. Each was a loud thunderclap, a sudden, affirmative whumping followed by puffs of black smoke. It was time to go. I jogged across an eerily deserted city, now deathly quiet, back to the relative safety of a motorway flyover, the old front line.

At that moment I wasn't much interested in the type of munitions raining down. There was a simple urge: to escape. My reporterly role—as I saw it—was to tell the human stories of those unwillingly caught up in conflict and to chronicle the end of Gaddafi's rule. I had used this method in colourful dispatches from Afghanistan and Iraq.

I brought to Libya the usual tools of a front-line correspondent: flak jacket, satellite phone, and first-aid kit, carried in a rucksack. And notebooks. As a cub reporter in the English provinces, I had learned a form of shorthand, devised a century and a half earlier by a bearded Victorian publisher, Sir Isaac Pitman. The internet hadn't quite been invented yet.

Someone called Eliot Higgins was following events in Libya too—not from the front line but from his home in the East Midlands. Specifically, from his sofa. It was a safer place to be. And, as it turned out, as good a perch as any from where to analyze the conflict and to consider questions that in the heat of battle were interesting but evidently unanswerable. Such as, from where did the rebels get their arms?

Higgins recalls growing up as a shy "nerd." According to his brother Ross, Higgins was an obsessive gamer and early computer enthusiast. He liked Lego, played Pong on an antediluvian

1980s Atari, and was a fan of Dungeons and Dragons. He spent hours immersed in World of Warcraft, where participants pooled skills and collaborated across borders. His instincts were completist: he wanted to finish and win the game. This would prove useful later on.

Higgins tried for a career in journalism and enrolled on a media studies course in Southampton. This didn't work out and he exited without a degree. Next he earned a living via a series of unlikely administrative jobs. One was with Barclays Bank. (Physically, Higgins looks not unlike a thirty-something bank manager— glasses, dark hair, sensible jacket.) Another involved processing payments for a ladies' lingerie firm based in his home city of Leicester.

He was interested in military matters but lacked formal training. Higgins grew up on air bases, thanks to his father, who worked as an air force engineer. A grandfather took part in World War II and was a torpedo loader with the British Royal Navy; a great-grandfather was a World War I veteran.

At a time when he was between jobs, Higgins logged on to the *Guardian*'s Middle East live blog. Libya was the centre of international attention. Higgins made his own contributions to the website under the name Brown Moses—a pseudonym from a Frank Zappa song. The blog featured videos uploaded by anti-regime fighters. There was fierce debate as to whether these live images were authentic or bogus.

One video showed a newly captured town. The rebels claimed that this was Tiji, a sleepy settlement with a barracks recently bombed by NATO jets, close to the border with Tunisia and on the strategic main road leading to Tripoli. There was a mosque, a white road, a few little buildings with trees around. The video showed a rebel-driven tank rolling noisily down a two-lane highway. There were utility poles.

Higgins used satellite images to see if he could identify the settlement and thereby win the discussion. The features were sufficiently distinctive for him to be able to prove he was correct: the
town was Tiji. "I'm very argumentative," he says. It was the first
time he had used geolocation tools. He realized he could collect
user-generated videos and later work out exactly where they had
been filmed.

Shortly afterwards his first child was born—a daughter.
Higgins combined his new child-care duties with online research.
Meanwhile, the uprisings in the Arab world spread. Soon Syria
was at war too.

What began as a way of scoring points over online adversaries
evolved into something bigger. Smartphones with cameras, social
media, Facebook, Twitter, Google Earth, Google street view,
YouTube . . . the digital world was multiplying at an astonishing
rate. This stuff was open source. Anyone could access it. By cross-
checking video with existing photos and Google maps it was possible to conclude what was going on in a faraway war zone.

These techniques offered interesting possibilities. Open-source
journalism might be applied to the realm of justice and account-
ability. Sometimes soldiers filmed their own crimes—executions,
for example, carried out on faceless terrain. If you could identify
who and where, this could be evidence in a court of law. The shadow
cast by a dead body was a strong indication of time of death.

At home, and surrounded by his daughter's discarded toys,
Higgins unearthed a number of scoops. He found weapons from
Croatia in a video posted by a Syrian jihadist group. The weapons,
it emerged, were from the Saudis. The *New York Times* picked up
the story and put it on the front page—an indication of how arm-
chair analysis might be as telling as dispatches from the ground.

Higgins documented the Syrian regime's use of cluster bombs.
He discovered that government soldiers were tossing DIY barrel

bombs out of helicopters and that rebels were fighting back around Aleppo with Chinese-made shoulder-launched missiles. His reputation spread. He became an authority on weapons. He began using his real name after *Foreign Policy* magazine suggested he write an article.

In summer 2014 Higgins launched a new investigative website. The idea was to consolidate pioneering online research techniques and to connect with a wider pool of international volunteers. The British journalist Peter Jukes supplied a name: Bellingcat. Bellingcat came from "Piers the Ploughman," an allegorical poem written in the fourteenth century by the English cleric William Langland. I read it as an English student at Oxford.

In its prologue a group of rats and mice discuss what to do about a tyrannical cat. They decide on an early warning system:

> We must buy a bell of brass or shining silver, attach it to a collar and hang it around the cat's neck! Then we shall be able to hear what he's up to—whether he's stirring abroad or having a rest or running out to play; and if he's in a pleasant, frisky mood, we can peep out of our holes and just put in an appearance, but if he's in a bad temper, we can take care and keep out of his way.
>
> The whole rat-assembly applauded this scheme.

The rats soon think better of the plan. The cat, in Langland's telling, appears to be a reference to John of Gaunt and his battles with the English Parliament. Gaunt was a powerful and unpopular figure, the son of Edward III and founder of the royal House of Lancaster, and a symbol of temporal power.

The fable could be applied to any individual or state that behaved in a predatory or arbitrary way, especially one whose lies might be easily disproved.

In its latest form the cat was the Kremlin.

The more often it was "belled," the angrier this Kremlin cat became.

In July 2014, three days after Bellingcat went live, MH17 was blown out of the sky. The incident grew into Bellingcat's first major investigation. Higgins's team discovered that the Buk missile launcher had come from the 53rd Anti-Aircraft Missile Brigade, based in Kursk. Video showed the launcher trundling across Russia as part of a military convoy. The system was filmed again by locals inside Ukraine after MH17 was brought down, heading back to Russia with one of its missiles missing.

Bellingcat tracked down social media posts by individual Russian soldiers and photos. It pieced together a chain of command. Later, Dutch-led international prosecutors confirmed Bellingcat's findings. (In June 2019 they charged three Russians and a Ukrainian with murder. The Russians were former GRU officers.)

Bellingcat got bigger. A key person was Christo Grozev, a fluent Russian-speaker and a Bulgarian from an anti-communist family. Grozev grew up in Plovdiv, Bulgaria's second city; his father was fired from his job as a teacher for growing a hippie-style beard. Later Grozev lived in Moscow, owning a series of popular radio stations there. A tall and formidable figure, he was based in Holland at one point and speaks English with a mild Dutch accent; currently he lives in Vienna.

Bellingcat also joined forces with the *Insider*, an independent website whose editor in chief, Roman Dobrokhotov, is a talented Moscow journalist.

This collaboration would prove useful. By summer 2018 the British police were confident they had identified the two Russian suspects who carried out the Skripal hit. Their names had not been made public. The hope was that they might travel to Western countries where they could be arrested.

There were discussions inside the British government as to what to do, my newspaper was told. One course was to demand the suspects' extradition—knowing Putin would refuse, as he had with Litvinenko's murderers. Another was to recognize that there was zero prospect of a criminal trial and to publish concrete intelligence.

That September Theresa May went with option two. She told the House of Commons that the two Russian assassins were Ruslan Boshirov and Alexander Petrov—adding that the police believed these names to be aliases. CCTV images from their trips to Salisbury were revealed. Also shown was the apparent murder weapon—the counterfeit perfume bottle containing novichok.

The bottle was discovered earlier that summer under tragic circumstances. A local woman, Dawn Sturgess, died after spraying novichok on her wrists. Her partner, Charlie Rowley, fell seriously ill. Police believe Petrov and Boshirov abandoned the bottle during their trip to Salisbury in March. Rowley thinks it was introduced later—possibly as part of an operation by a second Russian team to confuse Scotland Yard.

The new details were a boon for Bellingcat. Over the next few weeks its volunteer rats and mice would scurry all over the evidence. They would inflict a series of humiliations on the GRU cat—ones that may have contributed to the fall of its chief, Korobov.

IN THE TWENTIETH century Soviet assassins were able to travel around Europe using fake passports. Their movements were seldom discovered. They may have been better, more professional spies. Or lesser ones. It was an age before transparency.

The modern GRU was still using the old Soviet playbook when it came to covert operations, such as the murder of enemies outside the country. These analogue plots now took place in a digital environment. GRU officers earned their spurs in the Soviet "near abroad"—in places such as Tajikistan or Moldova or Ukraine. There were few CCTV cameras to worry about. And not much of a CIA or other American presence.

Western Europe was a different matter. Britain, in particular, was a counter-intelligence challenge. The UK had closed-circuit television cameras on every public corner—in railway stations, hotel lobbies, and airports. Any passengers arriving on a flight from Moscow would be logged and filmed. A port of entry database was available to Western security agencies.

Meanwhile, Russian markets sold CDs of mass official information: home addresses, car registrations, telephone directories, and other bulk indexes. For £80 or so you could buy traffic police records. With the right contacts, and a modest cash payment, it was even possible to gain access to the national passport database.

Paradoxically, this low-level corruption made Russia one of the most open societies in the world.

Corruption was the friend of investigative journalism.

And the enemy of government–military secrets.

After the Metropolitan Police published photos of Boshirov and Petrov, Bellingcat took up the hunt. It sought to unmask their real identities. The first step was to reverse-image-search their photos via online search engines. This yielded nothing. It looked for telephone numbers associated with the two names. Nothing again.

And so the online investigators tried a deductive approach. They spoke to sources in Russia and asked where a GRU officer operating in Western Europe was likely to have been trained. One answer was Siberia and the Far Eastern Military Command Academy in Khabarovsk, just across the Amur River from China. The men appeared to be in their late thirties or early forties. This gave an approximate date of birth.

Yearbooks from the academy gave no results. A photo of a group of graduates taken in Chechnya looked promising, however. One of the soldiers—woolly hat, uniform, standing in front of anonymous snow-covered hills—looked like Boshirov. The 2018 article said that academy students had gone on to become "heroes of Russia," Moscow's highest military award. Was it possible that Boshirov was among them?

The academy's website included a photo of its memorial wall. In its centre was a gold statue of the Soviet marshal Konstantin Rokossovsky, one among several top commanders who led the Red Army to victory in World War II. And a list of names, engraved in gold letters. Ten were "heroes of Russia." Most had earned their accolade fighting against the Nazis—or in Afghanistan. Two names were more recent. An online list said only that the pair had got the honour "by decree of the Russian president."

One was too old. The other looked about right.

The name was Anatoliy Vladimirovich Chepiga.

Bellingcat searched for further traces. Soon the evidence piled up. Chepiga featured in an old 2003 database. There was no address—merely a designation for a *spetsnaz* military unit from the GRU's 14th Brigade, based in Khabarovsk. He surfaced again in 2012, in Moscow. Bellingcat obtained Chepiga's old passport documents, together with his photo. They gave his place of birth: the village of Nikolaevka, in the Amur region, near the Russia–China border. And a date of birth: April 4, 1979.

At the age of eighteen Chepiga had enrolled in the military academy, twenty-five miles from his village. He graduated in 2001. His brigade served three times in Chechnya. At some point between 2003 and 2010 he moved to Moscow and was trained at the GRU's main academy, known as the Conservatory. In 2014 his brigade was deployed to Ukraine. It was there he earned his "hero of Russia" award. What he did is unknown. After that Chepiga travelled frequently to Western Europe and the UK.

The passport photo was a younger version of the assassin wanted by the British authorities.

Chepiga was Boshirov, and Boshirov was Chepiga.

Chepiga was married with a child.

The first Skripal poisoner, then, was a father, a husband, a soldier, and a would-be murderer. And a veteran of conflicts in Russia's restive southern and western borderlands. But what about the second?

Identifying Petrov was to prove a little more difficult. A reverse image search of his photo and a sweep of military academies yielded no results. But there were other possible directions in which to go, based on previous cases.

In 2016 a GRU officer, Colonel Eduard Shishmakov, tried to organize a coup in the tiny Balkan state of Montenegro. Montenegro's attempt to join NATO appears to have sparked Moscow's undercover effort. The operation was a spectacular flop. (Shishmakov paid his Serbian conspirators using his real name, the GRU's Moscow address, and Western Union.) Montenegro's special prosecutor showed off Shishmakov's two Russian passports—his actual one and his fake one, registered in the name of an Eduard Shirokov.

The passports gave clues. First name, date of birth, and city of birth were the same in both. It was therefore a reasonable assumption that there was some crossover between Petrov's cover identity and his hidden real one. The Bellingcat team obtained Petrov's cover passport. They took the first name and patronymic—Alexander Yevgeniyevich—and birth date—July 13, 1979—and searched through black-market databases.

Bingo!

There was only one match: Alexander Yevgeniyevich Mishkin.

From there it was relatively easy to piece together Mishkin's biography. Like Morenets and Chepiga, Mishkin was born on the fringes of empire. His career might be read as a tale of provincial ambition. He grew up in the village of Loyga, in the *oblast* of Archangelsk. The village sits on the main rail line between Vologda and Kotlas in northern European Russia. There are no paved roads—just wooden dachas, birch trees, muddy byways, and fewer than seven hundred residents.

Mishkin lived with his grandmother, Loyga's resident doctor, until the age of sixteen. He moved to St. Petersburg for further study, enrolling in the city's oldest school of medicine, the S. M. Kirov Academy, and training in its fourth faculty. His path seemed assured: a military doctor specializing in undersea medicine, with a career in the navy and submarines.

The GRU had other ideas. It recruited Mishkin between 2007 and 2010 and gave him the cover name of Petrov. Mishkin moved to Moscow and lived there with his wife and two children. He was formally registered at a fake address and at the GRU's headquarters. Travel records obtained by Bellingcat show Mishkin's schedule. In 2013 there are multiple trips to Ukraine and to the breakaway Russian-backed republic of Transnistria, a sliver of territory between Ukraine and Moldova.

Mishkin had an unusual profession for an assassin: he was a doctor.

BELLINGCAT REVEALED THE identity of poisoner number one in a message on its website. The story went around the world.

Having unmasked one assassin, it seemed likely that Bellingcat would succeed in identifying Petrov as well. Sure enough, in late September I received an invitation to a press conference. It was to be held in an illustrious location: the neo-Gothic Houses of Parliament in London, and an upstairs committee room, number nine. Its subject was Petrov's real identity.

By the time I arrived, the room was full. I spotted a reporter from the *New York Times*, Ellen Barry, together with leading representatives from the British and US media. It was hard to escape the conclusion that power in journalism was shifting. It was moving away from established print titles and towards open-source innovators. The new hero of journalism was no longer a grizzled investigator burning shoe leather, à la *All the President's Men*, but a pasty-looking kid in front of a MacBook Air with a skinny latte.

Higgins and Grozev were there, as well as a Conservative MP, Bob Seely. I found a spot on a Victorian bench and sat down. The mood was excited. And expectant. Seely set the scene. He described Bellingcat as a "truly remarkable group of digital detectives"— Sherlock Holmeses for our restless times. Their success was due to an explosion of digital technology and a rise in digital activism, he said.

Grozev explained how Bellingcat had identified Petrov as Mishkin. The search involved methods new and old. It found Mishkin in a car insurance database, as the owner of a Volvo XC90. The car was registered to the GRU's headquarters at Khoroshevskoye Shosse. Next, the website used Russian social media to get in touch with Mishkin's student contemporaries. Did any of them remember him from their St. Petersburg days?

Most didn't answer. Two did. One said Mishkin had been in a different class. And that Russia's security services had got in touch two weeks before and instructed graduates not to divulge any information about Mishkin under any circumstances.

Lastly, the *Insider* dispatched a reporter to Mishkin's home village. At least seven residents identified Mishkin from the photo produced by the British police. Mishkin's grandmother—now in her nineties—wasn't home. Her neighbours, however, said it was well known that Mishkin had received a hero of Russia award in connection with Ukraine. This, they said, was to do with the annexation of Crimea or the operation to spirit President Yanukovych to Russia.

There was a last remarkable detail. Mishkin's granny had a photo of her son receiving the award, residents said, and showed it to them proudly while never letting it out of her grasp. The person congratulating Mishkin and shaking his hand was a celebrated figure: Russia's president.

Putin, then, had met one and possibly both of the assassins sent to Salisbury. He may even have picked them for the mission.

President Trump's honoured friend—the individual to whom Trump gravitated at G20 summits, like an iron filing attracted irresistibly to a powerful magnet—was involved in the business of murder. Not in an abstract way, but—apparently—in an executive capacity.

The photo appeared to support the conclusion of the 2016 public inquiry into Litvinenko's teacup death: that Putin "probably" approved the operation. Putin's view of traitors was well known. Evidence that he supervised their extermination was circumstantial—there was no hard proof. But it was growing.

CHEPIGA AND MISHKIN'S world began to unravel even before Bellingcat outed them in Parliament. Their photos—as Petrov and Boshirov—had been sprayed all over the place. This presented a dilemma for the GRU. One option was to hide the pair away forever. Another was to double down and instruct them to give a media interview.

This strategy had worked sufficiently well in the case of Litvinenko's killers, Lugovoi and Kovtun. Lugovoi made regular appearances on Russian state TV. From a studio sofa, he railed against MI6, the British, and the late oligarch Boris Berezovsky. Lugovoi insisted he was a victim. He was articulate—plausible enough for ordinary Russians watching at home who knew nothing of the details.

Someone inside the Russian state decided to try this model again. It may have been Putin, who used a conference in Vladivostok to urge them to come forward. Chepiga and Mishkin agreed (or, more probably, were told) to speak to RT's editor in chief, Margarita Simonyan. Simonyan was a trusted person and Russian media star—a leading *apparatchik* who sat on top of a global propaganda empire. Putin had given her an award for "objectivity" for RT's coverage of Crimea. What could possibly go wrong?

As it turned out, everything.

Chepiga and Mishkin's joint interview on RT was a disaster. It was an unintentionally comic performance that made them and the GRU a laughing stock, not only among English-speaking countries but across Russia too.

They were professional spies and so lacked media experience. They appeared nervous, shifty, under pressure, timorous, idiotic, and craven. Unlike Putin—a grand master when it came to deceit—they were lousy liars.

The pair insisted that they were not GRU officers. And that their real names were indeed Petrov and Boshirov. As for the curious events of Salisbury—well, these might be explained:

SIMONYAN: What were you doing there?
PETROV: Our friends have been suggesting for quite a long
    time that we visited this wonderful city.
SIMONYAN: Salisbury? A wonderful city?
PETROV: Yes.
SIMONYAN: What makes it so wonderful?
BOSHIROV: It's a tourist city. They have a famous cathedral
    there, Salisbury Cathedral. It's famous throughout Europe
    and, in fact, throughout the world, I think. It's famous for
    its 123-metre spire, it's famous for its clock. It's one of the
    oldest working clocks in the world.

Chepiga/Boshirov's knowledge of Salisbury seems to have been gleaned from a cursory reading of Russian Wikipedia. The cathedral spire is impressive—built in the thirteenth and fourteenth centuries, the tallest in Britain, octagonal, with flying buttresses and scissor arches, and praised by Sir Christopher Wren and Malcolm Muggeridge as a marvel. Still, it seemed unlikely this spire had drawn the two spies all the way from Moscow.

How also to explain the fact that the Russians visited Salisbury twice?

Chepiga/Boshirov's answer: there was heavy snowfall the weekend they arrived, which played havoc with transport connections and made them "wet." So drenched, actually, that the pair said they were forced to abandon their sightseeing on day one, Saturday, and take refuge in the train station coffee shop. And to buy new dry shoes on London's Oxford Street.

The pair said they came back the next day and admired the "beautiful English Gothic buildings." Again, they were compelled to return to London from Salisbury because of "heavy sleet." Maybe they passed the Skripals' house, maybe they didn't, Chepiga/Boshirov said. He added, "I'd never heard of them before this nightmare started." By profession, they were "sports nutritionists." They sold vitamins and fitness drugs. This mini-business took them to Switzerland and elsewhere.

As the interview goes forward, two things are evident. One, Simonyan finds it hard not to snigger at the spies' all-round uselessness and discomfort, especially when she asks why two grown men would share a room together, insinuating that they might be in a (furtive?) gay relationship. Two, the GRU soldiers express zero sympathy for their victim.

They are concerned for themselves:

PETROV: If they ever find the ones who did it, it'd be nice if
    they at least apologized to us.
SIMONYAN: Who? The poisoners?

BOSHIROV: No, the British . . . you have no idea what it's done
    to our lives.
PETROV: Can't even go and fill up your car in peace.

The dominant note is self-pity. They say they are frightened,
scared, uncertain what may happen tomorrow, and generally
wretched, ever since their photos appeared in the media.

PETROV: One just wants to hide and sit it all out.
BOSHIROV: So that they get off our backs. . . . we simply wish
    to be left alone.
PETROV: We're sick and tired of all this.
BOSHIROV: Exhausted.

With that the heroes of Russia vanish. They are not seen again.
    For the GRU, the interview turned out badly. It was excruciat-
ing, in fact. It did nothing for the organization's domestic reputation. A cartoon video of Boshirov and Petrov made the rounds on
the Russian internet. The pair dance and sing an innuendo-laden
song about how much they love each other's "spires." (It was eventually deleted.) Seemingly, even RT joined in the fun. The channel
published an online transcript. It illustrated the text with British
police photos of the killers walking along a snow-free street.
    Meanwhile, the hunt for Mishkin and Chepiga led to some
astonishing discoveries. Bellingcat searched for all vehicles registered at the GRU's Komsomolsky Prospekt address. It got 305 hits.
There were names, passport details, dates of birth, and in many
cases mobile phone numbers. The 305 were likely GRU spies. If
Bellingcat could find their names, the CIA could too.
    The GRU officers registered their cars to their work address
to avoid paying bribes to Moscow's traffic cops. The same search
method could be applied to other buildings associated with GRU

espionage, as well as to premises used by the FSB and the SVR, which were no doubt enjoying the GRU's misfortunes.

A further weakness was the GRU's system for undercover travel. A special unit—770001—issued passports to serving intelligence officers and state VIPs. Chepiga, Mishkin, and Shishmakov, the GRU officer active in Montenegro, got their alias passports this way.

Alas, these passports had something in common. They were issued in numerical sequence. Petrov's and Boshirov's differed by just three digits. The passport files contained other clues. There were the words "Top secret," a black stamp saying "Do not provide information," and a telephone number in case of queries that went to . . . GRU HQ.

This was a grievous foul-up. Sir Rodric Braithwaite, a former UK ambassador in Moscow, compared it to a mistake made by the NKVD—forerunner of the KGB—in the 1940s. The Soviets used "one time" cipher pads to encrypt secret traffic. During and after World War II some pads were reused. This allowed American and other Allied code-breakers to exploit Soviet communications and to uncover the names and code names of KGB and GRU agents, more than two hundred of them working in the US alone.

By following the numerical trail the Russian website Fontanka was able to identify another officer who was in London at the time of the Salisbury poisonings—the "third man," as he became known. His passport had the same telltale number pattern as Chepiga's and Mishkin's. And a cover name: Sergey Fedotov.

The officer's real name was Denis Sergeev. Sergeev was a GRU major general. And something of a war hero—in August 1999 he had led a paratrooper battalion in the mountains of Dagestan against the Chechen warlord Shamil Basayev. This soldier of unusually high rank oversaw the murderous events of Salisbury.

By pulling his mobile phone records, using sources inside Russia, Bellingcat was able to reconstruct Sergeev's movements. He arrived in

London a few hours before Mishkin and Chepiga. He may have met them in Oxford Circus, while the pair were ostensibly buying shoes. Sergeev spent the weekend holed up at a Paddington hotel. While in London, he spoke exclusively to a single person in Moscow: "Amir."

Cellphone records show Sergeev's extensive espionage footprint. In early 2014 he went with Mishkin to Prague, possibly at a time when Skripal was talking to Czech intelligence. The following year Sergeev appeared in Bulgaria just as a prominent local arms dealer, Emilian Gebrev, was poisoned at dinner. Gebrev had been selling weapons to Ukraine. He survived.

Sergeev dropped into London in April 2016, soon before the EU referendum, flying in from Lyon. And popped up in Barcelona days before Catalonia's unofficial independence vote. The following month, October 2017, he was in the same building where Suzan LeVine—the US's recent ambassador in Switzerland—was giving a public lecture in Lausanne. Sergeev's purpose is unknown. The image of female diplomat and circling spy is chilling.

According to Bellingcat and the *New York Times*, Sergeev, Chepiga, and Mishkin were members of a secret military unit, 29155. Comprising about fifteen to twenty elite GRU officers, it specialized in subversion, sabotage, and assassination. Its commander was a major general, Andrei Averyanov; its headquarters, a building in the Skhodnya area of northwestern Moscow. Russia's special operations base—where Sergeev was a frequent visitor—is nearby.

The officers functioned as a diversionary cell, sent behind enemy lines, exactly as in Cold War times. Their base, according to French intelligence officials, was in the Haute Savoie region of southeastern France, close to the Swiss border. From there they set off on missions—destabilizing Moldova and Ukraine, hatching coups in Montenegro, and rubbing out "traitors" in Britain and Bulgaria.

The Skripal case was part of an operational pattern. There were surveillance trips, stays in inconspicuous budget hotels, and close shadowings of targets. And car hire. Off duty, the officers laid low in a series of villages and ski resorts in the French Alps: Annemasse, Évian, Megève. They were anonymous, blended with the tourists. The unit appears to have been hidden from the wider GRU. Western security officials discovered it only after the misfire in Salisbury.

Even assassins, though, need to relax. In July 2017 Chepiga and his family attended a waterside wedding. The father of the bride was Averyanov—Chepiga's GRU boss, and another hero of Russia. Video turned up by Bellingcat shows Chepiga and other guests. He is dressed in a checked jacket and black tie, a glass of wine in his right hand, smiling, clapping, and toasting the happy couple.

MOSCOW OFFICIALS DID their best to fight back against these embarrassing revelations. They used familiar tactics—disdain, innuendo, and ludicrous counter-claims. Beginning in October 2018 they purged Petrov, Boshirov, and other officers from their internal systems. The unit appears to have been mothballed after four years of hiding out in Europe.

The Russian envoy in London, Alexander Yakovenko, accused Britain's spy agencies of poisoning the Skripals and then kidnapping them. He summoned the media to his Kensington embassy and expounded his theory in lengthy press conferences. The ambassador described Bellingcat as a branch of the "deep establishment"—a phrase that echoed Trump's attacks on the FBI. (This claim was based on a "feeling," Yakovenko said. He pronounced Bellingcat as "Billin-Cat.")

Russia's strategy was to paint Bellingcat as stooges and spies working for MI6. This was an old Soviet trope, deployed by the modern Kremlin against opposition critics at home. The geeks of Bellingcat weren't secret operatives. Their methods were open. They were collaborative. And quick.

The attacks ignored a more interesting truth: that spying was no longer the monopoly of nation states. "Now it belongs to anyone who has the brains, the spunk and the technological ability," Jonathan Eyal, of the Royal United Services Institute, a security and defence policy group, told the *New York Times*, adding, "We are witnessing a blurring of distinctions."

In Moscow, the Kremlin tried to limit the damage. The State Duma passed a new law banning the use of social media for servicemen. Neither Mishkin nor Chepiga had an online presence, but plenty of soldiers had posted photos online—allowing Bellingcat to reconstruct their movements. As Higgins pointed out, the "horse had bolted." Meanwhile, the GRU sent the website spear-phishing emails, using the same fake security alerts that fooled the DNC.

I got one of them halfway through writing this book. In summer 2019 hackers sent phishing emails to about thirty journalists and researchers pursuing Russia. When I logged onto my account with ProtonMail—an encrypted Swiss-based email service—I found a curious message. It said: "Your privacy may have been compromised." The email recommended I change my password and encryption keys. It gave links.

The message looked real, apart from one slightly awkward sentence: "Also it will be better to scan your devices for malware." The phrase sounds more natural in Russian.

Grozev and Dobrokhotov received an identical email the same day—Tuesday, July 23—purporting to come from ProtonMail's support team. The Swiss firm said it was the most sophisticated phishing attempt they'd seen. Bellingcat found it was part of a larger ongoing hacking operation, using various methods and tools, and carried out by a state actor. It looked like the GRU again. I used the ProtonMail address with a handful of trusted contacts. Disconcertingly, the GRU had somehow discovered it.

Meanwhile, it was becoming evident that in the Skripal affair, Moscow had miscalculated. Despite Brexit, the UK still had allies. More than twenty Western countries expelled Russian diplomats in solidarity with May's government. About 150 embassy-based spies, mostly GRU officers, were forced to pack their bags. This was a serious blow to Russia's overseas espionage network. The GRU's ability to collect intelligence and recruit agents was set back.

Ironically enough, the biggest clear-out of Russian spies took place in the US. The Trump administration removed sixty Russian officials, including a dozen based at the UN in New York. It shut the consulate in Seattle, ending the Russian Federation's diplomatic representation on the West Coast. Was this a sign that Trump—someone who had shown no great enthusiasm for confronting Moscow or his friend Vladimir—was finally getting tough?

It would seem not. According to the *New York Times*, Trump reacted sceptically to Britain's request for punitive Russian expulsions. He viewed Skripal's poisoning as "distasteful but within the bounds of espionage" and "part of legitimate spy games." "Some officials said they thought that Mr. Trump, who has frequently criticized 'rats' and other turncoats, had some sympathy for the Russian government's going after someone viewed as a traitor," the *Times* reported.

Trump took action because of the persuasive skills of the then CIA deputy director Gina Haspel, it added. Haspel showed the president photos of nerve agent victims. She recommended a "strong" expulsion option.

A separate report in the *Washington Post* said Trump was furious when he discovered the US had turfed out more Russians than Germany and France, who expelled four each. Trump had instructed his officials to match the European response, the *Post* wrote—something his aides interpreted to mean total European expulsions, rather than those by individual countries. Trump subsequently accused his aides of misleading him.

"There were curse words," one official told the *Post*, "a lot of curse words."

THE GRU'S 2016 operation to interfere in the US election was a triumphant success. It began as an exercise in psy-ops sabotage. It was meant to instil cynicism in Americans towards their own political system. No one, up to and including Putin, had thought that Trump might actually win. There was a strong case for believing that Russian interference had tipped the balance.

A few years later, however, the agency found itself in deep crisis. There were expulsions, indictments, and staggering foreign mishaps, which dented the image of invincible Russian spycraft. In Bulgaria, the GRU went back to re-poison the arms dealer Gebrev—only to fail a second time. At home and abroad Putin projected a strongman persona. Now he looked a little foolish.

What had gone awry?

According to the defector Viktor Suvorov, the decline in GRU standards was part of something larger. Suvorov—real name Vladimir Rezun—was a former GRU officer who fled to the UK from Geneva in 1978. He had been a convinced communist and a brilliant foreign intelligence agent-runner. Gradually he became disillusioned with the Soviet system. In exile he reinvented himself as a best-selling author and historian.

Suvorov likened his old organization's failings to a nasty cancer-like illness. It was eating up Russia's entire body politic. This disease had affected spying, technology, and rocket production, he told me. It explained the abysmal roads, the dying villages. The country was literally disintegrating. Suvorov used the word "*raspad*": collapse or breakdown. The situation was akin to the

Titanic, he said—swapping to metaphor—with the rich looking to exit in a lifeboat.

The glory days of the GRU were in the 1930s and '40s, when its agents stole the US's atomic secrets, Suvorov said. After the USSR's demise the organization fared better than the rest of the country. Its leaders were less corrupt than their KGB counterparts, more idealistic and disciplined, and paranoid about the West. They did their best with limited budgets and few operations abroad.

Over time, though, the service was destroyed, physically and morally. When Putin's foreign policy turned aggressive and he needed covert-agent recruits, the GRU was rebuilt. But the quality was gone.

In Suvorov's day GRU officers were Moscow slicks with university degrees, unaccented foreign languages, and Soviet-posh manners. The most famous was probably Evgeny Ivanov, a Soviet naval attaché in London who in 1961 had an affair with Christine Keeler, forcing the British war secretary, John Profumo (who had also slept with Keeler), to resign. Ivanov was handsome, clever, witty, hospitable, and charming. Ivanov's modern-day successors, by contrast, were poorly educated and provincial. In their late thirties and forties, they came from villages nobody had heard of.

No wonder they got caught, left, right, and centre.

Suvorov said his former service had sunk into "idiotism." Its generals were incompetent and greedy. As for Salisbury, this was a "chain of stupidity," featuring not very professional assassins caught repeatedly on closed-circuit television. "In my time this would not have been possible! Such idiots!" he exclaimed.

Putin personally approved the novichok plot, Suvorov suggested, reasoning, "Nobody would take responsibility without him." Suvorov said the Russian embassy in London may have given logistical support but wouldn't have known the details, with these restricted to probably about fifteen or twenty people, including a technical expert and a handful of top Kremlin officials. The two assassins belonged to a small group of "dirty" specialists. They would have killed before.

After Suvorov left the USSR, both the Russian state and the GRU sentenced him to death *in absentia*. The GRU would never forgive a traitor, even if a civilian government did, he said. The Salisbury attack was carried out—in his view—to deter GRU colleagues who might be contemplating defecting to America. "The GRU is saying to its own, 'Boys, look at that!'" he said.

Was he sure the GRU did Skripal? "Of course," he replied matter-of-factly.

Suvorov joined the GRU in 1970. Back then it was a bitter rival to the KGB. The KGB's headquarters—the Lubyanka—was in the centre of Moscow and highly visible, reflecting the KGB's mission to protect the regime from home-grown enemies. The GRU was lower-profile and "somewhere in the dark," Suvorov said, which made the latest revelations of its staff's identities all the more painful.

Bellingcat had exposed a large number of officers. Certainly hundreds. Possibly thousands.

It amounted to the biggest compromise of top-secret Moscow information since the end of the Cold War, when the Soviet foreign intelligence officer Vasili Mitrokhin gave MI6 highly classified material. Mitrokhin had been entrusted with transferring the KGB's external archive from the Lubyanka to its new Greater Moscow office in Yasenevo.

Over twelve years he took voluminous notes, which he hid in a milk churn at his dacha. The archive showed that the Kremlin's modern attempts to influence American politics were nothing new. Nor were its targets. Back in the day, the KGB ran disinformation campaigns against the CIA and the FBI, smearing the FBI's legendary chief J. Edgar Hoover, for example. It also tried—without success—to stop Reagan winning a second term.

I met Suvorov in London, at the office of his literary agent. This was in December 2018, exactly a century after Lenin set up Moscow's first military intelligence service, following a proposal from Trotsky. The GRU was in poor shape, we agreed. Sure, it still sent kill squads to Europe and engaged in hybrid forms of warfare such as hacking. But it had failed to adapt to a twenty-first-century universe of total information.

As the Russian investigative journalist Kanev put it to me, "Everything is open. It's possible to follow everything. Where you go, whom you meet, where you work." He attributed the GRU's setbacks to a variety of factors, including drunkenness, unprofessionalism, and *bardak*—the Russian word for chaos. "The world is changing. They are doing everything like in Soviet times," he said.

Dobrokhotov agreed. "If you take any interesting topic and scratch at it a bit, you will find some GRU agents underneath," he said. "They are super-active. But not very effective."

Who was to blame for all this? Other than Putin, the most obvious person was Korobov, the GRU's top commander. Korobov got this job in February 2016. The outgoing Obama administration sanctioned him, together with Russia's two other spy chiefs, SVR head Sergei Naryshkin and the FSB's Alexander Bortnikov, for the DNC hack. All were banned from the US.

And yet in February 2018 the Trump administration invited the trio to Washington for counter-terrorism talks. Naryshkin and Bortnikov met with Mike Pompeo, the US secretary of state. It's unclear what Korobov did or whom he saw, but his trip took place a month before the GRU's botched hit on Skripal.

That autumn Korobov's standing inside Russia's elite fell sharply. According to Kanev, the Ministry of Defence was awash with rumours that the GRU was due for a clear-out, with generals likely to be asked to leave. There was talk of "deep incompetence," "boundless carelessness," and "morons." Korobov was tipped to be shuffled out.

Kanev's sources said Korobov was summoned in mid-September to a personal meeting with Putin. The colonel general set off from his apartment in an elite complex used for top-ranking officers on Starovolynskaya Street, next to Moscow's Victory Park. We don't know if the discussion with Putin was friendly. Or a dressing down. On his way home, Korobov felt unwell. The story of the general's sudden illness swirled around the ministry, Kanev wrote.

True account or not, Putin failed to mention Korobov during a speech at Moscow's military theatre to mark the GRU's hundredth anniversary. Instead he spoke of comrades who had died in battle. "As supreme commander in chief, I certainly know your, without exaggeration, unique capabilities, including in special operations," Putin said. Korobov wasn't among those invited to the gala ceremony. Was he becoming a non-person?

Seemingly, Korobov's errors had caused Putin to lose face.

Later that November Russia's Ministry of Defence made a sad announcement. It said that Korobov had passed away. He was sixty-two. His death was due to a "long and serious illness," the ministry said. Was he dead because he messed up? "Of course, it's pure speculation," Suvorov told me. "But everyone inside the GRU will understand 125 per cent he was murdered." He added, "Even if it was a natural death, people will say, 'Come on!' Nobody will believe. They know the nature of the organization."

The apparent price of failure was steep: eternal silence. From the grave, Korobov was in no position to tell what he knew or defect to a welcoming Baltic country. The reward for success, though, was considerable. With energy and ambition and a bit of luck you could rise a long way. From prison to the court of the czar, from the imperial city of St. Petersburg to distant treasure-filled continents.

CHAPTER 8
EAST INDIA COMPANY

Central African Republic–St. Petersburg
2012–2020

A state in the guise of a merchant.
EDMUND BURKE ON THE EAST INDIA COMPANY

The assignment was tough but doable. The brief: to shoot a documentary film about the activities of the Wagner Group, a notorious Russian mercenary outfit. Where to start? The group's ghost army was everywhere and nowhere. It had been seen in eastern Ukraine, in Syria, and in Sudan—fighting on the side of Moscow-backed rebels or shoring up Kremlin-friendly dictators. Now it was making inroads all across Africa.

Wagner's soldiers were elusive. They didn't work *officially* for the Russian state. In fact, private military companies didn't exist in Russia, at least not in any formal sense. As Peskov, Putin's press spokesman, put it, choosing his words with care, "*De jure* we do not have such legal entities."

And so everything Wagner's gunmen did was happily deniable. If they were killed while fighting overseas—something that regrettably happened in Syria, after a disastrous encounter with US forces near the city of Deir ez-Zor in 2018—that had nothing to do with Moscow! No need to explain to the press or answer questions in bilateral forums.

Nor could a direct link be drawn with the man who allegedly funded the Wagner Group and masterminded its myriad secret affairs. His name was Evgeny Prigozhin. He wasn't a government person. So far as the Kremlin was concerned, he was a talented entrepreneur from St. Petersburg.

Despite these disavowals, Prigozhin's mercenaries popped up in all of Moscow's wars. In 2014 they appeared in Donetsk and Luhansk, the rebel provinces of Ukraine whose anti-Kyiv "uprising" Moscow armed and propelled. In Syria they supplemented the regular Russian troops sent after 2015 to prop up Syrian president Bashar al-Assad. And in 2018 Wagner operatives and advisers worked closely with Omar Hassan al-Bashir, Sudan's Putin-backed leader.

Journalists seeking facts had few options. The Wagner Group didn't have a website or a press department. Its commander was said to be Dmitry Utkin, a GRU lieutenant colonel. Utkin's call sign was Wagner, a name chosen because of his enthusiasm for the helicopter scene from Francis Ford Coppola's *Apocalypse Now*. Other Wagner contractors had links with Russia's far right and the group Russky Obraz, I was told. Few knew how many armed men Utkin controlled. Was it 1,350, or perhaps 2,000?

The Russian journalists investigating Wagner decided on a logical approach: to find their subjects. They included Orkhan Dzhemal, an experienced correspondent; producer Alexander Rastorguyev; and cameraman Kirill Radchenko. The trio were working for the Investigation Control Centre (ICC), an independent media outlet set up in 2016 and funded by Mikhail Khodorkovsky, a former oligarch and Kremlin bête noire.

The first step was to shoot secret footage of Wagner's base near Krasnodar, in southern Russia. It was there that mercenaries were recruited, vetted, and trained. Regular Russian troops guarded the territory in the village of Molkino. It had a tank polygon (a crisscross of black tracks across a green field), multiple shooting ranges, and accommodation tents.

There was a small chapel on the road south from the base: a grey cube with a gold dome and arched window dedicated to fallen Wagner "volunteers."

Near it was a mawkish statue of a mercenary, dressed in full body armour and holding a weapon. A small girl clung to his right leg. The statue honoured Wagner employees who had died in Syria. On the base was a black cross set against a red background and the words "For blood and bravery." In 2018 the same mercenary shrine appeared in other cities where Wagner has been active: in a main square in Luhansk and at a regime complex near the Syrian city of Palmyra.

Military insignia, posthumous medals, statues, and chapels . . . the Wagner Group had all the symbols and rituals of a regular army. Except, of course, it wasn't one. It was a phantom brotherhood, made up of invisible killers working for money. They could be used for shadow state projects and then made to vanish, as if by witchcraft.

The Russian reporters wanted to track down Wagner soldiers to Syria or Sudan. Syria was problematic, though. Russian military intelligence staff were deeply embedded in Assad's military. The presence of journalists in the country might be swiftly detected. Syria was dangerous—for its long-suffering civilian population, first and foremost, but also for visiting TV crews seen as adversaries.

Meanwhile, there were intriguing rumours that Wagner had begun operating in one of Africa's most downtrodden states, the Central African Republic (CAR). In October 2017 the CAR's president, Faustin-Archange Touadéra, flew to Russia and met Foreign Minister Lavrov in Sochi. Moscow got permission from the UN to begin supplying the CAR with weapons as part of a peacekeeping operation. It would send trainers to the region.

Out of sight, the CAR delegation held talks with Prigozhin representatives. A deal was signed: a new gold and diamond mining company would be established in the prefectures of Lobaye and Haute-Kotto and guarded by Wagner staff. In return Wagner would take care of the president's personal security and provide in-country training for troops and gendarmes. Cut-price precious stones would flow in one direction; rifles and heavy weapons in the other.

A broke CAR was in the grip of a nasty sectarian war that was being fought by Christian and Muslim militias among dirt-poor rural settlements. Evidently Russia was seeking to boost its presence in a weakly ruled country and to squeeze out France, its former colonial power. It appeared to be part of a Russian push across the continent. From late 2017 Moscow began delivering arms to Touadéra's government and sending military personnel. The president got a new Russian national security adviser, a balding former intelligence officer from St. Petersburg, Valery Zakharov.

Signs of growing Russian influence were there if you looked carefully. According to South Africa's *Mail & Guardian*, an unmarked vehicle began to pay weekly visits to the Grand Café in central Bangui, the CAR's capital. The café served Western-style coffee and croissants. The occupants picked up their order—a delivery of baguettes—and quickly headed off. Their destination was Berengo Palace, which used to belong to the country's emperor, Jean-Bédel Bokassa. It was now home to 175 Wagner mercenaries, camped out amid crumbling grounds.

Senior Wagner staff rented an office in the capital. It was nicknamed the "Bangui Hilton." There was a large map of the Republic on the wall and a pile of weapons, just in case. From time to time, Zakharov would drop in for a snooze. One of Prigozhin's senior political advisers, Evgeny Kopot, posed for a photo holding a Kalashnikov. He's wearing aviator shades and a T-shirt with a logo in Arabic for RT, the Russian television channel.

The journalists decided to dump the Syria plan and fly to the CAR. For the trip to work, the team needed a fixer. In June 2018 they met a Moscow journalist, Kirill Romanovsky, who agreed to help. Romanovsky recommended a "local UN contact" called "Martin." The team got in touch with "Martin" via WhatsApp. "Martin" said he would arrange accommodation in Bangui and a driver who could translate.

In July the three Russians flew to Bangui via Casablanca. They arrived two days earlier than scheduled. "Martin" had agreed to provide a pickup from the airport. Strangely, there was nobody there to meet them. "Martin" wasn't responding to messages. The journalists made their way to the Hotel National. Eventually "Martin" got in touch and said he would send them a driver.

The journalists had a few days left to live.

The next day Dzhemal, Rastorguyev, and Radchenko set off for Berengo, some forty-seven miles from the capital. Inside the once-elegant palace Wagner mercenaries were training more than a thousand CAR soldiers. The trip was a disappointment: the guard on duty, who spoke Russian and English, refused to let them in.

On July 30 the group hit the road again. Their destination was Bambari, a town not far from gold mines guarded by Utkin's mercenaries. Maybe they would have better luck and be able to film the gunmen? The Russians told the receptionist they would be back in a few days and left a suitcase. By early evening they had reached the town of Sibut. From there they were supposed to continue east, towards Bambari. Instead their driver took them north, in the direction of Dékoua.

The scenery along the route was attractive: a vivid orange dirt road running between green forest and lush savannah, with an occasional village along the way. Dzhemal sat in the front, Rastorguyev and Radchenko in the back. At 7:00 p.m. the journalists exited Sibut and reached an army checkpoint. The local soldiers radioed the Russian base at Sibut and were ordered to let the car pass. Unbeknownst to the group, an SUV had crossed the same checkpoint minutes earlier. In it were five people, three of them white.

The ambush took place fourteen miles down the road.

The killers halted the journalists' vehicle. They dragged the passengers out. Dzhemal was beaten and then shot in the back seven times as he crawled along the ground. Rastorguyev was executed with a direct shot to the heart. Radchenko made a run for it, was caught, and then gunned down amid tall grass. His body was discovered yards away from Dzhemal and Rastorguyev, who were clumped together in death.

The murderers used AK-47s. They appeared to be seasoned professionals who—the ex-oligarch Khodorkovsky suggested later—had fought in eastern Ukraine and Syria. The journalists' personal effects, including Dzhemal's laptop, were untouched. The gunmen left behind three cans of petrol, loaded onto the back of the pickup—a valuable commodity in one of the poorest places on earth. The driver survived. He escaped.

At 8:00 p.m. the SUV recrossed the Sibut checkpoint, local soldiers said. It disappeared into the dark. The reporters' bodies were found the next day and taken to the morgue. Unknown persons set light to the ground where they had lain, destroying possible evidence and leaving behind black shapes.

IT TOOK A year before a team of investigators working for Khodorkovsky's Dossier Centre figured out exactly what had happened. The centre collected cellphone data and WhatsApp messages. It bought local Facebook ads asking for information. Private detectives recorded video interviews with villagers who lived close to the murder scene. There were autopsy reports. These allowed the killings to be reconstructed as graphics. Four to six gunmen had opened fire from close range.

The journalists were doomed from the beginning, it emerged. There were editorial blunders. The most serious was to rely on the Moscow journalist and cameraman Romanovsky. His elusive fixer, "Martin," turned out not to exist. "Martin" stopped replying to messages after the murders. He had been communicating with the journalists using a burner phone.

The Russians had walked straight into a well-planned trap, set before they even left home. In Bangui they were under surveillance. A member of the gendarmerie, Emmanuel Kotofio, monitored their movements. He had worked with Wagner instructors in Sudan. On the night of the murders he was seen sitting in the SUV that left Sibut ahead of the journalists' car. (When reached by the Associated Press, Kotofio hung up.)

There were links too between officials in the CAR and Prigozhin employees. Cellphone records show that Kotofio was in contact with the journalists' driver, who subsequently vanished. Kotofio made calls to Alexander Sotov, a Wagner instructor. Sotov spoke to other Russians inside the country, including the national security adviser, Zakharov.

The picture pieced together by Khodorkovsky's team was disturbing. Romanovsky worked for the Federal News Agency. The website was part of a sprawling disinformation empire funded by Prigozhin, the very person whose ambiguous activities the filmmakers were seeking to investigate.

The brutal slaying of the three Russians created a headache for the Wagner Group—and for Russia's Foreign Ministry. How to explain the murder of journalists probing a mercenary firm? Prigozhin's back office in St. Petersburg came up with an answer. It invented a different version of events: ten bandits speaking Arabic stopped the car and shot its occupants. The motive had nothing to do with politics. It was a robbery. Russian officials repeated this version, avoiding any mention of Wagner—the reason the team flew to Africa in the first place.

In the aftermath of the murders Romanovsky faced questions about his role in the affair and his apparent complicity in the cold-blooded executions. He gave evasive accounts of how he knew "Martin" and said he couldn't provide old chats because his phone "broke." He claimed to have met "Martin" ten years ago, later bumping into one of his friends in a Berlin supermarket.

This narrative was, frankly, rubbish. Romanovsky probably knew as much. He asked a senior colleague for help—Mikhail Burchik. On a Saturday evening in October 2018 the pair swapped messages. Romanovsky said he was being pressed for details. He asked Burchik how he might describe the supermarket. Burchik told Romanovsky to keep it vague.

> BURCHIK: [Say] a small supermarket in some sort of area no need to give any kind of further info.
> ROMANOVSKY: That will arouse suspicion. They will try and send me photos [of the building] from Berlin.
> BURCHIK: [Say] I don't remember something with a red roof.

Burchik wasn't a stranger to cover-ups; in fact, he was well versed in them. He was executive director of a Prigozhin shadow unit that was better known than the Wagner Group. It called itself the Internet Research Agency. It had recently carried out a stunning and successful campaign to influence an election result. Not in a broken-down African state, where you could buy a police chief for a few thousand dollars, but in the world's most powerful democracy.

THE CASE BEFORE Judge Abramov looked open and shut. It was a worrying sign of the times! The date was October 1981. The individual brought before the People's Court in Leningrad was a repeat offender. Two years previously he'd been convicted of theft. The Soviet state had treated him with leniency and ordered him to work for the national economy in a chemical factory. Instead of reforming, and doing his socialist duty, he'd embarked on a further round of breaking and entering.

The bold young hooligan sitting in the dock was called Zhenia. First name Evgeny, surname Prigozhin. He was twenty years old. His crimes were set out in a series of typed court documents, found many years later via the *Rosbalt* website. In February 1980 Prigozhin broke into the apartment of a citizen called Osipov. He made off with Osipov's modest possessions—wine glasses, a vase, and a napkin holder. The loss was put at 177 roubles. This was a little over a month's salary.

Weeks later Prigozhin went on another crime spree. Drunk, he clambered onto a first-floor window and was chased away. The next night he set out with a Leningrad friend and a teenage girl. They broke into an apartment. Their haul was a Soviet-made Orbita tape recorder, a denim jacket, and a woman's handbag and make-up. The gang was involved in other illicit activity, the court records say—selling jeans on the black market.

The end came after a night drinking cognac and champagne in the Ocean restaurant. On the way out, Prigozhin saw a young woman wearing an attractive coat. He and his accomplices followed her home. Prigozhin grabbed her by the neck, dragged her off the street, and threw her to the ground, the court was told; then his friend yanked off her boots and earrings. The police heard her screams. They arrested Prigozhin and found the handbag plus other items in his room.

Prigozhin didn't bother to deny his crimes. He was duly convicted of robbery, theft, fraud, and involving a minor in criminal activity. Abramov took a negative view of the case—besmirching as it did the reputation of the USSR. He sentenced Prigozhin to thirteen years in a penal colony. The young ruffian spent most of his twenties behind bars.

By the time he emerged, nine years later, stealing was not the crime it once was. Everybody was doing it—red factory bosses turned entrepreneurs, KGB officers, and twenty-something capitalists who began flogging everything from Xerox machines to ladies' tights. Prigozhin found a different niche: fast food. He became Leningrad's first seller of hot dogs.

Shady contacts helped, and an ex-classmate invited him to manage a chain of new private supermarkets. In 1996 Prigozhin opened St. Petersburg's first elite restaurant, the Old Customs House. Its menu of truffles, black caviar with pancakes, and Kamchatka crab salad was a hit with affluent diners. Two groups became his regular customers: city bureaucrats and ex-police and sports guys. The money rolled in. He set up a company, Concord Catering.

Prigozhin's next venture was another success. In 1998 a meal in Paris on the Seine inspired him to buy an old boat once used as a disco. He renovated it and moored it on St. Petersburg's Neva River. The floating restaurant, New Island, attracted Russia's leading politicians. In 2001 Putin had dinner on the boat with French president Jacques Chirac and their respective wives. Putin came back a year later with US president George W. Bush, and in 2003 celebrated his birthday there.

Putin—as everyone knew—was mistrustful. Especially about food and drink, the easiest way to poison someone, as the KGB well understood. How did Prigozhin gain Putin's confidence? Prigozhin said he impressed Putin by personally serving him and his VIP guests. Prigozhin was entertaining company, a good storyteller, and something of a court jester, his staff told Russian media. The talented caterer cultivated Putin's entourage too, including the president's security chief and judo partner, Viktor Zolotov.

This was only part of the story. St. Petersburg was Russia's most criminal city, a place where gangsters and politicians fraternized and did deals. This was Prigozhin's milieu. "Putin mediated between local criminal groups, local corrupt police, and other security agencies," Khodorkovsky told *American Interest* magazine. "Prigozhin was deeply involved in these communities and the two shared many mutual friends."

Putin's trusted associates fell into two categories, loosely speaking. The largest group was Chekists—former spies. The other was made up of thugs and mafia types. Prigozhin was never a Chekist. His time in jail and alleged underworld connections put him firmly in the second, gangster camp.

By the 2000s Prigozhin had become a member of Putin's inner circle. He acquired a nickname reflecting his favoured status: "Putin's chef." Prigozhin was rapidly becoming cook to the whole of Russia, a catering oligarch like no other, thanks to a raft of lucrative public contracts from his Kremlin friends.

He provided food to the St. Petersburg International Economic Forum, to which the Russian government later invited Trump and Cohen. Concord cooked the banquet for Dmitry Medvedev's 2008 presidential inauguration. It opened a restaurant inside the State Duma. And it began feeding Moscow schoolkids, despite protests from parents, who complained of lousy meals. In 2012 Prigozhin won a contract to serve the Russian army and perform other services in military towns—worth 200 billion roubles.

Prigozhin became a billionaire. The days of stealing Orbita cassette players must have seemed far away. He acquired a private plane, a yacht—the appropriately named *St. Vitamin*—and a collection of luxury cars, including a powder-blue Cadillac used by his mother. There were properties in St. Petersburg. His palace-like home featured a swimming pool, an orangery, a helipad, and a flagpole with the Russian tricolour.

There were plenty of reasons to thank Putin. Prigozhin's life was a picaresque tale: thief, jailbird, merchant, courtier to the czar. Prigozhin showed gratitude via a variety of projects. They had a national flavour and seemed designed to please the boss. They furthered the interests of the Russian state—and Prigozhin's business interests as well.

The boundary between the two was hard to distinguish. It was almost invisible.

OLGINO WAS A pleasant neighbourhood. From his studio apartment, Jay Aslanov could walk to the metro or drop in for groceries at the Auchan hypermarket. One of St. Petersburg's largest green spaces was on his doorstep. It was a park of culture on an island and named after Sergei Kirov, the murdered (whom the NKVD likely killed) friend of Stalin. There were canals, ponds, and a bright view of the Neva River estuary.

Aslanov's apartment, at 104 Savushkina Street, was on the same road as the office where he worked. This was a modern, anonymous, four-storey building, at number 55. A sign at the entrance said, "Business Centre." There were no indications as to what the building's occupants actually did. It resembled a regular office, except that the lights burned day and night.

The house was dedicated to something Putin viewed with suspicion: the internet. The online world posed an obvious threat to Putin's authority. Though he didn't use email himself, Putin was anxious to keep a grip on content and make sure that any data sat on Russian rather than US servers. The FSB was tapping the Russian internet via an intrusive spy system called SORM.

Russia may not have invented the web, but it was quick to understand that its leading platforms—Facebook, YouTube,

Twitter, Instagram—might be turned back against the country that devised them. America believed in an open model. Anyone could post content or contribute. Using paid operatives posing as real individuals, it was possible to push a conversation on social media in a certain direction. You could promote state-friendly attitudes and trash Putin-critical ones. The opportunities for influence were boundless. With a little ingenuity, the internet could be weaponized.

These operatives had a name: trolls.

The St. Petersburg building was home to the Internet Research Agency (IRA), run by Burchik and General Director Mikhail Bystrov. It became known as the "troll factory." Prigozhin—according to Mueller's indictment—funded its activities. Burchik—a young man of good looks and chestnut hair—joined in 2013. (Burchik called the US charges "gibberish.") Bystrov and Burchik met Prigozhin regularly. The Federal News Agency was based in the same office before moving elsewhere.

At first the trolls targeted the Russian-language internet. They posted pro-Putin comments on municipal chat forums and social networks such as Live Journal. Blogs would mix observations on innocent topics—"Signs that show you are dating the wrong girl" or "Europe's twenty most beautiful castles"—with politically partisan posts about Ukraine, or claims that opposition leader Alexey Navalny took money from the State Department.

Each morning the trolls were given "technical tasks," telling them what lines to take. They had to dream up their own non-political content. "The scariest thing is when you talk to your friends and they are repeating the same things you saw in the technical tasks, and you realize that all this is having an effect," one former troll told the *Guardian*'s Moscow correspondent, Shaun Walker. He—or she—spoke anonymously. All IRA employees sign a nondisclosure agreement.

In the summer of 2010 the FBI arrested a group of Russian deep cover sleeper agents. They were swapped at Vienna airport for Russian spies who had been working for the CIA and MI6. One of them was Sergei Skripal. After eight years in the UK, Skripal may have forgotten about his old employer in Moscow, Russia's GRU military spy agency. It remembered him. In March 2018 two GRU assassins tracked down Skripal to his home in Salisbury. They poisoned him with a Soviet nerve agent, novichok.
Handout

Skripal and his daughter, Yulia, survived. The incident traumatised the local community and sparked a political and health emergency. Downing Street blamed Vladimir Putin. Britain, the US, and their allies expelled more than 150 GRU spies. Donald Trump subsequently complained that Washington had overreacted.
Ben Stansall/AFP/via Getty Images

Heroes of Russia. Anatoliy Chepiga and Alexander Mishkin were colonels working for a super-secret GRU kill unit with a base in France. Using diplomatic passports issued under fake names, the two flew to the UK to murder Skripal. Their operation was an embarrassing failure.
Metropolitan Police

Back in Moscow, Chepiga and Mishkin made a disastrous appearance on the Kremlin's RT TV channel. They denied wrongdoing and said they had travelled to snowy Britain to see Salisbury's famous cathedral and spire. Few believed them.
TASS/via Getty Images

While in the Oval Office, Trump repeatedly praised Putin, the man who helped put him there. Their summit in Helsinki was arguably Trump's worst diplomatic moment. Putin said Russia didn't meddle in the 2016 vote—a lie. Trump believed it and said so at their joint press conference. Putin managed Trump in classic KGB style: as an asset to be flattered.

Chris McGrath/Getty Images News/via Getty Images

The most famous MI6 officer since James Bond. Christopher Steele spent twenty-two years working for British intelligence. He's pictured here (*left*) with business partner Christopher Burrows at a party to celebrate the tenth anniversary of their intelligence firm Orbis. Steele's 2016 dossier claims that Moscow has compromising material on Trump—something the president vehemently denies.

Orbis Business Intelligence

Putin's press secretary and long-time deputy chief of staff Dmitry Peskov, seen here on a night out with his Olympic ice dancer wife, Tatiana Navka. Peskov's job was to dissemble on behalf of his boss. He did it well, backing up false claims by Trump in 2016 over a proposed Moscow Tower.

Valery Shalifulin/TASS

The lovelorn spy. Aleksei Morenets (*below and right*) was part of a GRU "close access" team. His job was to hack into Kremlin targets around the world, including the World Anti-Doping Agency. Morenets's undercover career made it tricky to meet girls, so he took out an advert on a dating website. *Dutch Ministry of Defence*

Tuesday 10 April 2018
• Arrival from Moscow at Amsterdam Schiphol Airport

Caught in the act. In April 2018 Morenets and his GRU colleagues flew into the Netherlands on a routine mission. Dutch intelligence was watching. The Russian spies were arrested in the car park of a hotel in The Hague, while trying to hack the Organisation for the Prohibition of Chemical Weapons. *Dutch Ministry of Defence*

Viktor Suvorov was a star intelligence officer who defected to the UK during the Cold War. In his view, the GRU's mistakes over Skripal were one aspect of a wider malaise afflicting all aspects of Russian life, from science to espionage. Suvorov is the only living GRU insider to talk publicly. Moscow has sentenced him to death. *Sebastian Nevels/*Guardian

A geek and a sleuth. Eliot Higgins founded Bellingcat from a sofa in his home in the Midlands. The investigative website pioneered open-source reporting. It took advantage of this century's explosion in digital information, breaking a number of GRU scoops and earning the Kremlin's hate. *Prioschka van de Wouw/AFP/via Getty Images*

In the run-up to the 2016 EU referendum, businessman Arron Banks gave £8.4 million to Leave.EU, a pro-Brexit group. At the same time, Russia's embassy in London secretly invited Banks to invest in Siberian gold and diamonds. A special deal "not available to others" is how a PowerPoint slide put it. *From left to right:* Gerry Gunster, Arron Banks, Donald Trump, Nigel Farage, Andy Wigmore, Raheem Kassam.
Twitter/Leave.EU

A bald, bespectacled spy straight out of a Le Carré novel, Sergei Nalobin was based in London under diplomatic cover. He cultivated leading Tories, including future prime minister Boris Johnson, and ran an ill-fated pro-Kremlin parliamentary group, the Conservative Friends of Russia.
Twitter/Sergei Nalobin

Russian diplomat Alexander Udod wearing the ribbon of St George, a symbol of Soviet victory over fascism and a latter-day anti-Western emblem. Udod liaised with Brexit activists, including Banks and Nigel Farage, a friend of Trump and Steve Bannon. The government expelled Udod for espionage following Skripal's 2018 poisoning.
Russian Embassy

Evgeny Prigozhin, pictured in imperial costume with his family in a study for a painting. The hot-dog seller turned oligarch is known as Putin's chef. According to the FBI, he funded the "troll factory" in St. Petersburg, which backed Trump in 2016. Prigozhin is also behind Russia's recent push into Africa. *Dossier Centre*

Mikhail Burchik, a "troll factory" director, pictured at his 2008 wedding to his wife, Renata. The Internet Research Agency, or IRA, employed hundreds of trolls, some of them fluent in English. They posted pro-Putin content and denigrated critics. In 2016 they impersonated Americans on Facebook and Twitter. *Odnoklassniki*

In 2015 Burchik got a thank-you gift from Russia's military: a gold watch. The inscription reads: "From the chief of the main operational department of the armed forces of the Russian Federation." *Dossier Centre*

Jay Aslanov, a "troll factory" executive, posing against a moody sky. Aslanov lived on the same road as the agency's HQ, in the Olgino neighbourhood of St. Petersburg. He wrote analytical papers for the "boss"—Prigozhin—and claimed credit for Trump's 2016 victory in US swing states. *botsman.info*

Russian mercenaries from Prigozhin's Wagner Group on the move in the Central African Republic (CAR). The soldiers have been sent to Sudan, Libya, Syria, and Ukraine, a shadow army performing useful tasks. They are referred to internally as "musicians"—a pun on the name Wagner. *Dossier Centre*

Political adviser Evgeny Kopot, posing with a Kalashnikov inside Wagner's office in the CAR capital of Bangui. Kopot is wearing a Russia Today (RT) Arabic T-shirt. On the wall is a map of the CAR. Prigozhin's men provide security for the country's president and train local soldiers. *Dossier Centre*

At barely five feet tall, Konstantin Kilimnik (*far left*) was easy to miss. He was known as "Kostya from the GRU"—in other words, as a suspected Russian spy. Kilimnik spent a decade working with Paul Manafort (*seated, centre*) in Ukraine. In 2016 Manafort gave Kilimnik data on the Trump campaign. What Kilimnik did with it is unknown.
Handout

Special Counsel Robert Mueller spent almost two years investigating Trump and Russia. In contrast to Watergate, Mueller did not follow the money or consider whether the FSB spy agency had *kompromat* on the US president. Mueller's 2019 report cleared Trump of criminal conspiracy. It was a historic miss. *Win McNamee/Getty Images News/via Getty Images*

In 2019 TV comedian Volodymyr Zelensky became Ukraine's new president. It was a rise as improbable as Trump's own. Trump browbeat Zelensky into digging up dirt on his Democratic rival Joe Biden, as part of a shadow foreign policy. This unwise action led to Trump's impeachment and Senate trial, where Republicans acquitted him.
Saul Loeb/AFP/via Getty Images

Boris Johnson with his girlfriend, Carrie Symonds, on the steps of 10 Downing Street. Johnson celebrated his 2019 election victory at a party given by ex-KGB agent turned media tycoon Alexander Lebedev.
Reuters

IRA employees were divided into two sets. There were those who genuinely supported Putin and his anti-Western mission, and the rest, who viewed their work with indifference and cynicism and who couldn't find a job elsewhere, the ex-troll said. Supervisors carefully vetted the factory's output. They would fire anyone who went off script or failed to keep up an allegro comment rate.

Like Wagner mercenaries, Prigozhin's keyboard warriors were invisible and ubiquitous. They commented anonymously on the *New York Times*, *Guardian*, and other English-language news websites. Posts were shrill, blatant, and *ad hominem*—a wave of vitriol and propaganda endorsed by fellow trolls and bots. In the early days these contributions rolled out in clunky English. Over time the language improved, to the point where the trolls began to sound like Americans.

The trolls were especially active during Russia's 2014 war in Ukraine, where disinformation was deployed alongside tanks and artillery. Other correspondents and I drew thousands of abusive messages, posted at the bottom of our articles from the eastern front line. We were "Russia haters," "Russophobes," "liars," "spies," and "NATO shills." The *Guardian*'s readers' editor saw an "orchestrated pro-Kremlin campaign." Some comments were real. Most were not. They originated on Savushkina Street, churned out by Prigozhin's unsleeping drones.

Jay Aslanov headed Olgino's most important department, the foreign section. It was made up of fluent English-speakers whose salaries—65,000 roubles a month (£800)—were higher than the 45,000 roubles (£550) paid to those working on Russian-language internet sites. The two groups interacted rarely. According to former trolls, the foreign section got steadily bigger. It had its own coffee machine and separate area.

Aslanov's social media pictures show a confident young man posing in a forest against a charcoal and blue sky. In other photos he's standing on a bench in the snow, wearing furry boots and a pair of blue jeans, or sporting a khaki jersey and a Russian military cap. Aslanov was born in Ust-Kut, a Siberian town in the Irkutsk region. He moved to St. Petersburg and studied at the hydro-metereological university: another provincial kid on the way up.

The photos show Aslanov in London in 2011, standing in front of the Houses of Parliament. In one shot he's wearing a T-shirt with a Union Jack flag. He carries a camera. It's sunny and, according to Big Ben, late afternoon, 5:40 p.m. We don't know if Aslanov visited Britain as a tourist or a would-be spy.

Aslanov had an advantage over earlier comrades tasked with carrying out foreign influence operations during the late Cold War. He and his generation knew the West, had travelled there extensively, and had mastered its language and culture. On his VKontakte page—Russia's Facebook—Aslanov said he had spent several months in America in 2009, visiting New York and Boston.

In spring 2014 the foreign section embarked on an audacious new project. The objective was to sow discord in the US political system by boosting radical and polarizing opinions. These views already existed, independent of Russia. By using social media, you could feed internal division, with Facebook used as the kind of par-affin you might throw on a bonfire. More conflict meant a weaker enemy. A weaker enemy meant a stronger Kremlin.

The project was conceived at a time when Moscow and Washington were facing off over Ukraine. It was a war of sorts, fought not in the physical world but on the virtual fields of Silicon Valley, with one side caught supremely unawares and asleep.

IRA employees were instructed to *become* Americans. It was a new level of deception and mimicry. They set up social media accounts and Facebook groups. Unwitting US citizens interacted with "US activists," who were actually undercover Russians in St. Petersburg. Initially these contacts were low-volume. By the end, Aslanov's *perevodchik,* or translator department—responsible for US operations—was reaching hundreds of millions of people.

The US scheme was part of a bigger, interlocking project known as "Lakhta." The name comes from a St. Petersburg area where Prigozhin owns luxury properties and a hotel, next to Olgino. The translator operation involved online impersonation, the stealing of real US people's Social Security numbers, and old-fashioned spycraft.

Mueller's report sets out this operation in detail. In June 2014 four of Aslanov's colleagues tried to go to the US, claiming to be friends who met at a party. Two of them—Anna Bogacheva and Aleksandra Krylova, the IRA's number three—got visas; the other two were refused. The successful Russians toured America for three weeks, visiting Nevada, California, New Mexico, Colorado, Illinois, Michigan, Louisiana, Texas, and New York. It was an intelligence-gathering mission.

By 2015 the IRA was running multiple fake accounts. One of them, @ ten_gop, purported to belong to the Tennessee Republican Party. Other bogus accounts mimicked activists from the left and right—anti-immigrant and Tea Party groups, as well as Black Lives Matters and LGBTQ protesters, plus the United Muslims of America.

From at least February 2016 the IRA was ordered to help Trump and hurt Clinton. One document cited by Mueller says, "Main idea: Use any opportunity to criticize Hillary and the rest (except Sanders and Trump—we support them)." Aslanov's colleagues were appraised on their efforts. A review of an IRA-run Facebook page, Secured Borders, complained that there were too few anti-Clinton posts. "It is imperative to intensify criticizing Hillary Clinton," the message said.

The IRA organized and promoted political rallies, with an emphasis on swing states, including Florida. The trolls would announce a rally on Twitter and Facebook and—from among those who responded—find a real US person who would organize the event. (The Russian operator would say they were elsewhere in the US and couldn't make it.) The IRA would promote the rally, contact US media, and post photos and videos afterwards.

Some of these initiatives flopped. Others attracted hundreds of attendees.

Prigozhin may have concluded that Americans could be persuaded to do pretty much anything. In May 2016 Olgino organized a stunt outside the White House. It got a local to hold up a sign saying "Happy 55th Birthday Dear Boss." Prigozhin was about to celebrate his birthday; the photo was an in-house joke. On another occasion an American was hired to appear at an August 2016 rally in West Palm Beach dressed as Clinton in a prison uniform. The same person returned as Santa Claus with a Trump mask in New York.

The IRA succeeded in reaching the real Trump, as well as his aides, family, and campaign officials. In September Trump responded to a tweet that said, "We love you, Mr. President!" sent from the troll farm's @10_gop account. Donald Trump Jr., Michael Flynn, Kellyanne Conway, and others from Trump's circle reposted Russian content, sending dozens of tweets on themes such as voter fraud and claims that Clinton mishandled classified information. According to Mueller, they were unaware of the Russian connection.

Prigozhin expended considerable resources in wrecking the US election. The IRA's budget for its Lakhta operation was £900,000, or 73 million roubles, a month, concealed as payments for software support and development. It included 1 million roubles in bonuses for troll staff. Prigozhin's Concord sent the cash through accounts belonging to affiliate companies. Aslanov was general director of one of these St. Petersburg entities, Azimut LLC.

Facebook failed to notice that a foreign power had thoroughly hijacked its platform. In October 2017 it belatedly conceded that

Prigozhin had reached 126 million people, using 470 Facebook troll accounts and 85,000 posts. Twitter came up with more modest figures: 3,814 accounts seen by 1.4 million people. The Russians spent $100,000 on anti-Clinton ads, Facebook said.

This was a tiny sum compared to spending by the Trump and Clinton campaigns: $617 million and $1.2 billion respectively, including money donated from associated political action committees. Still, the IRA operation would have been seen in Moscow as wildly successful in a closely fought political race. The operation was secret, arrogant, brazen, and opportunistic—pumped into the American bloodstream like a slow-acting, stealthy poison. Russia's fingerprints were nowhere to be seen.

Aslanov and about eighty IRA colleagues took part in the 2016 election project, acting in clandestine style. There was a word for that: espionage. Traditionally, this was the job of Russian spy agencies, and of course the GRU had carried out its own separate hacking and dumping operation. But Project Lakhta amounted to something original: the outsourcing of a strategic intelligence task to a private company.

Asked in Helsinki about Russian interference, Putin said Concord had nothing to do with him.

"The company is being accused of interference, but this company does not constitute the Russian state," he said. Putin likened Prigozhin's subversive activities to those of George Soros, the philanthropist who supported democracy in Eastern Europe. Moscow saw Soros as a global troublemaker spreading hated liberalism—a conspiracy theory shared by many Republicans. Prigozhin didn't represent the Kremlin, in the same way that Soros wasn't the US government, Putin said.

Putin's insistence on Prigozhin's separateness was formally true but actually false—another lie tossed into the infosphere.

Of course, Russian businessmen might behave sycophantically

towards the man in the Kremlin and create schemes to please him. It was unwise to ascribe too much strategic value to Putin. At the same time, Prigozhin was a close and trusted member of Putin's team and a beneficiary of state largesse. It's inconceivable that Putin didn't know of Project Lakhta and the IRA's US operation. Or that he disapproved of it.

IN NOVEMBER 2018 a group of generals arrived in Moscow. Their leader was Khalifa Haftar, commander of the self-styled National Army and a man who controls two-thirds of Libya and much of its oil. Waiting for him was Russia's top brass. There was Valery Gerasimov, chief of staff of Russia's armed forces. And Sergei Shoigu, Russia's defence minister and a person whispered as a possible future president. Haftar and Gerasimov shook hands in front of a marble bust of Peter the Great.

All of those present, Libyans and Russians, were wearing uniforms. All except one. A video posted by the Libyan delegation shows a bald civilian, dressed in a suit and tie, waiting by the door. This anomalous figure joins the Russian army officers and takes a chair in the middle. It is Prigozhin, sitting in on a top-level government meeting, his prestige seemingly enhanced by the tumultuous events in America two years earlier.

For Haftar, the trip to Moscow was good PR and an opportunity to present himself as an international statesman. For the Russians, Haftar was one of several political partners in Libya. Another was Saif al-Islam, son of the late Gaddafi. Russia's goal was clear: to boost its influence in North Africa and the continent, from Sudan and the CAR all the way to South Africa and Madagascar.

Apparently, America's pushback against Prigozhin bothered him not one jot. The Obama administration sanctioned him over Ukraine. In 2018 Mueller indicted thirteen IRA operatives, including Prigozhin, Burchik, and Aslanov. The US Treasury blacklisted Prigozhin's media outlets, the Federal News Agency, USA Really, and other websites. Prigozhin reacted to these blows with amused disdain: "I am not at all disappointed I appear on this list. If they want to see the devil, let them," he said. (My own attempts to get Prigozhin to comment were unsuccessful.) The scandal of Russian interference may have shaken Washington. In Russia it had little practical impact. It was business as usual in St. Petersburg.

The IRA closed down its office on Savushkina Street. It moved to new premises in northwestern St. Petersburg, on the shores of the Gulf of Finland and adjacent to a glass Gazprom skyscraper nicknamed the "Eye of Sauron." From there the journalists of Prigozhin's "Patriot Group" carried on much as before.

Aslanov deleted his social media profiles, put his apartment up for rent, and got married. He appears to have become a father. He continued to pitch strategy papers on America to the "chief," as Prigozhin was known. In one, Aslanov proposed channelling disillusionment among African Americans into a separatist movement in southern US states. *Plus ça change!* In communist times the KGB had similarly sought to stir up American racial tensions.

Leaked messages show that Aslanov and his colleagues viewed their recent American activities as a professional coup. In January 2018 Aslanov wrote a note for Prigozhin on English-speaking African nations. Almost in passing, he cited an internal review of 2017. By all accounts the year before—2016—was an *annus mirabilis*. Aslanov said that the IRA had helped get Trump elected by "influencing the opinion of citizens in US swing states—Florida, Pennsylvania, Wisconsin." With troll assistance, a following wind, Trump had "outstripped" Clinton.

Russia's Ministry of Defence was grateful to the IRA. It gave key troll factory executives an engraved gift. Burchik received a commemorative plaque and watch with an inscription: "From the head of the main operative department of the general staff of the armed forces." Not much compensation, perhaps, for the fact that Burchik and Aslanov were indicted people who could no longer travel to the West. There was little chance Burchik would ever see his favourite rock star, Elton John, perform in Western Europe. (John's hit "The Circle of Life" was played at Burchik's wedding, I was told.) But the plaque was a pleasing sign of official recognition.

In the time immediately preceding the 2018 mid-term elections, the troll factory carried on with its US-facing operations. It released a video in which an IRA employee said Russia was seeking to fix the result. Unlike in 2016, US Cyber Command took action, shutting down the IRA's internet in the hours ahead of the November vote and for a few days afterwards. In 2019 the US Treasury hit Prigozhin again, targeting his yacht and private planes this time, one of them registered in the Isle of Man. The planes made multiple international flights. They went to Africa—Libya, Sudan, and the CAR—as well as to Syria and Lebanon. Plus Germany and Spain.

Meanwhile, Prigozhin's business empire flourished. Its operations were conducted under a cloak. The St. Petersburg back office was in an anonymous apartment. Employees in the field were given prepaid credit cards. Extensive use was made of front companies, designated with an "M." Staff sent messages via encrypted channels such as Jabber. There were old-school touches: Prigozhin approved invoices with a personal seal, stamping them with a vivid blue swirl in the manner of a colonial administrator.

Prigozhin's global operations were referred to internally by a potent single word: the "Company." The Company encompassed the mercenaries based at camps in Berengo, the Sudan, and in Libya, where a team of seventeen contractors was sent to fix up Haftar's broken tanks. It included the IRA, as well as employees working for other fake media outlets such as USA Really.

Prigozhin's multiple activities around the world were a form of hybrid warfare. They were simultaneously state and non-state, sanctioned and freelance. This twenty-first-century phenomenon was much discussed. In a chat with a colleague, Romanovsky made an eighteenth-century comparison, which perhaps better summed up the Prigozhin blend of public politics and rapacious private commerce. "Welcome to the new version of the East India Company," Romanovsky wrote in late 2018, in one of hundreds of messages and documents seen by the Dossier Centre in London.

The East India Company conquered large swathes of India and elsewhere in South East Asia, using a ruthless militia and local sepoys. At one point it controlled almost half the world's trade. As Edmund Burke put it, this mighty corporation was "a state in the guise of a merchant."

Now Prigozhin was attempting something similar in Africa and elsewhere. Like its celebrated English predecessor, Prigozhin's Company had a fuzzy relationship with power. And its own brute force component. His soldiers of fortune came from Russian military structures but didn't formally answer to them. The Company authored its own analytic papers and shared them with top-level contacts within Moscow's Defence and Foreign Ministries.

As well as mercenaries, Prigozhin dispatched political technologists to countries of Russian interest. These advisers brought with them methods—often crude ones—used at home. The aim was to shore up existing rulers and to damage their pro-Western opponents. Company documents show a desire to strong-arm the US, as well as the former imperial powers France and Britain, out of the region. And to establish a new generation of Kremlin-orientated African "leaders" and undercover "agents."

That was the theory. In reality Prigozhin's attempts to meddle in Africa weren't always as successful as in the US. In Madagascar, a group of Prigozhin political advisers turned up on tourist visas six months before the presidential election. They backed the incumbent and other candidates. All lost. The Russians eventually threw their support behind the eventual winner, Andry Rajoelina. In spring 2019 a different team travelled to South Africa to boost ANC president Cyril Ramaphosa and to smear his pro-Western opponents. Their impact was negligible.

Still, Russia was on the way to turning central Africa into a quasi-colony. Prigozhin employees drew a map showing the Company's activities, which the Dossier Centre showed me. I was struck by the range: it covered at least thirteen African countries, stretching from Zimbabwe to Comoros. (A team visited Comoros to see if a territorial dispute with Paris might be stirred up.) The Company claimed credit for removing CAR politicians sympathetic to France. It saw central Africa as strategically important, and a jumping-off point for future expansion.

In October 2019 Putin held a Russia–Africa forum, the first of its kind, in Sochi, which was attended by more than forty African heads of state. In the face of US and EU sanctions, Moscow was anxious to find new markets and strike new partnerships. It had signed military-tactical agreements with more than thirty African states, Putin told his guests. The summit confirmed Putin's conception of Russia as a great power, ready to take advantage of the Trump administration's weakness and retreat.

Election manipulation, alliances with dictators, arms deliveries, and a shadow army . . . Russia might be late to the superpower party in Africa but it was taking strides to catch up with Europe, the US, and China. Moscow's route in was a blend of capitalism and sneaky power politics.

Gold and diamond deals had advantages. Humans had mined gold since ancient times. Its appeal was universal. This was well understood in Russia—and in London too.

CHAPTER 9

MOSCOW GOLD

Amur River–London–Chicago
2015–2020

You Brits, what do you do? You take our black money
and wash it . . . You wring your hands when we poison
our traitors and you say please, please, dear Russian
friends, trade with us.
JOHN LE CARRÉ, *AGENT RUNNING IN THE FIELD*

From his office window, the governor could peer out at a mighty foreign land. On his side a municipal square, a fountain, a statue of Lenin. Beyond was the Amur River. In winter when the river froze you could walk across. On the far bank was an industrial town of high-rises and factories. It belonged to Russia's former enemy and now strategic partner the People's Republic of China.

The town of Blagoveshchensk is in Russia's Far East. It is directly opposite Heihe, a Chinese metropolis. In the late 1960s Beijing and Moscow fought a brief border skirmish over one of the Amur's islands. But relations between the two countries thawed, with agreements on international issues and enhanced military cooperation. Trade flourished. Russian tourists took river trips to Heihe. They came back with all sorts of items—fur coats, mobiles, even sex toys.

For Russia's central government, six time zones and 4,847 miles away, the Far East was a headache. It was a remote region of taiga forest and mountains, bears and mammoth tusks, bigger than Europe. There was a geostrategic fear that China might overrun it, if not with tanks then with money and people. And there were the local Russian politicians—a succession of jumped-up mobsters. Their main interest was stealing. Theft was usual, of course. But blatant enrichment annoyed the population and fuelled political discontent.

The solution, from Moscow's point of view, was to find loyal officials with few autonomous tendencies. One such reliable person was Oleg Kozhemyako. In 2008 the Kremlin made Kozhemyako governor of Amur Oblast, based in Blagoveshchensk, the provincial capital. Kozhemyako fired the town's mayor and fixed the power supply, no small thing in a place where winter temperatures fall to minus twenty-two degrees Fahrenheit.

In 2011 Kozhemyako got an adviser: Alexander Udod. The name sounds comic in Russian: it means hoopoe, a bird with a colourful crown. Udod was a tall young man with jet black hair and a pleasant grin. His job title said bureaucrat; his real role was spy and undercover FSB officer. The Far East contained abundant natural resources: fish, timber, coal. And precious metals such as gold. Kozhemyako had his own interests, including a trawler fleet; he was an enthusiastic biker.

Udod's shadow job, according to two sources, was to monitor Western businessmen seeking to invest. And to find out if they were sincere partners or perhaps foreign spies.

Udod worked with the local branch of the SVR, Russia's foreign intelligence bureau, the sources said. He got to know leading entrepreneurs in the region. One was Siman Povarenkin, the owner of gold mines in Yakutia, farther north. For a time Povarenkin was chief executive of Vladivostok's Far East shipping company. Udod's connections—to spying and to the world of mining and business—may have played a role in an intriguing story.

In about 2012 Udod was transferred to Moscow. This was an unusual step up for a provincial FSB guy. What happened next was unprecedented. A year or so later Udod reappeared in London. He was sent as a "diplomat" to the Russian embassy. He got a government passport and the title of first secretary, later bumped up to counsellor. His official job was bilateral relations and promoting Russian domestic policy in the UK.

Of all the foreign cities in the world, London was the most important to Moscow and a more significant espionage centre than even Washington or New York, citadels of the great enemy.

How come? It was close: a four-hour flight from the Russian capital. There were private schools and universities, regarded by elite Russian families as *the* places to send one's offspring. And British courts, seen as incorruptible. Wealthy Russians used them to settle their disputes, commercial and matrimonial.

Then there was London's welcoming attitude towards the international rich. The UK government was uninterested in how you acquired your fortune. It didn't bother to tax you on anything earned outside the country. It offered kleptocrats a special "non-domicile" status. This meant they could buy property and live for much of the year in London without paying tax—later changed in the face of public disquiet to a modest £30,000 charge.

An accountant might set up a firm at Companies House in London. A services outfit in a shady tax haven—the Marshall Islands, say—would manage the firm and appear on official documents. And *voilà*! You could use it to open a bank account, buy anything you wanted, and hide large amounts of cash. If money laundering was a multi-tentacled octopus, its suckers wrapped around the globe, London was its cephalopod brain and beak.

In theory Britain stood for fair play and the rule of law. In reality a class of professionals—lawyers, company formation clerks, estate agents—facilitated some dubious transactions. Not all were bad actors, of course, but many worked with corrupt and destabilizing forces emanating from the Kremlin. Banks and regulators paid little attention. In the event details leaked—to a journalist or other hostile person—London had libel and PR firms ready to assist. The media environment was chillier than in the US. There was no First Amendment.

The human rights campaigner Bill Browder described these well-paid intermediaries as a "Western buffer network." It enabled the Russian state to "infiltrate UK society and to conceal the underlying Russian controllers and their agendas," he argued.

A criminal Kremlin employed British professionals—some unwitting, others in the know—for massive money-laundering operations and to target critics and spread propaganda. In Browder's analysis—shared with the House of Commons' Intelligence Committee—Russian officials pretended nefarious private interests were "state" ones. They used their positions as cover and hired former UK diplomats, politicians, and intelligence officers to lobby on their behalf.

The shadow state functioned because Western agents masked its activities.

London attracted two classes of Russian émigrés. The first were the troublemakers and the dissidents. The tradition of Russian exiles settling in Britain went back to Lenin, at the turn of the twentieth century, and to the socialist writer and thinker Alexander Herzen a generation or so before that.

During the Putin years the oligarch Boris Berezovsky played the role of scheming revolutionary. Berezovsky was Jewish and a one-time ally of Putin's who decamped to London in 2000 and set up a Moscow-on-Thames. Berezovsky's base was a Mayfair office. His public goal was to topple Russia's president. Russian state media portrayed Berezovsky as a second Trotsky, in league with British spies.

By the time Udod got to London, most of Berezovsky's circle were dead. Berezovsky was found hanged in March 2013 at his ex-wife's Berkshire mansion. The police believed it was suicide; his family, murder. Five years later Berezovsky's friend Nikolai Glushkov—the most likeable member of the oligarch's circle—was found strangled at his home in New Malden, southwest London. Scotland Yard was unable to locate Glushkov's killer.

The second group comprised entrepreneurs and bureaucrats loyal to the regime. Some bought trophy houses and visited rarely. Others installed their families in London and commuted from Moscow. Vladislav Surkov, Putin's chief ideologist, was one such weekend traveller; Surkov's wife preferred the UK to Russia. Apparently there was no perceived contradiction between championing Russian nationalism at home and enjoying a cosy life in the West.

The Kremlin was intensely interested in both groups. It understood that Russian bankers and businessmen—once they fell out of power—typically fled to London. In exile they might reinvent themselves as victims of political persecution. Sometimes this was true; mostly it wasn't. It suspected exiles of collaborating with MI6, an organization Moscow viewed with neuralgic loathing.

Putin and his cronies, then, had a particular obsession with England. In Steele's view, this was because it was less corrupt than elsewhere; had a better understanding of the world than most; and was home to a large, influential émigré community. It was a love–hate relationship: love because London was a hiding place for illegitimate leadership wealth; hate because it was a refuge for anti-regime forces.

Povarenkin and Udod appeared in the UK at about the same time. In 2013 Povarenkin's wife, Irina, moved to London with their two small children. For the rich, the paperwork was easy. In exchange for £2 million Irina was granted a "tier one" investor visa. This gave her and her spouse the right to reside in Britain. The Povarenkins purchased an £11.3 million apartment in Ebury Square—one of London's smartest addresses—and enrolled their son and daughter in a fee-paying British school and nursery.

Meanwhile, Udod's career was on the up. He worked with a business council set up by Russian ambassador Alexander Yakovenko. Povarenkin sat on the council. Udod spent six weeks in America on a fellowship programme for diplomats from the former USSR. In Washington he spent time with a Republican member of the House of Representatives—Bob Latta, from Ohio's Fifth District.

Udod's public diplomatic activities seemed harmless enough. He met with British veterans who had served on Arctic convoys, delivering vital supplies to a wartime Soviet Union. The Kremlin gave them medals named after Fyodor Ushakov, an eighteenth-century naval commander. Few recipients were aware that Ushakov was the patron saint of Russia's strategic bomber fleet.

Udod took part in Remembrance Day commemorations, laying a wreath in Oxford and mingling with dignitaries and servicemen at a reception in St John's College. One detail hinted at the Kremlin's darker agenda. Photos show Udod sporting the orange and black St. George's ribbon worn traditionally for Soviet celebrations of Victory Day, marking the defeat of Nazi Germany by the Red Army.

Latterly, Putin had transformed the ribbon into a sinister and revisionist political emblem. In 2014 pro-Russian rebels and "volunteers" wore it in eastern Ukraine. It became synonymous with the Kremlin's aggressive anti-Western ideology. As the Russian writer Andrei Soldatov notes, it materialized on cars in Moscow, attached to the antenna, sometimes with a sticker saying "1945— We Can Repeat." The message: Russian soldiers might return to Berlin at any moment.

Udod and his fellow embassy intelligence officers tracked British affairs closely. In 2013 Prime Minister David Cameron announced that if re-elected, he would hold a referendum on the UK's future membership of the European Union. The move was a response to the growing political threat to Cameron's Conservative Party from UKIP, the far-right Eurosceptic party led by Nigel Farage.

It seemed unlikely that a referendum would ever happen, still less that Farage and his ragtag army of pound-loving fringe activists would prevail. Cameron had failed to win the previous election in 2010. He governed in coalition with the Liberal Democrats. Nobody expected him to get a majority the next time. As Farage saw it, the political "establishment" would see to that. More realistic was the prospect of Scottish independence, in a referendum set for 2014.

Still, these destiny-shaping plebiscites—one actual, the other theoretical—gave the Russian embassy plenty to think about. For Putin, Brexit was a highly desirable outcome. His pan-European objective was to break up the EU and weaken the UK and NATO. Brexit would do precisely that. It might estrange London from Paris and Berlin, do damage to Britain's economy, and inflame a promising little cultural war between cosmopolitans and English nationalists.

The same battle, in fact, that was about to define and shape America in the age of Trump.

The appeal to Moscow of Brexit grew after the EU and the US slapped sanctions against Russia for its theft of Crimea. Then in 2015 the unthinkable happened: Cameron won a general election with a majority of twelve. An in–out EU referendum would take place, Cameron said—by 2017 at the latest, and probably in 2016. Polls pointed to a Remain victory. The government said it would support staying in Europe.

For Moscow the route forward was obvious: to encourage Britain's destructive Eurosceptic political forces. The scenario was perfect for Udod and his embassy colleagues. In a fifty–fifty situation their efforts might have a dramatic effect on the outcome. The stage was set for Russia to interfere in Brexit, as it would with Trump in the US. The two espionage operations took place over the same time frame. The scene was often London. The dramatis personae knew each other. The plays overlapped.

IN NOVEMBER 2015 two men made their way along Kensington Palace Gardens. The street has a surprisingly rustic feel, given its location at the heart of a teeming world city. Old-fashioned street lamps lend it a touch of Narnia. At either end are police huts and armed guards. Cars are allowed beyond the barriers only with per-mission. A sign says NO PHOTOGRAPHY. There is little noise other than a low drone in the sky from planes on their way to Heathrow; cyclists, joggers, and pedestrians go past.

The street is home to a row of grand embassy buildings set amid plane trees. At the northern end is a large, attractive villa with a hedge and palms. Diplomatic vehicles are visible from the street; a two-headed eagle decorates a black-painted gate. This is the Russian Federation embassy, at numbers 6 and 7. The Israeli and Norwegian embassies are down the road, with the British royal family close by in Kensington Palace.

The visitors didn't go to the Russian embassy. They rang the buzzer at number 13, another dreamy classical villa, with an ornate wooden entrance and a large back garden, out of sight. This was the private residence of Alexander Yakovenko, in the 1980s a Soviet diplomat in New York, and since 2011 Russia's ambassador to the UK. It was where Yakovenko received guests. The pair had come for lunch. This followed an unusual invitation.

In late September Udod had been to the northern city of Doncaster to attend UKIP's annual party conference. The main speaker was Farage. The "Kippers," as the tabloids called them, were in buoyant mood. Also in Doncaster was Arron Banks, a Bristol-based businessman, and Banks's friend and sidekick Andy Wigmore. Banks was co-founder of Leave.EU, a new political group campaigning for Brexit. It differed from Vote Leave, the officially recognized campaign to exit the EU. Leave.EU was an insurgent outfit. It had an unapologetically anti-immigrant message. Banks, a former Tory party turned UKIP donor, was its main funder. He would give Leave.EU £8.4 million.

By US standards, the donation was small. In Britain the sum was huge. It was the largest donation in UK political history. In a country of ancient electoral laws, practically drawn up on vellum by a man in a ruff holding a goose quill, these millions might make all the difference, especially in the anarchic and unregulated world of online campaigning.

The question that would haunt the referendum and afterwards was this: where did Banks get this cash? Banks said it was his. Others were not so sure. In November 2018 the UK electoral commission said it had reasonable grounds to suspect that Banks was not the "true source" of the money. It referred the matter for criminal investigation.

If the money wasn't his, whose was it?

In Doncaster Udod introduced himself to Banks and Wigmore. Two weeks later he passed on an invitation to lunch with Yakovenko. Banks responded enthusiastically, telling Udod, "There is massive interest in the referendum in the USA as well, and we are shortly visiting Washington to brief key [people] on the campaign."

Banks gives an account of the lunch in a ghostwritten memoir, *The Bad Boys of Brexit*. The book portrays the two Brexit campaigners as plucky underdogs tweaking the noses of humourless lefty Remainers and the mainstream Conservative Party. Banks describes Udod as a "shady character," "Oleg." He writes that Udod was "introduced to us [in Doncaster] as the First Secretary to the Embassy—in other words, the KGB's man in London." Banks says he was cautious about seeing Yakovenko, but fortunately "we hit it off from the word go."

In Banks's telling, the meeting on November 6 turned into a boozy encounter fuelled by a bottle of special vodka. Yakovenko told his British guests it was "one of three in a batch made for Stalin personally." "I looked suitably impressed, secretly wondering whether he [Yakovenko] uses the same lines—perhaps the same vodka—on every guest," Banks writes. He continues, "Eventually, it was time to leave. We shook hands and promised to meet again." The ambassador gave them a parting gift: "a unique ambassador's blend of tea for special guests." "I hope it's not radioactive," Banks adds, in a pretty crass reference to Litvinenko.

The lunch, according to Banks, was a social event lacking in protocol. He acknowledges that the referendum came up. The ambassador "wanted the inside track on the Brexit campaign and grilled us on the potential implications of an Out vote for Europe," he writes. There is no mention of Yakovenko's own preferred referendum outcome, or if he agreed with Banks's prediction that Leave would win and "everyone's in for a shock."

And that, seemingly, was that.

Banks's Brexit campaign diary makes no further mention of the ambassador, who disappears stage left. It gives the impression that the meeting was inconsequential, a convivial one-off. For two years Banks claimed he met the ambassador once. There is no diary entry for November 17, 2015. If anything happened that day, Banks doesn't wish to tell us.

In fact, the meeting was the first of several. Before and after the referendum the ambassador extended multiple invitations to Banks and Wigmore. They were to musical recitals inside the Russian embassy, to business forums, and to the Valdai discussion club in Russia, whose meetings take place under the auspices of the Foreign Ministry. They were invited to a speech by the visiting governor of Kaluga province.

Banks and Wigmore reciprocated. They asked Yakovenko and Udod to drinks in a London pub and to UKIP's referendum night party—a wild victory celebration, as it transpired. There were regular emails between the Brexiteers and Udod, a live channel of communication in the crucial days leading up to the fateful EU vote, and one that would eventually loop across the Atlantic, all the way to New York and Trump Tower.

There was also gold—not the gilded variety seen in Trump's Manhattan elevator, but the real kind, from Moscow.

"Moscow Gold" was shorthand for the USSR's secret financing operations. During the Cold War the KGB bankrolled communist parties in the West, notably in Italy and France, as well as in America and developing countries such as India, a major KGB and GRU target.

Under Putin, the main vector of political influence shifted to the European far right. In the case of Leave.EU Moscow Gold wasn't a metaphor. The Russians were *literally* offering Banks gold. The gold came in the shape of a moneymaking opportunity to invest in Siberian mining.

The Bad Boys of Brexit leaves out this topic, discussed over lunch. The ambassador told Banks that an energetic Russian based in Moscow, and who visited London regularly, was seeking to create a large gold company. His name was Siman Povarenkin. The ambassador knew Povarenkin: they and their respective wives—Nanna and Irina—met socially. Povarenkin was on good terms with Igor Rotenberg, a prominent Russian whose billionaire father, Arkady, was Putin's friend and judo buddy.

Povarenkin, the ambassador said, was sounding out investors for what would be a lucrative opportunity. Might Banks be interested?

The book doesn't tell us, but we now know that Banks said yes, he would be ready to meet with this interesting tycoon.

A week after the lunch, on November 11, Povarenkin sent a seven-page document to Yakovenko. I saw it in 2018 while investigating Brexit together with Khodorkovsky's Dossier Centre. Its title was "Russian Gold Sector Consolidation Play." The PowerPoint presentation wasn't subtle. It features gleaming gold bars, piles of them, stamped with "Russia" in Cyrillic and a Russian flag, followed by charts and English text.

On November 17—eleven days after the lunch—Banks returned to Kensington Palace Gardens. Yakovenko introduced him to a diminutive person with dark, curly hair: Povarenkin.

Povarenkin had big ambitions, Banks discovered. His firm GeoProMining was one of Russia's smaller gold producers. Povarenkin aimed to create an $8 billion super-company the size of the market leader, Polyus Gold. He wanted to consolidate "six or seven" lesser firms, including his own. GeoProMining would start this process, helped by its "deep knowledge of the sector" and its "connections" with the major gold miners in Russia.

The final slide mentioned an extra inducement. It said that Sberbank Capital, a subsidiary of Sberbank, Russia's main state savings bank, was a shareholder in GeoProMining. The support of Russia's biggest bank had advantages. Or as the PowerPoint presentation put it bluntly, "It leads to certain opportunities not available to others." Sberbank was under Western sanctions. It kept cropping up in the Trump–Russia story and had sponsored the Miss Universe beauty contest. While in Moscow Trump had dinner with Sberbank's chief executive, German Greff.

The deal being dangled in front of Banks's nose—by no less a person than Putin's man in Britain—was being made to special people only.

A sweetheart deal.

Left unsaid was what the Russians might want in return. Or why they were anxious to offer Banks a proposition seemingly designed to suit his business interests, and comparable to the Moscow hotel deal waved before Trump.

The Banks–Povarenkin discussion came on the eve of Leave.EU's formal launch. A day after the secret gold meeting Banks began his campaign to take Britain out of the EU. The venue was a hall in Westminster, close to the House of Commons. Banks shared a platform with Gerry Gunster, a US campaign strategist, and Brittany Kaiser, a young American from a data company that would become notorious, Cambridge Analytica. The firm's vice president was Steve Bannon. Farage sat in the audience.

It was a busy day. According to emails seen by the *Observer*, Banks emailed Povarenkin, writing, "Dear Siman, Very nice to meet yesterday with the Russian ambassador." Banks told the Moscow businessman that he had given the gold presentation to Andrew Umbers, head of Oakwell Capital, a firm in which Banks said he had a "substantial stake." Banks copied it to his "partner" Jim Mellon, a fellow Leave campaigner "with an extensive interest in commodities," as Banks put it. Banks signed off, "I am very bullish on gold and so keen to take a look!"

At the same time as exploring Russian gold, Banks was reaching out to America. On October 24 he sent a message, copied to Bannon. It said that Leave.EU "would like CA [Cambridge Analytica] to come up with a strategy for fundraising in the States." This might involve US citizens with British relatives, Banks said. He floated the idea that "CA" could "look at the first cut of the data"—that is, information on British voters. (Banks later denied this was the case.)

By the end of 2015 Banks and Wigmore were plotting a trip to Russia. According to the *Sunday Times*, Wigmore emailed Udod on November 24, asking if he and Banks "could have a chat with you face-to-face about our plans to go to Moscow in the next few weeks." In Russia the pair would meet the "appropriate Sberbank decision maker."

On the small print of the deal Banks took advice from Nick van den Brul, an investment banker and friend of Wigmore's who had lived in Russia. Writing from South Africa, Banks said he would be back in the UK "next week." Could he meet van den Brul to discuss "Russian Gold Play"? Banks added, "I intend to pop in and see the ambassador as well." The message was copied to Udod. Meanwhile, Umbers wrote up a feasibility study ahead of a meeting with Banks and other potential investors in central London. In February he messaged Banks, asking, "Did you see the ambassador today?"

IT'S UNCLEAR IF Banks went to Moscow. In February 2016 Wigmore told journalists from the BBC and Sky News that Banks was away in the Russian capital. In 2018 Banks told the *Sunday Times* he had been to Russia—but on a sightseeing trip with his wife, featuring a visit to the Hermitage Museum and a river cruise. The answer was odd. The Moscow River is carpeted with ice in February, and the Hermitage is in St. Petersburg. Banks later said he wasn't in Russia that February.

Contact with Povarenkin continued. Povarenkin mentioned another tantalizing business opportunity that might interest the man behind Brexit.

Not gold, but gems.

In Soviet times, Moscow sold gold and diamonds to the West in exchange for hard currency. These transactions were routed via a non-transparent chain of Soviet banks. Precious commodities were easy to move—in the 1970s a Soviet passenger plane delivered gold regularly to Zurich, several tons per flight, the GRU defector Viktor Suvorov, who was based in Switzerland, told me, adding that the money was used to buy food from America—a humiliating exchange in his view.

Under sanctions, the Kremlin wanted Western investment in this crucial sector. According to the *New York Times*, Povarenkin told Banks that the Russian government was planning to reduce its holding in Alrosa, the world's largest diamond mining company, and to sell off 10.9 per cent of its shares. It would be a private offering to a restricted group of investors. The sale was expected to fetch about $800 million.

Banks expressed interest. Van den Brul emailed Wigmore saying that the Alrosa project "might open up some opportunities for Arron." Meanwhile, in March Yakovenko invited Banks and Wigmore to a private concert at the Russian embassy. The occasion was a recital by the Liverpool Philharmonic Orchestra and its Russian–British conductor, Vasily Petrenko.

In April Banks was approached with a third Russian offer. The prospective site was Africa and a gold mine in Conakry, Guinea, already a zone of extensive Russian excavation. Its owner was an "adventurous Russian" who "shares your passion for the yellow metal," an intermediary wrote to Banks. The Russian was Ilya Karas, the CEO of the Moscow-based Farafina Gold Group. Karas was described as an "inveterate entrepreneur" and "mini-oligarch."

Like Povarenkin, Karas lived an international life, with some time spent in London. In Guinea, he was seeking capital for exploration. He was looking for a $3.5 million investment to finance the production of two gold sites.

I emailed Karas asking him about Banks. To my surprise he answered. He said he knew nothing of the subsequent scandal that engulfed Banks over his bankrolling of Brexit. Karas told me he met Banks in "mid-2016" in Bristol to discuss a gold deal. Nothing came of it, he said, adding, "We didn't have any subsequent communications."

Still, the picture was unambiguous. In the period just before the EU referendum, Russians offered Banks at least three preferential business deals. These approaches were coordinated by Udod, an undercover spy based at the Russian embassy in London. All featured Russian middlemen. They were non-public. At the time of the referendum voters knew nothing of Banks's subterranean contacts with Putin's representatives.

How hard had Moscow pushed for Brexit? According to Steele's sources, the operation in "Foggy Albion" ebbed and flowed. Inside the Kremlin there were differing views on what to do in the UK, similar to the divisions in 2016 between those who favoured aggressive interference in US politics, in support of Trump, and others who took a more cautious and conservative line.

Some officials worried that Britain's EU exit would enhance power in Berlin and make Germany an even more dominant force on the Continent. German resurgence was an understandable area of paranoia for Moscow. Other senior Russian figures argued for all-out support in favour of Leave, the same sources said. The main person promoting interference was Igor Sergun, the GRU director and Korobov's predecessor.

Sergun's sudden death in January 2016 put the brake on operations, at least for a while. After three years in the job, the GRU chief was found dead in a seaside hotel room in Lebanon, possibly while on a secret assignment in Syria and at the age of just fifty-eight. (Moscow said Sergun died normally at home in Russia.)

Across Europe the Kremlin offered financial support to far-right political parties. Sometimes this was public; sometimes secret. In France, Moscow funded Marine Le Pen's National Front with a €9.5 million loan in 2014, granted by a Moscow bank. There was suspected cash too for the Alternative für Deutschland party in Germany, anti-EU forces in Hungary, and Matteo Salvini's far-right League in Italy.

Banks and Wigmore responded indignantly to the suggestion that their encounters with Russian officials amounted to anything furtive. There was, they said, nothing untoward going on. *Nyet!* No dark money had flowed into Brexit; to suggest as much was left-wing hysteria. And a betrayal of the 17.4 million who voted to leave.

The pair gave evidence in 2018 to Parliament's Culture, Media, and Sport Select Affairs Committee. It was a bad-tempered affair. The two witnesses walked out before MPs had finished their questions. Their message: they were the victims of a smear campaign by a cabal of die-hard Remainers, journalists and parliamentarians both, who were determined to invent a Russian conspiracy where none existed. In short, the same "fake news" stories that beset President Trump on the other side of the pond.

Wigmore, Leave.EU's director of communications, said that from the outset his side had realized that "referendums were not about facts." "It's about emotion," he said—a frank admission of the post-truth direction in which British and US politics were going.

And if the duo had misled reporters, so what? Yes, Banks said, he sometimes "led people up the garden path." Wigmore described himself as an agent provocateur who told fibs to wind his enemies up. There was a memorable exchange with Labour Party MP Jo Stevens. Asked why he told journalists in February 2016 that Banks was in Moscow, Wigmore said he liked "teasing" the media with wrong information.

WIGMORE: My job is to be provocative. That is my job. I am
    trying to give you— I have this sense of humour.
STEVENS: What is the difference between provocation and
    lies, Mr. Wigmore? Is there any difference?
WIGMORE: There is a difference. If you are trying to sell
    something or put a good case over to somebody, you will tell

the best story. If that is a provocation or a lie, if you want to call it that—

CHRISTIAN MATHESON, MP: Is that how your side, the Leave campaign, won the referendum?

Banks said he hadn't taken up the ambassador's offers. Media reporting of events was "sensationalized." "I have no business interests in Russia and I have done no business deals in Russia," he told MPs.

Besides, what was wrong with meeting Povarenkin (whose name, Banks said, he had forgotten)? "I am a businessman. Why shouldn't I? I thought it was interesting," Banks said.

In *The Bad Boys of Brexit*, Banks says Leave won because of its superior online campaign. He writes that "through the power of social media, we were creating an extraordinary mass movement, drawing in swathes of voters neglected by the main political parties." His co-workers took inspiration from Trump, "the ultimate political outsider," and deliberately bypassed the mainstream media, he writes.

What Banks doesn't say is that Putin *helped* in this cyber effort. Russian trolls pumped out the same strong anti-immigrant messaging, often based on bogus claims. They achieved a greater digital reach than the two authentic campaigns working to achieve Brexit, Leave.EU and Vote Leave.

The same Russian Twitter accounts that boosted Brexit were subsequently used to support Trump. They were among 3,841 accounts linked by Twitter in 2018 to Prigozhin's Internet Research Agency. This, at least, is what the parliamentary committee concluded in a 2019 report into fake news, which took evidence from the US digital expert Clint Watts.

One set of trolls working on Project Lakhta smeared Clinton. Another—sitting in the same building, and probably involving the same English-speaking "disinformation specialists"—attacked the

EU. Russian state media outlets, including RT and Sputnik, rolled out pro-Leave stories.

Moscow's playbook in the UK was the same as in the US. The goal was to promote divisive "hot button" issues that would warm the electorate's prejudices. Immigration, refugees from Syria, Muslim terrorism, attacks by ISIS sympathizers in Manchester and London . . . all were pushed remotely from Russia. There is evidence that Prigozhin trolls promoted Scottish independence, the committee found. When the independence referendum was defeated in 2014, the same St. Petersburg trolls spread claims that the vote was rigged.

In the end Banks didn't pursue Russian gold or diamonds.

But that wasn't quite the end of the story. Banks's business associate Mellon did invest in Alrosa. This was done through a fund managed by Charlemagne Capital, of which Mellon was a shareholder. The Kremlin sold its stake in Alrosa three weeks after the 2016 Brexit vote, at a heavy discount to the market price. The deal was profitable for those allowed to take part. Mellon says his fund, the OCCO Eastern European Fund, was able to participate because it had invested in Alrosa previously, in 2013.

(A spokesman for Mellon told the *Guardian* he was not involved at the time in investment decisions and had no management role. Nor was he a beneficiary of OCCO.)

And what of Udod? By summer 2016 he and Banks were on friendly first-name terms. Three days before the EU referendum, Wigmore wrote to Yakovenko and Udod—the ambassador and the spy from the Far East—inviting them to two social events. The message was seen by the journalist Peter Jukes. It says:

Alexander,
I hope your well
Arron Banks and I would like to invite you and the
Ambassador to 2 events if your free

Firstly, Arron is hosting a drinks event at the Bombardier pub in Notting Hill from 6pm and we would very much like to you to come, small gathering with a host of interesting people.

The second event is a party we have in Millbank Westminster from 8.30pm through to 6am in the morning to watch the results of the referendum come in.

your free we would love to see either or both of you

warm wishes

Udod replied, "Andy, Thanks a lot for the invitation, sounds exciting!" Udod said the ambassador was unavailable and flying back to Moscow, but that he would go to both events and looked forward "to seeing you and Arron there." He signed off, "With the best wishes, Alexander."

On referendum night Udod headed to the Millbank Tower party. There are no photos of the Russian spy, who is somewhere behind the cameras and the cheering Brexit supporters. Udod may have allowed himself a smile, as Farage proclaimed victory and celebrated what he called Britain's "Independence Day," achieved with Russian help. Yakovenko later told friends that his time as ambassador in London was a triumph. He had smashed the Brits to the ground. "It will be a long time before they rise again," he reportedly told a fellow diplomat.

IN THE SAME city, a bare few months earlier, a twenty-eight-year-old foreign policy aide, of Greek–American extraction, headed east, towards Holborn. The aide lived in Bayswater, in west London. He was on his way to a meeting. The young man's name was George Papadopoulos. Papadopoulos had just landed an important new job: foreign policy adviser to Trump.

Papadopoulos grew up in Chicago, did a master's at University College, London, and got an internship with the right-wing

Hudson Institute. His speciality was the eastern Mediterranean. Early efforts to join Trump were unsuccessful, but in March 2016, after a stint with the Ben Carson campaign, he got a position with Trump's foreign policy team, at that point little more than a blank space. Suddenly his career was going somewhere.

That month Papadopoulos went to a conference held at Link University in Rome. One seminar was on Italy's stance towards Libya. He got chatting to an older academic, Josef Mifsud. Mifsud was not much interested in Papadopoulos until he learned of the Trump connection. After this, he found the American intensely fascinating. The two discussed Russia, a place where Mifsud said he knew some top-level people. One was Yakovenko, whom Mifsud saw in 2014 inside the Russian embassy. They posed for a photo against a decorative wooden fireplace and a pair of striking Russian paintings.

Papadopoulos told me that his view of foreign affairs was shaped by realpolitik. There could be no progress on Syria, Ukraine, and other international problems without the Russians and the Chinese. Talking to Moscow advanced the cause of peace. And, of course, it advanced the cause of Papadopoulos. He might show off any Kremlin contacts to his Trump campaign colleagues and maybe even bring about a historic Trump–Putin conversation.

It was Mifsud whom Papadopoulos was now going to meet.

Mifsud—originally from Malta—taught at London's Academy of Diplomacy. He wasn't overstating his Russian connections. According to Mueller, Mifsud was friendly with an unnamed employee of the Internet Research Agency. In spring 2016 the two chatted about meeting up in Russia, and may have done so. Another of Mifsud's contacts was linked to the Russian Ministry of Defence, and in turn to Facebook accounts run by the GRU.

The London meeting took place in a Holborn hotel. Mifsud arrived with a young Russian woman called Olga Polonskaya, a former student. Papadopoulos believed, wrongly, that she was

Putin's niece. He told me she was "very nicely dressed." And accompanied by what he thought was .a bodyguard: a bald guy wearing jeans and a leather jacket. The bodyguard sat in a corner. He said little.

The approach to Papadopoulos looked like a typical Russian espionage operation, featuring as it did a pretty young woman, a bald spy supervising the encounter, and a shadowy professor of unknown allegiance—a combination that brought to mind the board game Cluedo. According to Papadopolous, Polonskaya told him she had friends at the Russian embassy in London. She said that Yakovenko was one of them and would like to meet him. She expressed enthusiasm for Trump, saying, "We really hope he wins." Olga didn't make much of an impression on Papadopoulos, who told me her English was "unfluent."

Nevertheless, a few days later Mifsud emailed "out of the blue" to say that she had loved the lunch and wanted Papadopoulos's number. She wished to invite him to a "family wedding in Saint Petersburg." The apparent aim: to get Papadopoulos over to Russia. In a note to the campaign team, Papadopoulos said he'd discussed US–Russian relations over the lunch with Mifsud and that the Kremlin leadership was keen to start a Putin–Trump dialogue, either in Moscow or in a "neutral" city such as London. Papadopoulos joined Trump a week later at a round table in Washington for the foreign policy team.

Through April 2016 Papadopoulos pursued the idea of meeting Yakovenko. There were messages to Polonskaya, with Mifsud copied in. The professor edited his student's emails and brushed up the English. Mifsud saw Papadopoulos again in London, ahead of what Mifsud said was a working trip to Moscow for a Valdai club discussion event and chats with Duma politicians.

The pair got together again on April 25, when Mifsud returned from Moscow. The venue was the Andaz Hotel, a Victorian building with red-orange brickwork darkened with soot next to London's Liverpool Street Station. The hotel once belonged to the Great Western Railway. There is a champagne bar, with marble-painted pillars, circular tables, and a fish mosaic. Glass office blocks loom over the area. There are commuters and pigeons.

Mifsud brought news. He said Kremlin officials had told him that Russia had obtained "dirt" on Clinton. It was sitting on "thousands" of emails. Papadopoulos told me he thought at the time that Mifsud was talking about Clinton's "missing" State Department emails, constantly referenced by Trump. Still, this information was interesting. And surely worth passing on?

As Papadopoulos continued his attempts to fix a meeting between the campaign and Putin, others in London were trying to figure out what a Trump presidency might mean. One of them was Alexander Downer, a veteran right-wing foreign minister and Australia's high commissioner in London. Downer was a Brexiteer interested in Trumpian thinking. One of his staff had come across Papadopoulos and suggested that Downer meet him. The junior staff member picked the venue, I was told—a Kensington wine bar, used by the high commission for social gatherings, close to the Russian embassy.

Downer saw Papadopoulos ten days after the aide learned about "dirt" from Mifsud. Over drinks, Papadopoulos mentioned the emails and said that the Russian government was in a position to assist the Trump campaign by anonymously releasing material that might hurt Clinton. Downer reported the chat to Canberra in a routine diplomatic cable. It was shared with Washington later, in July, after WikiLeaks' first dump of DNC data.

The Downer–Papadopoulos encounter was certainly fateful, and the subject of mythologizing much later.

It led directly to the FBI's counter-intelligence investigation into the Trump campaign and Russia, to Mueller, and to a ludicrous conspiracy theory eagerly promoted by the president and his supporters. The theory said that Downer had been sent to "spy" on Papadopoulos as part of the "deep state" plot. And that Mifsud wasn't a long-time Russian asset, as British and American intelligence believed, but . . . an FBI one!

There was no truth in this, as the report by Inspector General Horowitz made clear. Nevertheless, Papadopoulos keenly promoted this fictitious version of events, including in a memoir. His apparent goal was to rehabilitate himself with Trump—having once been scorned as a mere campaign "coffee boy"—and to run for Congress from California. Papadopoulos didn't come across as the brightest guy, but you couldn't fault his drive.

When I caught up with him in January 2018, over a late breakfast in his home city of Chicago, he was still semi-contrite. He had recently pleaded guilty to lying to the FBI about his interactions with Mifsud and the Russians. And to deleting his Facebook account in a dumb attempt to cover them up. "Pay no attention to that," he said, when I asked why he had misled the Feds. He was awaiting sentencing. (He eventually served fourteen days.)

Of Downer, he said there were "breadcrumbs" that led to their storied London drink. He added, "I'm not saying Downer set me up." I wrote Papadopoulos's answer in my black-and-red Oxford notebook. And what about Mifsud? "He was a shady businessman trying to sell connections in exchange for money. He was in the networking business," Papadopoulos said. (I called Mifsud to put these claims to him. He didn't get back to me.)

Papadopoulos wouldn't tell me if he passed the "dirt" tip on to the Trump campaign. He told the FBI that he "couldn't recall" whether he did. The bureau said he "wavered" over a possible conversation with Sam Clovis, Trump's chief policy adviser. Clovis said he "didn't recall" either. These evasions made little sense: why would Papadopoulos mention Russian "dirt" to a stranger in a Kensington wine bar, and to a Greek former foreign minister, while concealing it from his campaign colleagues, to whom it might be valuable?

Papadopoulos was energetic in his efforts to connect Moscow with New York. When it became clear that a Trump–Putin face-to-face was unlikely to happen, he pitched a different plan. The idea—per his notes—was to hold a shadow summit in September 2016 with Putin's representatives. This would be unofficial, with no message from Trump. Papadopoulos, Clovis, and Walid Phares, a member of Trump's foreign policy team, would participate. The proposed venue was London.

Meanwhile, Papadopolous spent much of that summer reaching out to senior Russian diplomats. Some were suspected SVR spies. On September 16 he got in touch via LinkedIn with Sergei Nalobin, a former colleague of Udod's from the Russian embassy in London and at that point based back in Moscow as a digital expert.

Nalobin had impeccable espionage credentials. His father was a retired KGB manager who supervised intelligence affairs at Moscow's Sheremetyevo Airport; his brother was ex-FSB. In London, Nalobin attended party conferences, posing with Labour and Conservative Party MPs. He was a ubiquitous figure on the right-wing scene, mysteriously gaining entrance to Tory fundraising balls, shaking hands with David Cameron. Nalobin was easy to spot: a dome-headed figure in his early thirties, wearing fashionable black-rimmed glasses and a tailored coat, a young spy straight out of a Le Carré novel. I once saw him lurking in the Red Lion pub, opposite Big Ben and the Houses of Parliament.

Nalobin's interest in British politics went beyond information-gathering or stalking reporters in crowded bars. It fell under the heading of "active measures."

His activities on behalf of the Russian state mirrored Udod's overtures to Banks.

In 2012 Nalobin instigated a new parliamentary group, the Conservative Friends of Russia. Its ostensible writ was to promote bilateral relations. The real objective was to rewire the Conservative Party, making it more Kremlin-friendly after the Litvinenko fiasco and identifying a new generation of Eurosceptic influencers. With time they might be encouraged to do Moscow's bidding or even become targets for recruitment.

The group launched at the Kensington Palace Gardens residence. Yakovenko gave a speech. Leading parliamentarians attended. Raffle prizes included a Putin biography. Also there was a young Conservative Party worker, Carrie Symonds, who would become Boris Johnson's girlfriend and in summer 2019 move with him to Downing Street.

Nalobin arranged for a delegation from the Conservative Friends of Russia to spend ten days in Moscow and St. Petersburg. The young right-wing activists went to the opera and visited the Duma. Rossotrudnichestvo, a Russian cultural agency seen by MI6 as an espionage outfit, paid the bills. One participant was Matthew Elliott, future Vote Leave chief executive, for which Johnson would act as effervescent front man. (Elliott said going on the trip was a "mistake" and that he had no subsequent contact with Russians.)

Another person in this milieu was Dominic Cummings, a political strategist who co-founded Vote Leave and became its campaign director. Cummings spent the years 1994 to 1997 in Russia. As prime minister, Johnson made him his senior adviser. He was a divisive figure, fanatical in his pursuit of Brexit. The opposition Labour Party questioned Cummings's "mysterious" Russian years and suggested that he knew Vladislav Surkov, Putin's chief ideologue. It asked what security clearance Cummings received prior to joining No. 10. Light fantasizing and smears, the government said.

There were a few embassy setbacks: after I wrote about Nalobin in the *Guardian*, the UK government refused to renew his visa. In 2015 he was forced to return to Moscow. By the following year he was back in business. His Twitter account linked to @TeamTrumpRussia, a pro-Russian network, according to the FBI.

Overall, though, these were golden years for Russian espionage. In Soviet times, the Kremlin tried to steal military-intelligence secrets. They were well defended. Latterly, the Putin regime switched targets. It now concentrated on the political systems in democratic countries. This was a genius approach. Moscow correctly concluded that Western politics was wide open—a soft underbelly. You could buy distressed newspapers, get émigrés to donate to certain political parties, and acquire troubled industries and infrastructure.

Seemingly without much resistance, Yakovenko's intelligence officers had glommed onto the key personalities behind Brexit and Trump. Not far from Kensington, the GRU had transformed the Ecuadorian embassy, where Julian Assange was holed up, into a publication hot spot. It was unclear if MI6 was across these giddy developments. Either way, it did little to stop them.

AFTER HELPING TO win the referendum, Banks moved on to his next political project: to launch Farage in America as "Mr. Brexit." Farage complained that he was "skint" and that there was no money in politics. Actually, this was wrong, at least for him. Banks funded Farage to the tune of £450,000 via one of Banks's companies, Rock Services Ltd. This paid for a house in Chelsea, a Land Rover, and a new shower curtain. In addition, Farage earned €100,000 a year as a member of the European Parliament, a body he was sworn to destroy.

Hundreds of thousands of pounds were spent on promoting "brand Farage" in the US. According to *Channel 4 News*, Banks underwrote Farage's business-class flight to Cleveland, Ohio, for the Republican national convention. There Farage dined with Roger Stone and radio show host Alex Jones and met John Bolton.

On Fox News Farage promoted the idea that Trump and Brexit were parallel insurgencies. They were people-led revolutions—bottom-up uprisings against "big banks" and "globalist insiders," as Farage put it, carried out by those left behind by mainstream politics. The Trump–Farage love-in was mutual. At a rally in Jackson, Mississippi, Trump introduced Farage onstage. Meanwhile, Fox News anchor Tucker Carlson interviewed Farage at a New York luncheon—in exchange for an £11,305.41 fee.

As Farage's US media profile grew, the Brexiteers were simultaneously in touch with their old friends, the Russians. On the way home from the RNC, Farage's twenty-two-year-old aide George Cottrell was arrested at Chicago's O'Hare International Airport. Cottrell was a UKIP fundraiser. The FBI charged him with twenty-one offences, including money laundering, fraud, blackmail, and extortion, dating from his time as a private banker. (The charges weren't linked to UKIP.) He would spend eight months in jail. "A spot of bother" is how Farage described the incident to me when I buttonholed him about it in London.

According to emails seen by the *Observer*, Wigmore gave Cottrell's federal indictment and other legal documents to the Russian embassy, emailing them to Udod, who was holidaying in Moscow. In Udod's absence, Wigmore swapped messages with another diplomat, Sergey Fedichkin. Wigmore was in Rio visiting the Olympics with Belize's sports minister. "Let me say how pleased I am that some Russian athletes will be competing at the Olympics," Wigmore began. He told Fedichkin that he was planning to visit the Russian delegation's hospitality house on Copacabana Beach.

The special channel of communication between Banks and the ambassador continued after Trump's victory. Days later Banks,

Wigmore, and Farage had what they called an unplanned meeting with the president-elect in Trump Tower. Also there was Raheem Kassam, the UK editor of Breitbart London. The moment was captured in a photo showing the five men with Trump in front of the gold-coloured doors of his Manhattan elevator.

According to Banks, Yakovenko got in touch after seeing the photo in the British press. He said the ambassador told him Moscow hadn't expected Trump to win. Did Banks have a number for him? As ever, the Brits were happy to help. They gave the Russians a number for the Trump transition team. After flying back to London, Banks again had lunch with Yakovenko. According to the *New York Times*, the two men discussed American politics and what role Jeff Sessions, then a senator, might play in Trump's cabinet.

ON BRIGHT, SUNNY days the Thames has a seaside feel. Small waves lap on a low-tide beach; there are gulls and pleasure boats, tourists and mudlarks. The river curls through the centre of London like a dark brown ribbon. The London Eye peers over the city.

Not far away, on the southern bank in Vauxhall, is an office complex. To get inside you have to show ID, sign in, and progress through a metal gate. This opens and closes behind you, pausing you temporarily, before a second gate opens, disgorging you into a concrete yard with several entrances.

This is the National Crime Agency, the NCA, Britain's equivalent of the FBI. A couple of floors up, officers in suits and ties sit in front of black computers. There is a glass-walled meeting room. The staff who work there form the international corruption unit.

In November 2018, following a referral from the Election Commission, the unit began a criminal investigation into Banks. It was, to say the least, a politically fraught mission. And an overdue one: more than two years had elapsed since the EU referendum, an event every bit as divisive and unhappy as the 2016 election of Trump. The NCA was trying to answer the commission's unresolved query: from where did Banks's Brexit cash come?

The possible answer led in numerous directions. These included Moscow, obviously, but also non-permissible donors who lived abroad and were therefore not allowed to finance UK politics. One trail pointed across the Atlantic. It went to Banks's American supporters and ideological co-strugglers and back to Russia again.

"From what we've seen, the parallels between the Russian intervention in Brexit and the Russian intervention in the Trump campaign appear to be extraordinary," Adam Schiff, the top Democrat on, and chairman of, the House Intelligence Committee, told the *New York Times*. In similar remarks to the *New Yorker*, Schiff pointed to the parallel roles played by Russia's ambassadors in London and DC. Both were conduits of "malign influence," he said.

To the left of the NCA building, along the embankment, was a green ziggurat-shaped temple with satellite dishes on the roof: MI6. Remarkably, British intelligence had not, I was told, launched a comprehensive investigation of its own into Russian meddling and Brexit. It had done some modelling work, written a few analytical conclusions. Yes, one MI6 source told a *Guardian* colleague, the Russians were "on manoeuvres." How much was unclear. MI6 hadn't carried out a full-blown inquiry. To do this, it needed instructions from Downing Street. And the government of Theresa May was distinctly unwilling to give such orders, or to go down a road that might lead to the conclusion that the Brexit vote was invalid.

May's attitude was perplexing. As prime minister she was bold in her condemnation of Russia's plot to murder Skripal. Her statement to the House of Commons—across the Thames from the NCA—pointed the finger at Putin and the GRU. Her government expelled twenty-three diplomats from the Russian embassy in Kensington Park Gardens. All were known intelligence officers. They included Udod, the embassy's man on Brexit, who was outed as a spy and given days to pack up and fly home.

May's decisiveness over Skripal stood in contrast to her lack of action over Russian mischief in the referendum. *Guardian* columnist Jonathan Freedland called her stance "Janus-faced." "Noisy about Salisbury, hushed about sabotage of the 2016 vote," Freedland wrote. In the US the special counsel was trying to get to the bottom of what happened in 2016. His inquiry identified dozens of Russian conspirators. May refused to carry out a similar exercise in Britain. Ministers said there was no evidence of "successful" Kremlin interference. They refused to explain what "successful" meant. Or how the government might be sure of this without a similar Mueller-style probe.

Broadly, the British political class and the BBC ignored Russia's possible role in the Brexit vote. May regarded delivering the "will of the people" as a quasi-religious duty, at least until her own party ousted her in summer 2019.

Meanwhile, opposition Labour Party leader Jeremy Corbyn and his closest advisers appeared to be closet supporters of Brexit—or Lexit, a left-wing Brexit that might undo neo-liberalism and usher in radical change. There were party considerations, of course. The Tory grass roots were overwhelmingly Eurosceptic. Many northern Labour Party constituencies voted Leave. Independent-minded MPs asked in Parliament about the Kremlin's role. They were lone voices.

In the absence of a British Mueller, it was left to investigative journalists to fill this civic gap.

The *Guardian* and *Observer*'s Carole Cadwalladr doggedly pursued Farage and Banks and explored their transatlantic ties to Bannon and Robert Mercer, the billionaire hedge fund owner behind Breitbart and Cambridge Analytica. She discovered that Cambridge Analytica was spun out of a bigger UK company called SCL Group, which specialized in "messaging and information operations" during conflicts. Wigmore told Cadwalladr that Cambridge Analytica used Facebook as a "potent weapon." "Likes" allowed ads to be tailored to individual voters. Wigmore said the company gave its services for free. Asked why, he told Cadwalladr in 2017, "Because Nigel [Farage] is a good friend of the Mercers."

(Banks later insisted that Leave.EU never hired Cambridge Analytica: "We had two or three meetings with them and it became clear to me that—as is true in a lot of politics—there is a lot of sizzle and sometimes not a lot of substance.")

Cadwalladr was trying to pull together the bigger picture. Dark data, dark money, billionaires with radical right-wing agendas, and coordination across national borders . . . the phenomenon was new and disturbing. There were profound questions about whether elections could be free and fair in an age of anonymous online influence. Seemingly, Bannon regarded Britain as a jumping-off point for spreading far-right Trumpian populism across Europe. The scale of the problem was enormous, and neither governments nor Silicon Valley wished to address it.

It was Cadwalladr who broke the scandal of Cambridge Analytica's illegal harvesting of personal data taken from Facebook users—at least eighty-seven million of them. Her exposé led to a $134 billion slump in Facebook's market capitalization and underwhelming testimony from Mark Zuckerberg on Capitol Hill. Cadwalladr earned a Pulitzer nomination with the *New York Times*.

And much opprobrium. Banks, Wigmore, and their pro-Brexit supporters trolled her remorselessly, tweeting a gif from the movie *Airplane!* in which a woman—with Cadwalladr's face pasted on it—is repeatedly punched around the head. In the background the Russian national anthem plays. Whatever your views on Brexit, this campaign of bullying looked nastily misogynistic. Farage and Banks praised Putin's political agenda. (Banks described Crimea as being as Russian as the Isle of Wight was British.) From time to time Leave.EU's official account retweeted Yakovenko's denials of Russian involvement in Brexit.

The NCA's task, therefore, was an unenviable one, the equivalent of being sent into a minefield with a compass and a breezy message of good luck. Where should it look?

A good place to start was Banks and Moscow. His second wife, Ekaterina (Katya) Paderina, came from Russia's Urals. They married in 2001; their three children had joint citizenship. Paderina's background was colourful. In the 1990s she moved to the naval town of Portsmouth and married a merchant sailor forty years older than she was. Local MP Mike Hancock subsequently helped Paderina in a dispute with the city council.

Colleagues in the European Parliament told me Hancock had a series of young Russian and Ukrainian assistants whom they believed to be "swallows." The MP, who chaired Parliament's Russia group, later had an affair with his twenty-four-year-old Russian researcher. A spy, according to MI5, who tried to deport her. (The aide, Katya Zatuliveter, appealed successfully against her removal.)

Banks went to Russia regularly. In March 2015 he flew to Moscow and then to Yekaterinburg to celebrate his mother-in-law's sixty-fifth birthday. The question for the NCA was whether these trips were exclusively family affairs or business opportunities, something Banks firmly denies. Of interest were other Russian contacts. One line of inquiry was whether Mrs. Banks knew Irina Povarenkin, wife of the Russian gold tycoon. Another was if the two women met in Moscow—where the Povarenkins lived in a mansion in the village of Borodki—or at the Povarenkins' chateau in the French seaside resort of Deauville. Povarenkin flew into and out of Deauville on a private jet. Had Banks been in it?

Equally puzzling was Banks's corporate empire. Much of it was offshore: in Belize, the British Virgin Islands, the Isle of Man, and

Gibraltar. These was nothing illegal about these structures. Maybe they contained the secret of Banks's fortune.

The Panama Papers gave us a few clues. I found Banks's firms among 10.5 million leaked files from the offshore law firm Mossack Fonseca. There was a gas bill from Banks's home in Bristol, a certified copy of his passport, and a "declaration of wealth/income" form in which Banks wrote "business trade." Plus a 2010 cutting about Hancock and Paderina. Povarenkin was in the Panama Papers too. I found his passport and discovered next to a grinning photo that he was "born in Omsk, USSR."

Banks's offshore arrangements were complex and opaque.

A key firm, PRI Holdings Ltd., was registered in the British Virgin Islands, an international tax haven. Banks said he didn't make the law and that any businessman would use similar structures. He said that he paid tax in the UK, a lot of it—£1.8 million in 2015. I found a flow diagram in the Panama Papers that helped make some sense of this maze. It showed "Arron Banks," with an arrow pointing to PRI Holdings, and further arrows to four companies. They included security and intelligence, wealth management, and mining rights—African Strategic Resources Ltd. Banks's main business was insurance. He also owned a 30 per cent stake in a financial group on the Isle of Man.

But it was his foray into diamond mining that appeared to be at the centre of the NCA investigation.

By 2015 Banks had acquired four diamond mines in South Africa and a licence to a mine in Lesotho. What motivated him to buy them was unclear. Many were at the end of their productive lives, with few if any diamonds to be found. Banks said the mines were profitable, with "significant finds." But was he interested in mining in Africa, or in the *appearance* of mining in Africa? The suspicion—vehemently denied—was that the mines provided a cover story for infusions of cash. Cash from somewhere else.

This, at least, is what Banks's former business partner alleged in court documents filed in South Africa and given to the NCA. Chris Kimber claimed that Banks had "unrealistic expectations" for the mines. And "had been dealing with Russians." Kimber alleged Banks "attempted to marry . . . illegally gotten diamonds" from other sources with the scant yield from his own holdings. One alleged diamond source was Zimbabwe, where Alrosa had a joint venture with the country's state-owned mining company. The theory—fantastic though it seemed—was that illicit or smuggled diamonds might have funded Banks's mining operations—and, perhaps, Brexit.

Such claims were "far-fetched," Banks told the *Sunday Times,* which published details of Kimber's lawsuit. It cited a 2014 email in which Banks told Kimber he was flying to Hong Kong with an uncut diamond and didn't have the necessary paperwork. He said his email account was hacked and that he was confident—correctly, as it turned out—that the NCA's probe was "going nowhere."

Remainer hopes that the NCA might pause or even cancel Brexit were wishful thinking, similar to expectations in the US that the Mueller probe would see Trump dragged from the White House. The NCA's investigation was narrowly defined, I was told. It had to meet criminal standards. Banks might be an unpalatable guy— horrible, even—but this was beside the point without prosecutable evidence, sources said. There was recognition that the government had been too slow to act. And that Britain's ancient electoral laws weren't fit for purpose.

In September 2019 the NCA acquitted Banks of criminal wrong- doing. It found that he was "legally entitled" to loan Leave.EU £8 million—a major victory for Banks against his critics. It added, "The NCA has not received any evidence to suggest that Mr. Banks and his companies received funding from any third party to fund the loans, or that he acted as an agent on behalf of a third party."

Seemingly, this was the end of the matter. A postscript, however, hinted that the NCA was still delving into South Africa and Banks's assets there. It said, "There have also been media reports alleging that Mr. Banks has been involved in other criminality related to business dealings overseas. The NCA neither confirms nor denies that it is investigating these reports."

The Electoral Commission was unhappy with this outcome. "We are concerned about the apparent weakness in the law which allows overseas funds into UK politics," it said.

It had previously fined Leave.EU for overspending during the 2016 vote. The Metropolitan Police declined to press charges. The Electoral Commission found Vote Leave guilty of similar allegations after the campaign channelled £675,000 into a pro-Brexit group that pretended to be independent but wasn't.

Meanwhile, the cabal of politicians who made Brexit happen, breaking electoral law along the way, were now encamped in Downing Street. In July 2019 Johnson won a vote of Conservative Party members to succeed May. He immediately appointed a hard-right cabinet, all committed to an extreme, ideologically pure version of Brexit, involving a possible EU crash-out. Johnson's behaviour was ominously Trumpian. It was characterized by populist slogans designed to fire up Brexit voters and a breezy indifference to truth. The US president made the comparison himself, making clear his approval for Johnson and dubbing him "Britain's Trump." Johnson's own priority was to suck up to Trump big time, in the hope of a US–UK trade deal.

Johnson was the culmination of what looked like a Bannonite project to bring about the creative destruction of the traditional Conservative Party. The strategy was to force out moderate Euro-friendly Tories and to empower a radical fringe, similar to the takeover of the Republican Party. Some suspected that Bannon was counselling Johnson behind the scenes and urging him to cause mayhem with provocative ideas. *Guardian* columnist Matthew d'Ancona said Johnson consulted Bannon before describing Muslim women in *niqabs* as "looking like letter-boxes" and "bank robbers." Bannon's closest comrades in the UK were Farage and Breitbart's Kassam, a vocal supporter of the far-right activist Tommy Robinson.

Britain's new prime minister had his own curious links with Russia.

In April 2018 passengers at Italy's San Francesco d'Assisi Airport were startled to see a crumpled figure, evidently utterly hungover, lining up on his own for a budget flight to London—Johnson, at this point foreign secretary. He had spent the night at an opulent palazzo in Perugia belonging to the ex-KGB agent Alexander Lebedev and his son Evgeny. The Russians owned London's *Evening Standard* newspaper. They were known for throwing extravagant parties for actors and celebrities. Johnson had left his government security detail behind. This was unorthodox, akin to Trump's refusal to allow US officials to listen in on his private fireside meetings with Putin.

What were Johnson and the Lebedevs discussing? We don't know. It was a strange time for Johnson to be hanging out with Russians; the previous day he had held talks in Brussels with Mike Pompeo about the Salisbury novichok attack. A year after the mysterious Italy trip the *Evening Standard* endorsed Johnson as the best Tory candidate for prime minister—a view at odds with its Remain-voting metropolitan readership.

As Britain's political chaos continued, Yakovenko exited London. After eight years the ambassador was moving on. The pro-Brexit forces he had done much to encourage were in government.

On August 24, 2019, the Russian embassy in London tweeted a valedictory photo of Yakovenko's home in Kensington Palace Gardens. It said the ambassador had relinquished his duties and returned to Russia. His new job: rector of Moscow's Diplomatic Academy.

If he looked out of his aeroplane window, Yakovenko might have felt content as he took off for Moscow. Below him was a troubled land beset by destructive forces and on the brink of Brexit. Britain was febrile, weak, and at war with itself. Meanwhile, an actual war—in which thirteen thousand people had died, shot and ripped apart by shellfire—was taking place in the borderlands of Europe.

CHAPTER 10

TONTO

Lucca–Kyiv–Washington, DC
2012–2019

Off to collect my paycheck at KGB :))
KONSTANTIN KILIMNIK, IN AN EMAIL TO THE AUTHOR

The venue was a private villa near the Italian city of Lucca. There was a view of the Tuscan hills, a swimming pool, terrace, olive groves. The house was furnished with tasteful pieces picked up from a local flea market. It was an idyllic place for conversation and good wine.

In the summer of 2012 a small, cosmopolitan group gathered there. One guest was a Russian national—elfin in appearance, with short dark hair. His name was Konstantin Kilimnik. He spoke marvellous English. Kilimnik was inconspicuous, polite, charming, and very smart, colleagues said—more anxious to listen than to ask questions, more low-key than some of the vaudeville characters who would figure in the Trump story. Kilimnik arrived at the villa with his Russian wife, Ekaterina, a medical doctor.

The host was Alan Friedman, a US journalist of distinction. In a successful career Friedman had written for top-end newspapers— the *Wall Street Journal*, the *Financial Times*, the *International Herald Tribune*. He penned columns and books. He was a gun for hire who used his literary talents as a PR guy and lobbyist. The villa belonged to Friedman's girlfriend, Gabriella Carignani, an Italian countess.

The two-day meeting was an informal strategic retreat. Its goal was to solve a problem besetting Viktor Yanukovych, the then leader of Ukraine. In 2010 Yanukovych narrowly beat his rival Yulia Tymoshenko in the presidential election. An American political consultant—Paul Manafort—masterminded Yanukovych's victory and his comeback from defeat and disaster in the election of 2004.

At home, Yanukovych was all-powerful. His Russophone political bloc, the Party of Regions, controlled Ukraine's parliament, the Rada. Yanukovych cronies pulled the levers of power: the prosecutor's office, the Ministry of the Interior, the courts. Most of the media and TV was under his control, either directly or via friendly billionaires. One was Rinat Akhmetov, who introduced Manafort to Yanukovych.

The problem was abroad. Yanukovych's early act as president was to jail Tymoshenko, the defeated opposition leader and former prime minister. She was accused of abusing her office by signing a bad gas deal with Putin. One further person who loathed Tymoshenko was Dmitry Firtash, the oligarch who together with Gazprom owned the country's gas transit industry. Other charges followed. Yanukovych insisted that Tymoshenko was in no way being persecuted and that his prosecutor general was simply applying the law.

The international community didn't buy this—not unreasonably. The Tymoshenko case looked to the EU and to Western governments suspiciously like selective prosecution, with misogyny thrown in. The claim of graft could be made against practically all Ukrainian politicians, including Yanukovych, whose crooked proclivities grew blatant once he took power. By the time the guests got together in Tuscany, Tymoshenko had just come off a hunger strike, her plight a matter of deepening concern in the Obama White House.

The challenge, then, was to convince the world that Tymoshenko deserved her fate. A surreptitious media strategy was under way. Its objective was to influence public opinion in Europe and America, especially on Capitol Hill, via newspaper articles, social media posts, YouTube videos, and sneaky Wikipedia edits. Black PR, in short—done deftly and anonymously by Yanukovych's American advisers. To carry this out Manafort had subcontracted Friedman and Friedman's business partner Eckart Sager, a former CNN producer living in London.

In summer 2011 Friedman and Sager had mailed a confidential strategy paper to Manafort and to the president's team, which I saw in 2018. It proposed "deconstructing" Tymoshenko and projecting a positive image of a European Ukraine under Yanukovych's wise rule. Manafort signed off on the plan. Details were sent via password-protected files. Yanukovych's chief of staff, Serhiy Lyovochkin, provided funds—$1.4 million to Friedman's company, according to the *New York Times*, put into tropical offshore accounts. (When payments were late, which they often were, Friedman would complain that the weather was "cloudy." When the cash arrived the weather was "sunny," I was told.)

One element of this strategy was to set up a bogus think tank in Prague: the Centre for the Study of Former Soviet Socialist Republics. The centre's website would publish "long-form international affairs articles that have in-depth analysis and commentary," as well as "small news snippets" and "quick news commentary." Posts could have a formal "op ed" style and a more casual "bloggy" one, Sager suggested. Academic "fellows" would dignify the centre's output.

Social media was crucial, the private paper added. Twitter, Facebook, YouTube, and news websites with open-thread comment sections . . . all might be exploited. Collectively, this online space offered "great opportunities for guilt by association," Friedman wrote. The hapless Tymoshenko could be depicted as "reckless," "unstatesmanlike," "malicious," and even "anti-Semitic." Twitter users—"both those known to us and strangers"—would retweet hostile content.

This clandestine operation complemented efforts by Prigozhin and the troll factory to use Twitter and Facebook to disparage and rip apart another powerful woman: Clinton. Used correctly, anonymous social media posts might mess with the heads of Americans.

Moscow's playbook in action.

In Ukraine's case, a Mafia-style regime was exploiting the open nature of Western society and its tech platforms—and finding willing American enablers and apologists happy to pile in for a fat fee.

By the time of the Tuscany meeting these dark arts were having an impact. At least this is what Friedman and Sager claimed in updates sent to Manafort, Manafort's deputy Rick Gates, and Kilimnik. Friedman took credit for arranging sit-downs between Yanukovych's foreign minister, Kostyantyn Gryshchenko, and European newspapers—Italy's *La Stampa*, Spain's *El Pais*, Germany's *Süddeutsche Zeitung*, Poland's *Gazeta Wyborcza*.

There were media successes in America too. Among them was a profile of Tymoshenko written by the *Wall Street Journal*'s Matthew Kaminski and done "as a result of our work." (Kaminski told me Friedman had nothing to do with his piece.) Plus a Tymoshenko-bashing blog in Breitbart, a Yanukovych opinion piece in the *Journal,* and favourable coverage in the conservative website *RedState*, under the fake byline of "Matthew Lina."

Meanwhile, Manafort and Kilimnik hired a leading New York law firm, Skadden Arps, to write a report into the propriety of Tymoshenko's trial and conviction. Did it meet US standards? Officially, the investigation was independent. And cheap—costing just $12,000. In fact, a Ukrainian oligarch paid Skadden Arps $4 million. The operation was secretly coordinated with Ukraine's

Justice and Foreign Ministries. Two more Washington lobbying firms, Mercury and the Podesta Group, were recruited too.

Despite these efforts, Yanukovych was some way from being viewed as a virtuous and respectable international statesman, as he might have wished. Around the villa and over dinner, a further gambit was discussed. Why not hire former politicians to lobby on Yanukovych's behalf? The operation might be subtle and discreet—a whisper here, a private word there. Germany's Angela Merkel was an especial target. Nobody need know that there was cash swirling around.

Sitting in their Italian retreat, the participants agreed on a name for these roving dignitaries. They were to be called the "Hapsburg group"—a nod to the nationalities of the ex-politicians, led by retired Austrian chancellor Alfred Gusenbauer. A key figure was Romano Prodi, the former head of the European Commission and twice Italy's prime minister. Ex-ministers from Silvio Berlusconi's cabinet were mooted as possibles.

Manafort didn't go to Tuscany. He missed an excursion led by Friedman to nearby Lucca, with its ruined Roman amphitheatre, palaces, Renaissance piazzas, and seventeenth-century walls. Manafort was looped in, though. In an "eyes only" memo written the same month as the meeting—June 2012—he set down how this "super VIP" effort might work.

The objective, Manafort wrote, was to "assemble a small group of high-level European highly influencial [sic] champions and politically influential friends who can act informally and without any visible relationship with the Government of Ukraine." An arm's-length agency would be created to retain these "endorsers," who would act "at our quiet direction." A shadow scheme. Manafort would handle the cash. There was plenty of it: €2 million routed offshore.

The Europeans eager to top up their pensions were part of a much larger multimillion-dollar lobbying operation. Its tentacles stretched as far as US members of Congress, officials in the executive branch, and their staffs. This was an under-the-table attempt to influence American politics and decision-making. Manafort should have registered with the US Department of Justice as a foreign government agent. He didn't. That wasn't merely unethical; it was illegal.

Lurking in the background—just out of the frame—was Kilimnik. His friends called him Kostya, a diminutive of Konstantin. Back in the 1990s he was known as "Kostya, the guy from the GRU."

IN PERSON AND over email—with me and others—Kilimnik denied that he was a Russian spy. The charge was preposterous, ludicrous, fanciful, silly, jejune! And wrong, a made-up narrative, he protested. Kilimnik styled himself as a victim of the "political game"—a martyr to the strange and surreal "agenda" that gripped the US after Trump became the Republican nominee in 2016, and then the country's forty-fifth president, and in the long years afterwards.

Kilimnik's assessment of the decade he spent at Manafort's elbow was self-effacing. His role was trivial! He was, he told me, "a little tiny screw in a toy car." Or, as he explained to me in an email, he had performed the minor part of Tonto—"faithful Indian scout and interpreter"—alongside Manafort's Lone Ranger.

How seriously should we take Kilimnik's playful denials? They failed to convince Mueller. In 2018 the FBI identified Kilimnik as a person with links to "a Russian intelligence service." Specifically— though this wasn't spelled out—to Russian military intelligence. Plenty of clues supported this assertion.

One was the scrupulous care he took to avoid being photographed. A couple of images exist. Neither is recent. Such caution indicates professional counter-intelligence awareness. The career

GRU officers and hackers who worked out of the Khimki Tower behaved in the same crepuscular way: they mostly avoided social media.

Another clue was Kilimnik's CV. He was born in April 1970 in Soviet Ukraine and grew up in the steel city of Kryvy Rih, in the Dnipropetrovsk region. In the final years of the USSR he moved to Moscow, and in 1987 joined the Military Institute for Foreign Languages, now a part of the Kremlin's Military University and attached to the Russian Ministry of Defence.

The institute had an illustrious history going back to the communist revolution. Its recruits wore uniforms and military caps. During World War II Red Army soldiers piled hundreds of volumes of looted foreign-language works onto carts and transported them from Europe and Asia back to Moscow: poems, novels, works of military doctrine. Most were burned in the 1950s, when Nikita Khrushchev decided to reshape the service.

By the 1960s the institute was educating a generation of linguists and future military spies. Its boss—Colonel General Andrei Andreev—hinted to recruits that they would soon be involved in intelligence work. "There's no point in denying that you are all *razvedchiki* [intelligence officers]," Andreev said in a speech, according to Igor Golovko, an Arabist and journalist who was in the audience and who later wrote a history.

The GRU defector Viktor Suvorov told me the institute was unique—a privileged establishment, with many students coming from high-ranking Soviet military families. It was frequently a stepping stone to the KGB and the GRU. Suvorov said that when he arrived at the Soviet Military Academy—the name given to the GRU's undercover training school—about "20 to 25 per cent" of his year came from the languages institute.

Suvorov was assigned to the first faculty, which prepared officers for undercover spy work using civilian cover. As a GRU trainee,

Suvorov said he was instructed never to allow himself to be photographed. "It was forbidden," he said. "If you are photographed in a group, you don't know what will happen fifteen or twenty years later. Someone might say, 'Ah, that's you! You are standing with a famous spy!'" Joining the shadow intelligence world from the languages institute wasn't "automatic," but the "majority" did.

Would a spy ever admit he was a spy? "Never, never, never," Suvorov answered.

So inevitably Kilimnik would have rubbed shoulders with current and prospective GRU officers. In 2017 the Russian acknowledged this in an interview with the Kyiv-based journalist Christopher Miller, telling Miller that the GRU had hired several of his contemporaries. But not him, he said.

His old institute produced liberals and intellectuals, linguists and philologists, Kilimnik told associates, complaining that he was collateral in someone else's intrigue. One name he mentioned was Soviet author Arkady Strugatsky. Strugatsky studied English and Japanese and worked as a military interpreter after World War II, becoming a successful science-fiction writer together with his brother Boris.

At the institute Kilimnik learned English and Swedish. He spent seven years working in the Russian army as a translator, and then joined the Russian arms industry, using his Swedish to negotiate the contract for a consignment of tanks. In 1997 he got a visa to travel to the US for a Russian diplomatic passport. This was another compelling clue. Why would a translator have diplomatic status—unless, of course, he actually worked for a secret government agency?

In 1998 Kilimnik got a job in Moscow with the International Republican Institute (IRI). The IRI was a Republican Party outfit that promoted democracy in Eastern Europe—a mission that Putin would criticize as aggressive US State Department-funded meddling.

Kilimnik's American IRI colleagues thought he came from Russian military intelligence. How else to explain his flawless, idiomatic English? Western intelligence experts describe this level of fluency as "velvet" and associate it with spy training. Kilimnik didn't dispel the idea that he had an intelligence background. According to one IRI colleague it was well known he had Kremlin links.

He did translation work and low-level office administration. Then in 2004 he got involved in events in Ukraine. Yanukovych, the prime minister, ran in the presidential elections against a pro-Western reform candidate, Viktor Yushchenko. Yanukovych was an uninspiring campaigner—clunky and Soviet and gaffe-prone—but with powerful friends.

Moscow technologists helped. On the night of the vote exit polls put Yushchenko ahead. Yanukovych's team hacked into Ukraine's central election commission and added 1.1 million votes to his tally. He was declared the victor. This trick prompted mass demonstrations, and an impromptu tent city took shape in Kyiv's Independence Square: the Orange Revolution. Putin didn't much like Yanukovych, regarding him as slow-witted and uncouth. There was no doubt, though, that he was Moscow's candidate. When Yanukovych lost a rerun vote this was Putin's humiliation.

In the aftermath of his election disaster, Yanukovych hired a veteran US Republican Party adviser who had worked with Ronald Reagan, George W. Bush, and Bob Dole: Manafort. Kilimnik began moonlighting for Manafort while still at the IRI. In April 2005 Stephen Nix, the Russian-speaking head of IRI's Eurasia programme, learned of this. "I fired him," Nix recounted to me. His intelligence links may also have figured in his dismissal. Kilimnik became the head of Manafort's Kyiv office. His employer was Manafort's consulting firm, Davis Manafort Partners.

The office was a simple affair, at 4 Sofia Street. It was a short walk from where pro-Orange activists had camped out along the city's chestnut-tree-lined Khreschatyk Boulevard. Inside, a map of Ukraine hung on the wall; flags were pinned against different regions. The most significant for Yanukovych was Donbas in the Russian-speaking east, dominated by industrial mining towns—including the one where Yanukovych was born, Yenakiyevo—and the cities of Donetsk and Luhansk.

Kilimnik kept an apartment in Moscow and a house in Kyiv. Manafort and Gates travelled frequently to Ukraine from the US. Manafort's de facto home was the Hyatt Hotel—a glassy five-star edifice on the main square, next to the pistachio-coloured St. Sofia Cathedral and a monument to a Cossack hero riding a horse. The Foreign Ministry was within walking distance.

The two men, Manafort and Kilimnik, became inseparable, former associates said. The ministry nicknamed them "the Kazakhs" because of consulting work they had done in the former Soviet central Asian republic. Kilimnik was essential during meetings, since Manafort couldn't speak Russian beyond a few basic words such as *spasibo* and *dosvidanya*. They rode around Kyiv in a second-hand Mercedes with a Ukrainian driver—Tonto and the Lone Ranger, on hired wheels rather than steeds.

"They were a funny pair, like something out of comedy club," one associate recalled. "You have a tall guy and a small guy. The difference in height was almost a meter. Paul was always dressed in a good US suit and tie. Very often he was sleepy because of jet lag. Kostya was going with him everywhere. When they met Yanukovych, Kostya acted as interpreter."

By the time I saw Manafort in Kyiv in September 2007, Yanukovych was prime minister for the second time. Manafort had transformed his client's political fortunes and reframed his public image. Yanukovych now blow-dried his hair, undid the top button of his shirt at election rallies, and stuck to vague but uplifting slogans such as "I will hear everyone." He was an uninspiring speaker, but no longer quite the dolt of 2004.

Ahead of parliamentary elections, the Party of Regions was reaching out to foreign media. I met with Lyovochkin, the head of Yanukovych's private office. Lyovochkin told me that the prime minister had changed, played tennis with the US ambassador, was learning English, and had "become a democrat." Our meeting took place in the Cabinet of Ministers, a short walk up a cobbled hill from Manafort's headquarters and on the same road as the Rada, Ukraine's parliament.

Manafort was a tall, imposing figure in a dark suit and tie, with glowing chestnut hair. He was anxious to dispel the idea that Yanukovych was the candidate of Russia—this was bad, lazy reporting, he told me. Yanukovych couldn't ignore Ukraine's powerful neighbour but had made "more overtures to the West." He was a strong leader and his own man. "There is no Russian influence in this campaign," Manafort assured me.

There was no sign of Kilimnik. It was clear that Manafort's tactics were paying off. The US embassy in Kyiv was on friendly terms with the consultant and observed in a cable that Yanukovych's political bloc—"long a haven for Donetsk-based mobsters and oligarchs"—had undergone an "extreme makeover." It was competitive again and profiting from Orange disarray after Tymoshenko and Yushchenko fell out.

"Paul is a very smart guy," Kilimnik told me in 2016. "He's a genius strategist. He always ran his elections in a free and fair way. He refused to play games with the system. He brought campaign technology to Ukraine. He developed a strategy based on polling." Kilimnik praised Yanukovych's party as strong, the best in the country. "If a party is organized, it's successful," he observed.

This may have been true. What was false—a lie, in fact—was that Yanukovych was in any way a reformed character. Or a democrat. After becoming president in 2010, his despotic tendencies came to the fore. As well as jailing Tymoshenko, Yanukovych bribed deputies to switch sides, enriched his family, and pocketed billions. He pivoted between Russia and the EU, screwing concessions from both. Then in late 2013, and under intense pressure from Putin, he abandoned Europe and embraced the Kremlin. The strategy plunged his country into flames.

I HAD BEEN reporting from eastern Ukraine for a week. It was April 2014. The events of the previous months had been grimly dismaying. There had been protests against Yanukovych and his corrupt rule. The previous November he had torn up an association agreement with the EU and accepted a financial bailout from Moscow. The move was symbolic. It signified that Ukraine would be under de facto Kremlin control, at least with regard to foreign policy and NATO membership. Its citizens would live under coercive Putin-style conditions, with Yanukovych Moscow's de facto viceroy.

The protests grew. Brutal force met them. They got bigger. At this moment of turmoil Kilimnik jetted off to Washington. The well-known journalist Serhiy Leshchenko saw him at a DC restaurant, sitting next to Lyovochkin. They were due to meet US officials to discuss the Ukraine crisis. The meetings were put off because of heavy snow.

By February Kyiv resembled an apocalyptic medieval hell as ant-like protesters armed with home-made shields and helmets battled riot police and flung stones with catapults. Yanukovych's security forces opened fire, killing more than a hundred civilians. The president fled to Russia, possibly with the help of the GRU's Chepiga and Mishkin. Putin dubbed the uprising a "fascist coup."

His response—carried out by the GRU and Russian special forces troops—was to invade and annex Crimea.

The following month I flew to Donetsk, where a pro-Moscow uprising was taking place. In the city and surrounding towns, youths were occupying municipal town halls and seizing police stations. These anti-Kyiv manifestations enjoyed local support. They were largely amateurish in nature; teenagers built roadblocks from tyres. Pro-Ukraine residents organized counter-protests. They waved blue and yellow flags.

There was a strong sense that behind the scenes Russia was involved—coordinating events, unveiling new pro-Moscow political "leaders," and activating an underground network of military veterans, sports club members, and law enforcement agents. I set off with a driver for the town of Kramatorsk. The Ukrainian army had recaptured a small military airbase recently seized by separatists.

At the Kramatorsk train station I discovered a crowd surrounding several armoured personnel carriers. Sitting on top of them were armed men in fatigues. Some wore balaclavas. They had orange and white ribbons—the symbol worn by Udod. There was nothing amateurish; this militia was well armed with Kalashnikovs, flak jackets, a grenade launcher. Flying from the top of the APC was a Russian tricolour.

The gunmen, it turned out, had seized the military vehicles from terrified Ukrainian soldiers. This new anti-Kyiv army posed for photos and set off. It rattled past the station and turned right, over a steep, dusty bridge. I drove after it—following a cloud of diesel smoke and white tread tracks left in the tarmac. After a little over six miles the column turned left and drove into the town of Slavyansk, parking around the back of the city hall and the White Nights Café.

The soldiers got out. They took up positions in a sunny green park. It was evident they had military experience. The hall had been turned into a fortified command post, complete with sand-bags and sniper posts on the roof. Curious locals were uncertain what their arrival meant. "I heard the sound of tanks approaching. I thought the Ukrainian army had come," Vladimir Ivanovich told me. Asked who the masked men were, he replied, "I don't know."

The gunmen, I discovered, were Russian. They appeared to be special forces—GRU, or a similar special unit under Moscow's control. One soldier told me he had come from Simferopol, Crimea's regional capital, where Russian troops without insignia had recently seized the regional parliament building. How were things there? "Excellent," he said. "The old ladies are happy. Because of Russia their pensions have doubled."

Back in Donetsk, the situation was fluid. The city's new pro-Ukraine regional governor, Serhiy Taruta, was trying to assert control. He had taken up residence in the Victoria Hotel, an attractive white-painted building with a large swimming pool. In the main square, the freshly proclaimed Donetsk People's Republic was running its own parallel government from the city's eleven-storey administration building, which was decked out with Stalin flags and anti-Obama slogans. Across the square was the art gallery. Several portraits were by Boris Pasternak's father Leonid.

Taruta's unenviable task was to hold local elections and to stop the Russia-backed insurgency from spreading. "The number of aggressive protesters is quite small," he told me, putting the number at about three hundred. A billionaire industrialist who looked uncannily like Woody Allen, Taruta was one of several oli-garchs appointed by Ukraine's post-Yanukovych president, Petro Poroshenko, to deal with the crisis.

I watched as a gang marched through the city, ripping down Ukrainian flags. Their destination was the regional TV centre. The crowd burst inside. The separatists brought a technician. He switched off Ukrainian channels and replaced them with Russian state TV. Masked men in fatigues supervised; three had guns. A peaceful protest about the status of the Russian language and the failures of the Ukrainian state was being turned into an ominously armed affair.

At this critical moment in Ukraine's fortunes a Russian political expert turned up in the east, unannounced and uninvited—Kilimnik, who presented himself to Taruta's team in Donetsk. He offered to assist. "We knew he worked for the Party of Regions. We thought, *The more the merrier*," Alex Kovzhun, who advised Taruta and had travelled with him from Kyiv, told me. "Kilimnik was one of the backroom boys. He was polite, smiling, and calm."

Kovzhun—himself a media adviser—took a dim view of Kilimnik's election talents. "He was a hack. He provided documents very fast. They were blunt, of the type 'You should say good things and not say bad things,'" Kovzhun said. "There was no insight or strategy. At the time I thought Kilimnik was just a guy who worked for bastards. We had won the revolution. He was on the losing side and we felt a bit superior."

Kovzhun said Kilimnik was efficient and unobtrusive. Might he also have been a spy? "It's incredible in a world of smartphones that only a couple of photos of him exist. You have to be able to evade that professionally. Someone has to train you." He added, "His Russian is native. He doesn't have a regional accent. It's as if all the traces of region were wiped." And, "He's quite comfortable in himself."

Two days after arriving in Donetsk, Kilimnik disappeared. These were hectic times, Kovzhun said, and his departure went unremarked. I left on the penultimate flight, just before fighting consumed the city's airport. A few weeks later Taruta escaped. He set up base in Mariupol, a port on the Azov Sea, and soon to be the front line. Chechen gunmen turned up at the Victoria Hotel, where Taruta and his staff had been staying, shouting, "Where are those faggots?"

By summer Donbas was a full-blown war zone. Russia supplied the rebels with heavy weapons, artillery, and tanks. Its soldiers, disguised as "volunteers," streamed over the border. The Ukrainian army evicted the militia from Slavyansk and soon found itself crushed by superior Russian firepower. The Donetsk and Luhansk People's Republics became political and geographical facts—run by disposable puppet warlords and functionaries answering to Moscow.

In Kyiv, and against a backdrop of conflict and shelling, Kilimnik continued to work with Manafort. The Party of Regions became the Opposition Bloc. Kilimnik was kept on at his old office. At some point the oligarchs who funded Manafort and Kilimnik's activities ceased paying their bills. According to *Politico*, in late 2015 Manafort flew to Ukraine, hoping to chase down some of this outstanding cash. At the Hyatt Hotel, the landlord who owned the office building ambushed him, demanding unpaid rent.

The office contained a safe. Inside were documents and a framed sketch, signed by Yanukovych and apparently put there by Kilimnik for safe keeping. Plus an invoice that appeared to show a mysterious $750,000 payment funnelled through an offshore account in Belize.

There was an application by Kilimnik's daughter Larissa—then fifteen—to study at a private school in Germany. It described Kilimnik as a "political/strategic consultant: [he] took part in over fifty election campaigns in Russia, former Soviet Union countries, and Europe. Currently serves as an adviser to Ukraine's president, Viktor Yanukovych." Home was a street in Moscow, close to the Oktyabrskoye Pole metro station and the GRU's conservatory.

Larissa had inherited her father's flair for languages, the application said. She was interested in international politics. She spoke "very fluent English" and some German and Chinese. She had travelled extensively—visiting "almost every country in Europe," as well as Korea, China, and the US.

IN SPRING 2016 a mood of excitement gripped Kilimnik's oligarch contacts in Ukraine. Yes, the Party of Regions was out of office. It had scant chance of finding a way back. But over in the US there was good news. Manafort had begun working for an exciting new client: Trump! In March the two men held talks at Trump's Mar-a-Lago estate in Florida. Trump unveiled Manafort as his new convention manager. Gates got a job as Manafort's deputy.

"When Paul popped up next to Trump a lot of our guys became very enthusiastic. They saw it as a chance," one senior Party of Regions former adviser told me. "The Ukrainian oligarchs who had paid for Paul were unhappy because of the change of government [in Kyiv]. They thought, *Paul is again in the game.* And, *If Paul is influential in the US Republican Party, he can lobby some relief for us.*"

Manafort's rise certainly opened new opportunities for Kilimnik. And, it appears, for Kilimnik's backers in Moscow. Kilimnik's multiple meetings with Manafort in 2016, 2017, and 2018 would be central to the FBI's collusion investigation.

What might be said of them?

One, they were secret.

Two, they appeared to advance Russian state interests.

Three, Manafort subsequently lied about these encounters, seeking to cover them up, not once but on several occasions, according to Mueller.

Four, if Kilimnik was indeed a GRU asset, as the evidence suggests, he was a good one.

Manafort's own ties to Russia were extensive. Between 2005 and 2009 he worked for the oligarch Oleg Deripaska. His remit included improving the international image of Putin's government. According to testimony by Gates, Manafort installed "friendly political officials" in countries such as Montenegro, where Deripaska had business interests. Manafort's company earned tens of millions of dollars from Deripaska, and borrowed millions more from him. Relations between the pair spoiled in 2009, when Deripaska invested in a Manafort fund, Pericles. The fund failed. Deripaska sued to recover his cash.

Manafort's role in the Trump campaign offered him a chance to make it up with Deripaska—or to "get whole," as he phrased it. His interactions with Kilimnik can be read as business, as an opportunity to make money. And also as espionage. After getting his Trump job, Manafort sent a memo containing articles on his appointment to Kilimnik. Kilimnik forwarded it to "friends" in the Opposition Bloc—Akhmetov, Lyovochkin, and Boris Kolesnikov, a senior party figure. And to Deripaska in Russia.

Kilimnik's line of communication to Deripaska went through the oligarch's deputy, Victor Boyarkin. In the 1990s Boyarkin had served in the office of Russia's defence attaché to Washington, reportedly as naval attaché, and based out of the Russian embassy. Such a posting could mean only one thing: Boyarkin was GRU. Subsequently he joined Deripaska's company, Basic Element. Boyarkin was a spy, then—a former one, perhaps—though as everyone in Moscow knew, former officers never really cut ties with their old service.

When he joined Trump, Manafort brought with him his pollster Tony Fabrizio. Beginning in April 2016, he instructed Gates to send Fabrizio's data and other Trump campaign updates to Kilimnik. Gates pinged the data to Kilimnik via WhatsApp, taking care to cover his tracks afterwards by deleting his chat history on a daily basis. Kilimnik in turn gave the polling to the three Ukrainians and—Gates understood—to Boyarkin/Deripaska.

This was extraordinary! Manafort anticipated future money-making opportunities and wanted to ingratiate himself with Deripaska, who might in return drop litigation, Gates told the FBI. Whatever his motive, Manafort was handing sensitive internal Trump campaign information to people in Russia—the same place that was busy sabotaging and taking apart Clinton.

It was a real-time back channel, connecting New York to Moscow and involving not one but two GRU agents.

It was hard to think of a more glaring example of conspiracy, stretching into treason.

Mueller's cautious reading of it was one of many disappointments from his inquiry.

The US State Department was also in touch with Kilimnik. During the Yanukovych years officials met with him from time to time to discuss the Party of Regions and the regime in Kyiv. He offered them frank and illuminating insights. These were described to me as Cold War-style tête-à-têtes. The State Department knew of Kilimnik's connections in Moscow but were naive about his intelligence side.

In early May 2016 Kilimnik flew to the US. He met two US officials in a bar a couple of blocks from the White House. It was the last meeting of its kind. Two days later, on May 7, Kilimnik caught a 3:00 a.m. train to see Manafort in New York. Soon afterwards Manafort became Trump's campaign chairman. At the Republican Party's national convention in July, a motion calling for lethal aid to be delivered to Kyiv was watered down—shades here of Trump's future impeachment scandal. This decision mystified some delegates, who believed that Russia posed an existential threat to Ukraine and regarded Moscow in traditional Reaganite terms as an "evil empire."

In July, according to the FBI, Kilimnik flew to Moscow. He spent five hours in conversation with Yanukovych.

In a coded email to Manafort, Kilimnik wrote:

I met today with the guy who gave you your biggest black caviar
jar several years ago . . . I have several important messages
from him to you . . . It has to do with the future of his country, and
is quite interesting.

The reference was to a lunch where Yanukovych gave Manafort
a $40,000 jar of caviar.

In another email Manafort asked Kilimnik if there had been
movement on resolving the "issue" of his failed Deripaska investment. Kilimnik said that "our friend"—Boyarkin—was optimistic.
Manafort then said of Deripaska, "If he needs private briefings we
can accommodate." No briefings happened, Manafort said.

Kilimnik flew to JFK in early August and had a late-night dinner with Manafort and Gates at the Grand Havana Room, an up-
market New York cigar bar near Trump Tower. The discussion, in
a mahogany-panelled private room, went "very much to the heart
of what the special counsel's office is investigating," the prosecutor
Andrew Weissmann told a federal judge in 2019.

The release by WikiLeaks of hacked Democratic Party emails
dominated the campaign. The obvious culprit was Russia.

According to Gates, however, Kilimnik said that it was Kyiv, not
Moscow, that was behind the hack. Manafort subsequently "par-
roted a narrative" that the Ukrainians were to blame. He shared
this theory with Gates and others, Gates told the FBI. This version
appears to have reached Trump's adviser Michael Flynn, who was
adamant the "Russians" weren't involved, Gates said.

Later Trump would espouse this conspiratorial view—
which exonerated the Kremlin—with disastrous and incriminating results. Fresh from Moscow, Kilimnik delivered a secret
proposal—the Mariupol plan. It envisaged that Yanukovych might
be brought back from exile in Russia and installed as prime minister of an autonomous Donbas region. His return could boost the

local economy and revive the prospect of a negotiated settlement to Ukraine's turmoil. Yanukovych wanted Trump to come out in favour of the plan and for Manafort to sell it in Kyiv and Europe.

There was an obvious beneficiary here: Putin. The proposal effectively legitimized the Kremlin's shadow invasion of eastern Ukraine, and the new separatist territories. A deal would be a crucial step towards the removal of US and EU sanctions on Russia—Moscow's foreign policy priority. Manafort said he told Kilimnik the plan was crazy and that they didn't discuss it further.

This wasn't true—Kilimnik pressed the idea subsequently, until summer 2018. But Manafort was correct that it wouldn't work. It was hard to see how anyone in Kyiv would negotiate with Yanukovych, a coward who used lethal force against protesters and then made off. Nor would any Ukrainian government accept partition. In interviews, Trump appeared to have swallowed Moscow's line. He told ABC's George Stephanopoulos that Putin wasn't "gonna go into Ukraine" and the "people of Crimea, from what I've heard, would rather be with Russia."

Over dinner in the cigar bar, Manafort filled Kilimnik in on his campaign messaging, his plan to beat Clinton, and the latest internal polling data. He briefed on the "battleground" states he considered key to victory: Michigan, Wisconsin, Pennsylvania, and Minnesota, according to Gates. They also discussed finance—the unresolved Deripaska lawsuit and how Manafort might get back money owed to him by the Opposition Bloc.

The three men were anxious that their meeting remained under wraps. They left the club via separate exits. There were no photos.

Kilimnik dismissed it afterwards as nothing—a chat about "bills" and "current news." As for the polling data—well, this was pretty much open information and not different from what you could find on RealClearPolitics or other websites, he told the *Washington Post*.

Manafort's six months at Trump's side ended abruptly in the same month, when documents surfaced suggesting he earned $12.7 million from his consulting work in Ukraine, paid out of a Party of Regions slush fund. In Kyiv, Leshchenko gave a press conference. He produced evidence—a black ledger—recovered by protesters who ransacked the Party of Regions headquarters. Manafort denied wrongdoing and quit the campaign.

Kilimnik was becoming the object of growing media speculation. Two weeks after the cigar bar meeting—about which I knew nothing—I sent him an email.

It began, "Dear Konstantin, Might you talk about your work with Paul in Ukraine?"

Kilimnik wrote back affirmatively. He was in Kyiv. He suggested that we chat, on Viber or WhatsApp. He was sceptical that he had much to say. "Doubt I can tell you anything new," he wrote.

After a couple of false starts—he was in a meeting—we spoke by phone. Kilimnik was friendly, confiding, and to the point. Manafort was not a Russian stooge, he said. Rather, he had "done significantly more" to bring Ukraine to the EU than "all the people in the current government combined." He didn't want Ukraine to be vulnerable to Russian attacks. It wasn't Manafort's fault if Yanukovych had proved incompetent: "There was a lot of bad judgement around."

Kilimnik sounded almost elegiac about his time with Manafort and predicted that this happy era might come again. "Manafort cared about this country. He really loves it. I won't be surprised if he's back. He's a campaign professional," he told me. There was another interpretation: that Manafort cynically exploited Ukraine's Russian-speaking east as ballot-box fodder, pitting it against the Ukrainian-speaking west, and thereby feeding radical Ukrainian nationalism and division.

Days later, *Politico* ran a long profile of Kilimnik. It set out his intelligence connections. I emailed him. Was he a Russian operative?

Kilimnik replied in droll style:

Thank God *Politico* hasn't figured out that I taught Colonel Putin German and judo. And that visit to Dallas in November 1963— phew, how could they have missed it.:))

It really boils down to 2 versions. Both of which have all chances of being true.

First—this was all a double agent game. Manafort and I were just pretending to be Russian agents but we were really working for US intelligence. Sometimes we would get confused, because the orders from Washington were so incredibly stupid that we naturally assumed they must have come from Moscow.

Second—it was probably a black op from the Deep State in the basement of the Pentagon which wants to know what the hell the State Department is doing in Ukraine and the trail of stupidity leads inexorably to the Trump campaign. Which explains why the US sent the Lone Ranger and his faithful Indian scout and interpreter Tonto who would never be suspected. It all fits.

Seriously though—nobody gives a shit here about such stuff because it is so insane. It is well understood by everybody that the real goal of this whole campaign is to push Manafort away from Trump and annihilate his chances of winning, which are there as long as Manafort runs his campaign. My guess is Trump understands this well and HRC's [Clinton's] strategy has not worked so far.

People who matter here, including the President himself, understand very well Manafort's role here and do not buy into all the gibberish about the black ledgers etc. Manafort will make billions on this free PR working for the same people he used to work. And probably get a lot of new clients with his newly found fame.

I am just a minor casualty in the US political game, which honestly has nothing to do with Ukraine or its future. If I am the biggest issue this country has—then we are all seriously in trouble.:)) But now I could write spy novels.

Off to collect my paycheck at KGB.:))

K

Kilimnik's answer was funny—a masterpiece of deflection and amused outrage. As a guide to what would happen next, it was inaccurate. In a follow-up email, he predicted the "silly attention to Manafort would go away." As for the black ledger and rumours of cash being given to "Paul": "To me the whole thing sounds like a big scam aimed at undermining Manafort and gutting Trump. Pretty stupid."

I wrote back and suggested that Kilimnik should tell his own story. It was an interesting one. If not now, I ventured, then perhaps a first-person account once the US election cycle was over?

Kilimnik wasn't convinced. He riposted:

Or maybe even write a script for another movie with DiCaprio and the bear who rapes him. All organized by Manafort and KGB, of course, and paid for by the Party of Regions black cash.:))))

Believe me—there is no story. As they say in Russian, зацепило прицепом. Scratched by a cargo trailer. There is nothing in that story other than bad spin.

Apparently Tonto and the Lone Ranger had ridden off into the sunset, their adventures over. In fact, Kilimnik continued to see Manafort. Manafort was formally outside the campaign, but was plugged in still and communicating with Kushner, Bannon, and Trump. On December 8 Kilimnik mentioned the peace plan idea in an email to Manafort, writing that "[a]ll that is required to start the process is a very minor 'wink' (or slight push) from DT

[Trump]." Manafort might be appointed "special representative." He could travel to Moscow, be received at the "highest level," and deliver peace in Ukraine within months, Kilimnik wrote.

In January 2017 Kilimnik and Lyovochkin attended Trump's inauguration. They met Manafort at the Westin Hotel in Alexandria, Virginia. As a foreigner Kilimnik wasn't allowed to buy a ticket. Three years before, he had set up a lobbying and consulting company with Sam Patten, a former IRI colleague. Patten found an American "straw purchaser" who bought them tickets.

Manafort had declined a job in the administration and was instead cashing in—advising foreign governments on how to deal with the new Trump administration. In February he met Kilimnik in Madrid. Kilimnik flew in from Moscow. Manafort initially denied the meeting but later acknowledged that it had taken place after the FBI showed him evidence that Kilimnik was there at the same time.

Kilimnik was a will-o'-the wisp, a small, ghostly person who flitted over the bogs and swamps of American politics, half seen. In 2017 he decided to disappear. The FBI was investigating Manafort and his connections with Russian intelligence. In Kyiv, Kilimnik packed up his belongings. He told the *Kyiv Post*'s Miller he was sorry to leave Ukraine.

There was an inevitability about his next move.

Kilimnik went to Moscow.

One person who knows him well told me that Kilimnik never showed direct sympathy towards Russia or signs he was playing a double game. The person conceded that Kilimnik's biography looked suspicious, adding that once you were on the radar of Russian intelligence you stayed there: "They help you build your career and wait until you reach a certain point where you become useful." And, "If he is GRU, he's a top-class operator."

THE SPECIAL COUNSEL'S inquiries had a remarkable effect on the Americans who had worked closely with Kilimnik. All of them followed the same impulsive course when confronted with Mueller's questions. They dissembled, equivocated, told false stories, and did their best to cover up and delete incriminating traces. Their attempts at concealment—born no doubt from panic—were foolish and unfortunate.

One unwise course of action was witness-tampering ahead of trial—a deed that was likely to bring the scales of justice crashing down on one's head. The same trait was, of course, visible from inside the White House, where the president browbeat witnesses, hinted—to Manafort and others—that if they did the right thing they might expect a pardon, and urged hanging tough.

In 2018 I got hold of documents that revealed the black PR operation against Tymoshenko. They included Friedman and Sager's strategy papers, updates sent to Kyiv, and details of meetings with Manafort. Seemingly, any foreign government with an image problem could—for regular monthly sums—buy positive editorial content and favourable posts in the US and European media.

I drafted a story. I sent emails seeking comment. Lyovochkin texted that it was "better to ask Manafort." Sager didn't reply. From Tuscany, Friedman wrote to say that he had "never worked as a lobbyist for Ukraine." He added, "I never registered as a foreign agent because I never was one. I was a communications guy, doing PR media strategy work in Europe for a client, like dozens of PR companies that work for a variety of governments." The single aim was to move Ukraine closer to the EU, he stressed.

I wasn't the only person sending Friedman messages, it turned out. That February Mueller's newest indictment revealed Manafort had paid large sums to the Hapsburg Group. Its members agreed to take positions "favourable to Ukraine, and to lobby in the US." (Gusenbauer, the Austrian ex-chancellor, and Prodi, the Italian former prime minister, deny wrongdoing.) The same day Manafort phoned Friedman twice and sent him a WhatsApp message saying "This is Paul."

Friedman didn't respond. This was arguably ungrateful: in summer 2016 Manafort had fixed a one-on-one interview for Friedman with candidate Trump, which took place on Trump's private jet while it was parked in the cargo zone at Houston's George Bush Intercontinental Airport. Manafort tried again, chatting, "We should talk. I have made clear that they worked in Europe."

This failed to elicit an answer. Next it appears that Manafort asked Kilimnik to help. From Moscow, Kilimnik reached out to Sager—or "Person D2," as he appears in a legal exhibit—writing, "hi! How are you? Hope you are doing fine.;))." He explained that Manafort wanted to brief Friedman and to give him a "quick summary" that "our friends never lobbied in the US." Kilimnik kept trying, sending further messages via telegram. In April he got in touch with Friedman directly, writing, "Hi. This is K."

All these approaches were in vain. What Manafort didn't know was that Friedman was already cooperating with the FBI. Friedman told the bureau that his former colleagues had been in touch and were trying to "suborn perjury." This was true: as part of his Hapsburg duties Prodi had met in 2013 with Congress representatives in the US. Friedman had even ghosted an opinion piece for Prodi that appeared in the *New York Times*.

Mueller duly charged both Manafort and Kilimnik with two counts of obstructing justice. Manafort already faced five charges of money laundering and bank fraud. The pair tried to "corruptly persuade" Friedman and Sager and to "influence" their testimony, the special counsel said. The judge hearing Manafort's case, Amy Berman Jackson, was unimpressed with these shenanigans. She revoked his bail and said, "I'm concerned you seem to treat these proceedings as another marketing exercise."

From here on, Manafort's plight worsened. In August 2018 a jury convicted him on eight counts. The charge sheet spoke of white-collar crimes: bank fraud, tax fraud, failing to disclose foreign bank accounts. Some $75 million of Ukraine-derived income went through Manafort's accounts. He hid this from the IRS. Much of it was deposited in Cyprus, a favoured destination for illicit Moscow cash. Among other extravagant purchases, Manafort used it to buy a bomber jacket lined with ostrich—a fitting symbol of his greed and bad taste.

Apparently chastened by his conviction, Manafort said he was going to cooperate with law enforcement. He pleaded guilty ahead of a second trial in DC. His repentance was insincere. In November the special counsel's office revoked Manafort's deal on the grounds that he had lied repeatedly about virtually everything. He failed to tell the truth about his meetings with Kilimnik and much else, it said. (Manafort's lawyers said he may have forgotten details amid the pressures of a hectic presidential campaign.) In spring 2019 Manafort was sentenced to ninety months. Judge Jackson remarked, "Court is one of those places where facts still matter."

The sentence looked lenient. Still, at the age of almost seventy—and after a career spent working for bad guys and dictators, with Trump the pick of the crop—Manafort was likely to spend his twilight years in jail. A pardon was on the cards, but he faced fresh charges of fraud and conspiracy in New York state, where the president didn't have the power to amnesty him.

The episode revealed the impressive scope of Mueller's investigation—and its painful limitations. His attorneys carried out numerous interviews, seized emails, and—we imagine—used material from intelligence sources. Sometimes subjects lied. This too had evidentiary value. Dubious testimony might be matched against statements from more plausible witnesses, such as Gates.

Sitting in Moscow, Kilimnik was tidily out of reach. He might as well have been on the dark side of the moon. Much of the Russian side of the story remained opaque. Investigators never discovered what Kilimnik did with the polling data. Or what other information might have been swapped.

Still, it was clear Kilimnik had an uncanny knack for getting close to people with intelligence value. First Yanukovych, then Taruta, and finally Trump. Thanks to Manafort, Kilimnik had an insider's view of the Trump campaign as it unfolded—a unique perch from where he could watch events and shape them.

Kilimnik enjoyed being rich and had his own interests. Ultimately, though, he served Moscow.

He said nothing about the downfall of his friend. When the *Guardian*'s Moscow correspondent Andrew Roth called in late 2018 at the gated development where Kilimnik lives, security guards shooed him away. Reporters from the Russian website Projekt reached Kilimnik on the phone. At first he denied being Kilimnik. He phoned back on a different number, and said of his work with Manafort—more than a decade of conversations, meetings, car rides, breakfasts, and dinners—"I'm not interested in discussing this issue."

Kilimnik lived in a $2 million Scandinavian-style house, with a balcony and a forest backdrop of mature pine trees, in northwestern Moscow. The district is Novogorsk, the area Khimki. A short drive away is the ring road, the Moscow Canal, the GRU's glass tower, and the Skhodnya base, belonging to the GRU's murder unit 29155.

The FBI didn't get access to all of Kilimnik's communications with Manafort, many of which were encrypted. Mueller admitted his office was "limited" in its ability to gather evidence from inside Russia. Meanwhile, Manafort was "unreliable": a polite way of saying he was a serial liar. The upshot of all this: the FBI didn't "establish" whether Manafort coordinated with Moscow over its espionage activities.

We are unlikely to ever find out if the data reached the GRU or other Kremlin actors. Kilimnik said it didn't. And added, to the *Washington Post,* that Mueller never got in touch. The special counsel couldn't establish a connection with Russian election interference.

If there *were* a link, the Russians were hardly going to tell him.

On this, and on much else, Mueller fell short.

CHAPTER 11

RECKONING

Antigua–London–New York–Montenegro–Washington, DC
2019

*If we live long enough, it's all going to turn out
to be completely true. I have some hope that
history will be kind to us.*
GLENN SIMPSON ON THE TRUMP–RUSSIA INVESTIGATION

In early 2019 Chris Steele and his wife, Katherine, went on vacation. It was their first break for two years. Steele might be forgiven for wanting to escape. There was abuse from Trump—a regular occurrence bordering on obsession. And, as Steele admitted to friends, being a hero of the resistance was in its own way pretty exhausting. Mueller's long-awaited report lay just around the corner.

Their destination was the Caribbean and the island of Antigua. Perhaps there they could finally relax. Steele made no effort to hide his identity. He booked the trip under his own name and talked about it online. The only precaution was to pick a luxury resort with security. They would be there for a week.

Antigua turned out to be a good choice. There were white beaches and forested hills. The hotel, in English Harbour, looked onto yachts and a smooth, turquoise sea. One of the boats appeared to belong to Dmitry Rybolovlev, the Russian billionaire who bought Trump's Florida mansion.

On their final day the Steeles went on a speedboat trip to the west, snorkelling in Carlisle Bay, splashing amid wrecks and tropical fish. Later that evening, and back in their apartment, they dressed for dinner.

And then something strange.

Steele's wife went to her toiletries bag. Inside she found two wedding rings. They hadn't been there before. The rings didn't look expensive: one was well worn, a man's; the other, a small, shiny platinum band, a woman's. Someone—it appeared—had broken in. And left the rings behind as a sinister calling card.

As Steele knew well, only one secret service had a history of creepy intrusions. As a young British spy in Moscow the KGB had slipped into his apartment on several occasions, leaving behind similar clues. The message: "Watch out! We can fuck with you anytime!" Steele removed the rings gingerly, using tissues. You couldn't rule out poison. Or a set-up, with the rings reported stolen. He handed them to hotel reception.

It was disconcerting, an episode designed to be unsettling and carried out by persons unknown to ruin a vacation mood and replace it with one of foreboding.

IN JUNE 2019, two months after Mueller's report was published, guests gathered in a back street close to Buckingham Palace. They had come for a party. Rather an exclusive one. A cream invitation had gone out, featuring five champagne flutes and a corporate logo. It said: "Orbis Business Intelligence Requests The Pleasure Of Your Company To Celebrate Its 10th Anniversary." Orbis had come a long way since Steele and his partner Christopher Burrows came up with the idea of stepping out from the shadows. In 2009 both were experienced MI6 officers. Their plan was to leave government spying and apply their skills of investigation and analysis to the realm of private business. Their new firm would supply high-level Russia-facing intelligence.

It was a risky career move. The sector was crowded. And their timing was poor, coming as it did a year after the global financial meltdown. Moreover, both Chrises had just been through momentous personal challenges: in Steele's case the death of his first wife at the age of just forty-three; in Burrows', a prematurely born son.

Could they make a living? Would anyone notice them?

London's Goring Hotel was a favourite of the Queen. Sometimes Her Majesty dropped in for lunch. By the time the guests assembled outside its front entrance in June 2019—Union Jack flags, frock-coated doorman—these Orbis questions had been answered. Trump's attacks on Steele had become part of the cosmic fabric. Steele was, according to Trump, a low-life, a fraud, and a fake. The dossier continued to torment the president, like an incurable itch. Since *BuzzFeed* published it in January 2017 the leader of the free world had tweeted about it fifty-seven times.

The special counsel's now public investigation into Russian interference in the 2016 presidential election had intensified Trump's rage. He was as choleric as ever. Four days earlier the president had taken to Twitter to express his feelings about Steele, in dossier tweet number fifty-eight:

When will all the Fake News media start asking Democrats if they are OK with the hiring of Christopher Steele, a foreign agent, paid for by Crooked Hillary and the DNC, to dig up "dirt" and to write a phony Dossier against the Presidential Candidate of the Opposing Party.

The sentence was the usual gloopish Trump stream of consciousness; it only made sense because Trump had written similar things before. Thanks to his enduring antagonism, Orbis had become one of the world's best-known private intelligence outfits. And despite what the president claimed, the dossier—post-Mueller—looked more right than wrong.

Mueller confirmed Steele's thesis: that Russia had carried out a multifaceted operation in support of Trump. In many respects, though, the report was a disappointment, a bracing let-down— at least as far as Steele's friends and colleagues were concerned, together with liberal Americans and progressive citizens in Britain, Europe, Australia, and elsewhere.

The moment of catharsis that Trump's critics had fervently expected for almost two years failed to materialize. Mueller didn't discover a bigger story. Or, to use his precise words, he didn't "establish" one. On the evidence available he concluded that Trump hadn't coordinated or conspired with the Russian government or been a criminal player in Moscow's election-wrecking activities. The dossier said differently. Orbis's sources believed that Trump's close aides, notably Manafort and Cohen, had directly plotted with Russians.

The discrepancy between empyrean expectation and bathos-filled end product might be explained in different ways.

First, Mueller had adopted a lofty standard of proof. In an introduction he explained his "evidentiary considerations." The word that best summed up Trump's dealings with Russia— "collusion"—wasn't considered, Mueller said, since it didn't exist in law. Instead he looked for something else: coordination with Moscow. Mueller described this concept as "*more than* the two parties taking actions that were informed by or responsive to the other's actions or interests [my italics]".

It was a high criminal bar. It meant that to establish a conspiracy case Mueller had to find evidence of the Trump campaign working *directly* with agents of the Russian state. Foreign intelligence services rarely put their active agents in direct contact with government actors. The Russians preferred to use "cutouts." These were persons who had no direct and documentable relationship with Moscow, and who were also possibly unaware of the manner in which they were being used.

Mueller's approach was ultra-conservative. It was not characteristic of charging practice in the Eastern District of Virginia and the District of Columbia, the two most relevant legal jurisdictions, I was told. Or with prosecutorial practice around the Espionage Act. Additionally, Mueller failed to challenge prior Justice Department rulings upheld by Attorney General Barr that a sitting president couldn't be indicted. This—per the Justice Department—was on the grounds that prosecution would have a chilling effect on the president's ability to conduct his or her duties.

The Justice Department therefore narrowed Mueller's options. The special counsel closed them down further with his own interpretation of law. And by an apparent deep reluctance to go face-to-face with his elusive quarry, Trump. As one law professor, Scott Horton from Columbia University, put it to me, "Mueller was extremely gun-shy." Horton pointed out that previous independent counsels—Ken Starr, who pursued Bill Clinton in the 1990s, and Leon Jaworski, who went after Nixon in the 1970s—had been way more aggressive.

Collusion might not be a legal term, but a reading of Mueller's redacted record gave us plenty of examples of it. There were secret meetings, offers of dirt, encrypted messages, hints, and whispers. They included the notorious 2016 encounter with a Russian lawyer inside Trump Tower featuring Trump Jr., Kushner, and Manafort. The Russians comprehensively penetrated Trumpworld, we learned. There were few occasions when campaign officials pushed back against Kremlin outreach. At no point did anyone tip off the FBI.

This behaviour—by Trump and his subordinates—was deeply unethical. It was troublesome and unpatriotic. It gave rise to profound national intelligence and security concerns that went beyond the parameters of Mueller's inquiry. According to Mueller, the many contacts linking Moscow to the Trump operation weren't criminal. There was insufficient evidence to establish a broader conspiracy, he said. A shared motive undoubtedly existed between the American and Russian camps to damage and destroy Clinton. But for Mueller this wasn't quite enough.

OVER CHAMPAGNE AND canapés, Steele's guests mulled over the report and the unsatisfactory place where Mueller's investigation had washed up. Horton told me later that Mueller left him "negatively impressed": "I thought at this point we would be much closer to knowing the truth. I see Mueller doing almost nothing to advance the story. He brought us almost exactly to where we were. He didn't answer the big questions."

The party took place in the Goring's downstairs room. It opened onto a modest paved terrace where you could smoke. Those who attended had, in lesser and greater ways, played a role in the dossier. They included Americans, Brits, and Germans. Glenn Simpson and Peter Fritsch—co-founders of Fusion GPS—had flown in from DC. There were barristers, diplomats, ex-spies. And family and friends. Had Trump wandered in, he would have taken the gathering as proof that there was indeed a well-developed Anglo-American conspiracy against him, as Fox News said. In fact, the event was just a party—a jolly one, to celebrate Orbis's success against the odds and toast the next ten years.

Amid the sense of anticlimax, there was some praise for Mueller. His report at least confirmed the key Russian element of Steele's reporting. The naming and exposure of Moscow's spies was half the battle, Steele remarked.

"My early takeaway on day one was 'Oh, thank God,'" Simpson told me. The dossier's broad assertions had been stood up, Simpson felt. The actors identified in 2016 by Steele's sources figured prominently in Mueller's 2019 narrative. The Russian espionage operation delineated by Steele had actually happened. It involved "willing" Trump people. If anything, it was even worse than the dossier said. "All these things are true in great detail," Simpson said.

Three years on, his verdict on the dossier was that many of its allegations had been borne out, with some remarkably prescient. Others remained stubbornly unconfirmed. A few—such as Cohen's trip to Prague—looked doubtful but were not yet disproven. Ultimately Simpson was confident that history would vindicate the decision to investigate Trump and Russia and expose what was by any standard a well-developed intelligence operation.

In the meantime the mood was one of frustration.

Mueller, in Simpson's view, had failed to heed the main lesson of Watergate: follow the money. He hadn't clarified the president's murky relationship with Deutsche Bank. Nor had he examined Trump's real-estate deals around the world and the millions from Russian buyers that had flowed into the president's accounts. Had this Moscow cash put him under any kind of obligation? Mueller didn't ask the question, and we never got an answer.

Another shortcoming was literary, we agreed. Mueller had fallen short as a storyteller and communicator to the nation. His findings were written in legal prose. The language was stuffy and at times impenetrable, at least to many. "The thing is so understated and legalistic it leaves itself open to malicious misinterpretation," Simpson said. There was a "disconnect" between the report's percussive content—a series of booms!—and its muffled delivery. In the end, most voters didn't read it.

This problem of language was glaring at the end of Volume Two, the finale. Had Trump obstructed justice? Mueller declined to answer this. He fell back upon Department of Justice guidelines, which said indicting an incumbent president with a federal crime would be unconstitutional. "We did not draw ultimate conclusions about the president's conduct," Mueller wrote. "Difficult issues" would need to be resolved "if we were making a traditional prosecutorial judgement."

So Trump was in the clear? Well, no—he wasn't. Mueller's point, implied but unfortunately never expressed, is that *were* Trump anyone but the serving US president he might well face criminal prosecution.

Indeed, most prosecutors thought he was highly likely to do so. Hundreds of them signed an open letter arguing that there was sufficient evidence to bring "multiple felony charges" for obstruction of justice. They cited Trump's attempts to fire Mueller and to falsify evidence. Plus the president's blatant attempts to stop witnesses from cooperating with investigators and his efforts to ensure his personal behaviour fell outside the inquiry.

Mueller ended his investigation with the words "If we had confidence after a thorough investigation of the facts that the President clearly did not commit obstruction of justice, we would so state. Based on the facts and the applicable legal standards, we are unable to reach that judgement. Accordingly, while this report does not conclude that the President committed a crime, it also does not exonerate him."

This crucial passage doesn't reveal itself on a second reading. It gets lost amid a fog of double negatives and subjunctive phrasing. This occluded payoff created an opening—exploited masterfully, you had to admit, by Barr. Almost four weeks before the report was published he sent a four-page letter to Congress with a précis of its findings. It said Mueller cleared Trump of obstruction and collusion. The summary was wrong and deliberately misleading. Trump was able to proclaim his "total exoneration," while Barr sat on the contents.

There were other deficiencies, not all of them the fault of Mueller. The report was arguably the most damaging official

political document ever written about a US president. If you had
fallen into a coma in December 2016 and awakened in March 2019,
you might have assumed that the Mueller revelations would lead to
Trump's swift removal, with the president cuffed and led away into
a waiting police vehicle.

By the time Mueller's document emerged, much of the story was
known. His team had charged thirty-four people. They comprised
twenty-six Russians, Flynn, Manafort, Cohen, and other individuals. The indicted Americans pleaded guilty to federal crimes.
The most scandalous facts were out; the GRU's cyber operation in
Moscow had been extensively revealed; we knew the names of Putin's
military spies. It was a long-running saga, with multiple characters
and a hard-to-follow plot line. As Simpson put it, many people were
tired. An exhausted nation had lost its capacity for outrage.

The report roamed little beyond these earlier indictments.
Contrary to expectations it did not include additional charges—for
example, against Donald Trump Jr., an obvious potential candidate. Mueller said he hadn't taken action against Trump Jr. because
he couldn't be certain of his mental state.

The biggest enigma of 2019 was why Mueller had ended his
probe that spring.

One reason: Barr and his deputy Rod Rosenstein had put the
special counsel under enormous pressure. Their message: wrap it
up. One Orbis guest told me that Mueller "wimped out" under
assault from Trump and the president's attorneys. "Pretty medi-
ocre" was Steele's own view, according to friends. These comments
may have been harsh. But it was reasonable to wonder if this pressure had succeeded, at least to some degree. The report's publication felt abrupt, as if a pupil had been told to put down his pencil at
the end of a public exam.

In May Mueller made a rare public appearance at the Department
of Justice—a grey-haired figure, bowed, his voice a little tremulous.

He announced that he was shutting the office of special counsel and going back to private life. Mueller summarized his report. Russia had sweepingly interfered in US democracy via cyber attacks and remote impersonation. This should concern every American, he said, including—the rebuke was implicit—President Trump.

As he read his statement Mueller looked weary, a distinguished public servant now in his mid-seventies. At times he stumbled and had to repeat a line he had just read. Former FBI colleagues spoke of Mueller's acuity, of his zeal in previous investigations for "in the weeds" detail, and his prolific work rate. But the sharpness appeared to have gone. In his nine-minute address Mueller said he didn't intend to comment further, to Congress or to anyone else, or to elaborate on his published text—"my testimony," as he called it. His chief desire, it seemed, was to become invisible.

After two years in the spotlight, Mueller may simply have had enough. It had been a gruelling, remorseless period for him. The former FBI chief faced daily vilification. He had become a synecdoche for the fate of the American republic and for Trump's continuation—despised by the president and his fans, mythologized by Trump's political opponents. In the end, Mueller proved to be a man, not a superman. He was scrupulous, fair-minded, and careful, a virtuous soldier-bureaucrat. He did everything cautiously, by the book.

The delinquent subject of Mueller's probe was none of those things. For more than a year the special counsel's office sought a sit-down interview with the president. He declined. Instead in November 2018 Trump gave a series of written answers. They appear in the report's appendix. These are so grudging, perfunctory, and unhelpful that they might be read as a form of executive trolling. On more than thirty occasions the president claimed he didn't remember or couldn't recall pivotal events—what he knew of the Trump Tower meeting, when he learned of the DNC hack, and so on.

Ultimately Mueller didn't subpoena the president. He argued that to have done so would have delayed his report because of "potentially lengthy constitutional litigation." His office had already acquired a "substantial amount of information." This was enough to make "factual conclusions on intent and credibility."

The argument didn't convince. As one of Steele's guests put it to me, before we stumbled, a little tipsy, into the street, me clutching a Putin/Trump 2020 T-shirt, in the final analysis Mueller was unequal to the great and unreasonable task put before him. It was a historic miss.

THE SUSPECTED GRU spy Kilimnik wasn't the only important Russian whom Mueller was unable to find.

During 2017 another Moscow-connected translator vanished from his New York home. His name was Sergei Millian. When precisely Millian went to ground is unclear. At some point that spring he left his apartment on 18th Street in Astoria, Queens—a brown-brick building, not far from the East River and Astoria Park. He didn't return, vanishing as if into air.

Similar to Kilimnik, Millian had laughed off accusations that he worked for the Russian government. Yes, he had friends in Moscow, including high-ranking ones and presidential advisers! No—he wasn't a spy, he said in 2016. Millian was president of the Russian–American Chamber of Commerce in the US. This was a small, mysterious trade group whose purpose was to bring Russian and American businessmen together. One person Millian claimed to know well was Trump.

How Millian ended up in America was as vague as his own personal story. He grew up in Belarus. Or was it Russia? In one version he studied languages and diplomacy at Minsk State Linguistics University. And worked as a military translator. In a 2009 résumé, however, Millian said he graduated from Moscow State Linguistics University and was an interpreter with the Russian Foreign Ministry.

Even Millian's name was a source of confusion. When he immigrated to New Jersey, in about 1999, he was known as Sergei Kukuts. And as Siarhei, Sergey, or Siahiey. He said the fictitious Millian name he used in America came from his grandmother's side of the family.

None of this amounted to proof that Millian was Russian intelligence. There were tantalizing clues, though.

In 2006 Millian registered his trade body in Atlanta, Georgia. Within a short period it was hosting visiting Russian politicians. Five years later, in 2011, he was part of a delegation that took American executives to Russia under the auspices of Rossutrudnichestvo, the cultural agency that brought young conservatives to Moscow from London. The junket aroused FBI suspicion. The bureau interviewed US participants when they got back. The diplomat in charge of these arrangements, Yuri Zaytsev, quietly left Washington and went home.

The FBI was making uncomfortable discoveries during the Obama era: that the number of active Russian spies was higher than they might have imagined; and that they were being organized along classic KGB lines. Cultural exchange was a form of espionage cover. So too was commerce. During the Cold War, trade missions in America or Europe were stuffed full of Soviet intelligence officers operating under a business legend.

Millian appeared on Steele's radar in April 2016, a small, curious blip. By this point he was a naturalized American. He talked publicly and enthusiastically about his support for Trump and of how a Trump presidency might transform US–Russian relations. Millian gave an on-the-record interview to the Moscow news agency RIA Novosti. His knowledge of the then candidate went beyond mere acquaintanceship; they had done business together for years.

In an interview with ABC News Millian said he met Trump in 2007. The encounter happened via a "mutual friend." This was when Trump was expanding his contacts with Russia. The unnamed friend helped Trump launch his brand of vodka at the Millionaire's Fair in Moscow. The event was held at the Crocus Expo Centre—owned by Agalarov, the 2013 Miss Universe host. Millian said he was invited to watch a horse race from Trump's private box at Gulfstream Park in Hallandale Beach, near Miami.

Beginning in 2007 Millian began identifying buyers from the post-Soviet world for Trump's Florida properties. He said he was Trump's "exclusive broker." The volume of Russian business amounted to hundreds of millions of dollars, Millian said in 2016. Some of the Russians were famous, such as the billionaire oligarch Rybolovlev. Others were rich and obscure.

Millian, then, was someone who knew about Trump's private affairs and his non-transparent financial dealings with influential figures in Moscow. He said Trump visited Russia "more than ten times." The last trip, to Millian's knowledge, was in 2013. The purpose? To popularize Trump properties, promote the brand, and pursue the Moscow City skyscraper deal. Trump felt warmly towards Russians, Millian suggested. They gave him recognition, respect. Those and lots of cash.

"He [Trump] knows that a lot of Russians love his properties. They buy his luxury residences. So it was a good, very good business for him," Millian said.

These were things Millian was willing to express openly. What did he know of Trump's off-duty behaviour in Russia? And could he be persuaded to talk about it?

Steele considered how to approach Millian, a potentially useful source. A direct attempt wouldn't work, so Steele sent an intermediary. Millian spoke at length and privately to this person, believing him or her to be trustworthy—a kindred soul. The conversation was relayed to Steele. Millian was the main source for the dossier's most eruptive claim: that Trump was filmed with Russian prostitutes in November 2013, while staying at Moscow's Ritz-Carlton Hotel.

Millian is "source D."

It was Millian who said that Trump employed two women to perform a golden showers show in the hotel's presidential suite. The FSB had fitted out the room with microphones and concealed cameras.

How seriously should we take Millian's tales? Talking to the FBI, Steele described Millian as a "boaster" and an "egotist" who "may engage in some embellishment." The remarks appear in the report by Inspector General Horowitz.

It would be easy to dismiss Millian as a fantasist were it not for the fact that other independent sources corroborated his gossip. The story was part of a much larger *kompromat* file on Trump compiled by the Russian secret service. Steele's informants included a "senior Russian Foreign Ministry figure," a "former top-level intelligence officer still active in the Kremlin," and a "a senior Russian financial official." Plus a female hotel staffer and another unidentified source: E. Source E said that hotel staff were "aware" at the time of the episode.

Trump denies Millian's account.

Nevertheless, circumstantial evidence says we should take it seriously. Millian's unguarded remarks in summer 2016 were made at about the time he talked to ABC News. It was his only sit-down interview with a US TV network. The transcript is revealing. It fits with what Millian said to Steele's undercover contact.

Millian talks in detail about Trump's 2013 Moscow trip—of the beauty pageant, the official party and after-celebration; the Russian billionaires who were there; of Putin's tardiness when it comes to meetings. And of the lacquered decorative box given by the Russian president to Trump by way of apology, after Putin blew off their scheduled chat. Millian says he didn't go to the pageant. He says he was in Moscow at the time.

ABC NEWS: So he [Trump] likes Russia because there is money to be made there?

MILLIAN: He likes Russia because he likes beautiful Russian ladies. And he likes talking to them of course. And he likes to be able to make a lot of money with Russians, yes, correct.

ABC NEWS: Does he have a Russian girlfriend?

MILLIAN: No.

Then the channel asks Millian repeatedly if he's involved in Russian espionage. He says he is not.

ABC NEWS: But you have friends inside the Russian government, don't you?

MILLIAN: Of course.

ABC NEWS: Do they ever ask you what's going on in American politics?

MILLIAN: Yes. Because usually, if I meet top people in the Russian government—they invite me, let's say, to Kremlin for the reception—so of course I have a chance to talk to some presidential advisers and some of the top people.

Mueller can scarcely have been unaware of Millian, a person of interest when the special counsel began his 2017 probe, taking over from an existing FBI counter-intelligence operation. The Russian was at the centre of two lines of inquiry. One covered Trump's financial dealings with post-Soviet buyers. These were extensive. And non-public.

The other was whether Moscow had material that might damage

and embarrass Trump. The question had national security implications. If Trump—despite denials—knew Moscow possessed *kompromat* on him, this might affect foreign policy. And explain his complaisant treatment of Putin. These twin issues were of the same magnitude as the question of Trump's relations with Moscow during the 2016 election. Money, *kompromat*, and collusion converged.

Mueller chose not to pursue either of the first two strands. In a 2017 interview with the *New York Times* two months after Mueller was appointed, Trump warned that his business affairs were a red line. Mueller appears to have peered at the line and retreated.

The special counsel offers no assessment of whether the dossier's Ritz-Carlton story is credible. Most intelligence professionals think it is. In summer 2019 one former head of a major Western European foreign intelligence service told me, "I believe this to be true." The ex-chief—on first-name terms with his Russian counterparts at the top of the FSB—said surveillance would naturally have taken place. "If someone like Trump goes to Moscow, it's normal FSB behaviour," he said.

The most high-profile former Soviet intelligence officer living in the US—Oleg Kalugin—agrees. Kalugin had a stellar KGB career. He ran agents in New York, duelled with the CIA around the world, and rose to become deputy chief and then chief of the KGB's Foreign Counter-Intelligence Directorate—one of the KGB's youngest generals. He ran moles from Beirut to Helsinki. After ten years in Moscow, working closely with Yuri Andropov, he fell out with his own organization, exposed it, and left for America.

Kalugin confirmed that the KGB had a dossier on Trump. How did he know? Kalugin said that he had read it. The KGB took an interest in all foreign visitors to Moscow, especially ones who were very interested in everyday life and "Russian girls." "They were always noted and observed," Kalugin said.

Trump was "rather friendly" towards "Soviet female comrades,"

Kalugin added drily, speaking in summer 2019 to the Russian–
American historian Yuri Felshtinsky.

> FELSHTINSKY: The KGB watched Trump?
> KALUGIN: Certainly.
> FELSHTINSKY: Because he was seeing some girls?
> KALUGIN: Yes.
> FELSHTINSKY: How do you know that?
> KALUGIN: I know that since the time when I still worked for the
> KGB.
> FELSHTINSKY: And you remember Trump?
> KALUGIN: Yes, I remember. It was a long time ago and he was
> noted even back then.

Kalugin said he perused the Trump file when he was the KGB's
counter-intelligence chief. "There were some documents," he said.
"The KGB for sure had a dossier on him." It was one reason for
Trump's "friendly disposition" towards Putin. Such papers would
be lodged in a special archive off-limits to all but senior intelligence
employees, he added. Was Trump aware that Putin had this material? "Yes, he [Trump] knows," Kalugin replied. Kalugin, of course,
couldn't know this as fact but offers an insider's understanding of
the system.

Mueller's report fails to explore Moscow's tradition of *kompromat* and scarcely mentions Millian. He makes a fleeting appearance on pages 94 and 95—a bit-part player swallowed up in the
bigger drama. The FBI, we learn, lost track of him. "Sergei Millian
remained out of the country since the inception of our investigation and declined to meet with members of the Office despite our
repeated attempts to obtain an interview," Mueller writes.

With no person to see, Mueller falls back on the electronic
record. The report gives us Millian's interactions with Trump's

foreign affairs aide Papadopoulos. In July 2016 Millian contacts Papadopoulos via LinkedIn, stating in brazen terms that he has "insider knowledge and direct access to the top hierarchy in Russian politics." The pair meet twice in New York. Like his Russian counterparts in London, Millian tries to bring Papadopoulos over to Moscow and invites him to energy conferences.

The two stay in touch; that August Millian sends the aide an intriguing message, the report says. He promises to share a "disruptive technology that might be instrumental to your political work for the campaign." Mueller doesn't identify what the technology is or what its significance might be. (Papadopoulos tells Mueller he can't remember this.) It's an investigative dead end.

The morning after Trump's victory, the two men message again. Millian floats the possibility of doing business deals with Russian billionaires "who are not under sanctions." This offer to Papadopoulos looks like an inducement made towards someone who might soon be working inside government. There is a further meeting at the Trump International Hotel & Tower Chicago.

According to Papadopoulos, Millian talks about private-sector deals, but "cools" on Papadopoulos after learning he isn't going to join the new administration. They continue to communicate. They agree to meet up in a DC bar when they attend Trump's inauguration.

And with that, Millian disappears from the narrative. In real life, as soon as he learned that he might be in legal jeopardy, Millian slipped out of the US. For a little while longer he was on social media. In November 2017 he appeared at a conference in Singapore; a short video clip shows him banging a gong. After that, his posts on Facebook and Twitter grow strange. They are written in Guccifer-style English—as if someone has taken over his account.

Millian's absence from Mueller's investigation is one of several gaping holes. The lead Russians in the story—Millian,

Kilimnik—are nowhere to be seen. The Americans are less than cooperative. Often they don't tell the truth. Manafort promises to help. He doesn't. Trump and Trump Jr. refuse FBI interviews. Trump works furiously behind the scenes to obstruct the special counsel and suborn witnesses.

IN JUNE 2017 Oleg Smolenkov flew with his family from Moscow to the Adriatic. There was nothing unusual about the trip. In high season thousands of Russians go on vacation to Montenegro, a small country in southeastern Europe and a favourite Russian destination. It has a coast, mountains, good food, sunshine, and beaches. There are four or five flights a day filled with Russian-speaking tourists.

Smolenkov, his wife, Antonia, and their three children—ages fifteen, twelve, and seven—checked into a hotel in the town of Tivat. A few days later Smolenkov got into a cab. He set off for the nearby port and harbour.

In the mid-1970s Tivat's deep-water bay was home to a Yugoslav naval dockyard. Soviet submarines from the Black Sea resort of Odessa came to the yard for a refit. Russian sailors would disembark, wander along the promenade with its palm trees and restaurants, and admire a country that was a part of the socialist family and yet distinctly Western.

Yugoslavia's president, Josip Tito, took a pragmatic approach to Cold War relations. After falling out with Stalin, he reached an understanding with later Kremlin leaders. Red Moscow was allowed to send its ships to be repaired. At the same time, Tito permitted US planes to operate from his territory and launch reconnaissance flights over Hungary and other Warsaw Pact nations.

Tito's successors carried on with a policy of sitting on two chairs, as local journalist Jovo Martinovic put it to me. Days before

Smolenkov left Russia, Montenegro joined NATO. It had an American presence. At the same time, Russia's security services and oligarchs were highly active. They had connections with the ruling party. A former KGB general, Viktor Ivanenko, owned a sprawling seaside hotel.

In theory Montenegro was a democratic EU candidate state; in practice an old-fashioned and clannish Balkan autocracy.

Meanwhile, the old communist-era naval base was transformed into a luxury resort, Porto Montenegro. In summer the marina was home to dozens of super-yachts owned by international tycoons. Naturally enough, all sorts of illicit activities took place. Prostitutes and cocaine, wild parties and orgies, champagne and vodka . . . consumed as the sun set over mountains and sea.

The authorities turned a blind eye to Porto Montenegro's goings-on, regarding them as a price worth paying to bring in big-spending clients. The marina was an extra-territorial zone. Little effort was made to check on its transitory guests. Petrol was exempt from VAT. It was a perfect place for smuggling—goods, people, class A drugs. This happened in both directions, in and out.

At the marina Smolenkov emerged from his taxi—a middle-aged figure approaching fifty years of age, with gold-rimmed glasses and neatly parted sandy hair. It's uncertain if his family was with him. He climbed onto one of the marina's many yachts. He disappeared.

From there, the Russian's most likely route was out into Kotor Bay and west across the Adriatic. It would have been a smooth four-hour crossing to the Italian resort of Bari. Smolenkov's yacht wasn't a regular boat. His new minders and crewmates were from the CIA. According to sources at the US embassy in nearby Albania, the agency uses Bari Airport for sensitive extractions.

Smolenkov was a high-ranking Kremlin diplomat. And a covert American spy who for at least a decade had been secretly passing information to the CIA. He appears to have been recruited at some point in the 1990s—at about the same time as Skripal, in a period that was a happy hunting ground for Western intelligence. Smolenkov occupied a series of government "adviser" positions, initially low-grade ones.

Over time he grew into a highly placed super-asset. He spent five years as second secretary at the Russian embassy in Washington under Ambassador Yuri Ushakov, who would go on to serve as Putin's chief foreign affairs adviser. What did Smolenkov know? Peskov's version: not much; he was fired in 2016. US officials say Smolenkov had access to secret documents. Even, they add, to papers put on Putin's desk.

Russian intelligence sources told the Moscow daily *Vedomosti* that Smolenkov didn't see classified material but was able to glean "sensitive" details from conversations with colleagues. According to CNN, he was a source for the assertion made by US agencies in 2016 that Putin personally authorized the sweeping plan to tamper with American politics.

Russia's own agencies appear to have had no clue that Smolenkov was a faithless fellow. In September 2017 an investigative committee launched a criminal probe into the civil servant's disappearance after he failed to return from vacation. Their assumption was that he could have been murdered. Or suffered an accident. His family didn't go back to Russia either. The US mission to exfiltrate the Smolenkovs worked.

But why remove Washington's foremost mole inside the Kremlin, a source of unique information from an otherwise closed place?

One answer: Moscow had launched an urgent counter-spy investigation of its own, in the wake of the Steele dossier and the Russia scandal. Clearly someone had been leaking to the Americans. Finding that person or persons—and dealing with them—was a priority.

There was another compelling explanation, at least in part. This was Trump's erratic behaviour towards the Russians and his reckless handling of sensitive and classified information. There was a fear that Trump might reveal the existence of the source, thereby putting him in terrible danger.

According to CNN, quoting senior US intelligence officials, Smolenkov turned down an initial request to leave Russia. The exfiltration operation went ahead following Trump's meeting in May 2017 with Moscow's two top diplomats: Foreign Minister Sergei Lavrov and Dmitry Kislyak, then Russia's ambassador in DC. The previous day Trump had fired FBI director Comey. "I faced great pressure because of Russia. That's taken off," he told his guests in the Oval Office.

Trump gave them details of a highly classified intelligence briefing. It concerned an Islamic State plot. The intelligence wasn't actually Trump's to share—it had come from the Israelis via a secret source deep inside ISIS. The agent appears to have supplied details of an attempt to smuggle explosives concealed in laptops onto a plane. Trump told the Russians the name of the Syrian city from where the intel had come.

There was more. According to a *New York Times* report, the president said that he didn't mind that Russia had interfered in his election. The US did the same thing in other countries, Trump assured Lavrov, whom he met again in the Oval Office in December 2019. Trump's private acknowledgement of a debt to Russia was at odds with his public rubbishing of a Moscow connection. The Russians would have interpreted Trump's remarks as a green light. The president's message: interfere again in 2020.

Trump was a counter-intelligence horror show.

IN JULY 2019 Mueller testified before Congress. He was a reluctant witness—dragged before the House Judiciary and Intelligence Committees against his wishes. In back-to-back sessions stretching over seven hours, he was unwilling to go beyond his original report. Mostly his answers were minimal. We got a series of staccato "nos" and "trues" mixed with "accurate," "speculation," and "I presume."

For Democrats the public hearing was a chance to reaccuse Trump of various crimes, especially obstruction; for Republicans it was an opportunity to trash the FBI, Mueller, and the "Russia hoax." The flow of politics was predictable, along highly partisan lines.

Still, there were moments of illumination along the way. And a vivid sense from Mueller that the Russians remained a potent twenty-first-century threat—one still largely underestimated by the American public at large. "It wasn't a single attempt. They are doing it as we sit here," Mueller said of Kremlin God-playing in US democracy.

Mueller made it plain that he expected the Russian government to meddle again in the 2020 US presidential election, sixteen months away at that point. "I hope this is not the new normal. But I fear it is," he said frankly. More needed to be done to prevent hostile foreign powers from influencing politics, he warned.

The session touched on Trump's truthfulness, or lack of it. "I think there's probably a spectrum of witnesses in terms of those who are not telling the truth and those who are outright liars," Mueller said. And where might the president sit on this spectrum? Mueller said it was "generally" correct to conclude that Trump's written answers were neither complete nor wholly truthful.

There was also the question of blackmail—whether Moscow was in a position to exploit information it held on public officials and, through this, compel them to make certain choices. Trump wasn't mentioned explicitly; Mueller's exchanges with Adam Schiff on this theme were the day's most interesting to and fro.

Schiff mentioned Flynn's conversations with Ambassador Kislyak, about which Flynn lied to the FBI; Cohen's call to Peskov's office in Moscow, which the Russians probably "taped"; and Trump's backroom Moscow Tower project. All were "counter-intelligence nightmares," Schiff suggested. Mueller agreed. The special counsel said they showed the need for a "strong counter-intelligence entity."

But where was that entity?

The status of the FBI's counter-intelligence inquiry into Moscow—something that had gone on during the Cold War and afterwards—was an enduring mystery. On page 13 of his report Mueller recognized that his investigation threw up "foreign intelligence and counterintelligence information." This information lay outside Mueller's brief. It was relevant to what he called the FBI's broader national security mission.

For more than a year FBI personnel had been embedded in Mueller's office. These officers reviewed the results of the special counsel's crime probe and sent written summaries to the FBI's headquarters at Pennsylvania Avenue and to FBI field stations. Most of this information didn't find its way into Mueller's report—a text, as he made clear, that dealt primarily with "prosecution and declination" decisions.

The FBI's counter-intelligence division met regularly with Mueller and his team. The nature of its work—and whether any sort of probe was still ongoing or had been shut down—remained frustratingly unclear.

Attempts by Schiff and others to get to the bottom of this failed. Schiff told the *Washington Post* that quarterly counter-intelligence briefings stopped in 2017 after Comey got fired. There were no further updates to the Gang of Eight—the senior-ranking Democrats and Republicans in the House and Senate. And no answer to an unresolved query: whether Trump was—or wasn't—a foreign asset. The Justice Department didn't engage, Schiff said. All of which left open the possibility that an outside power might "warp" US policy through some sort of coercive hold or "compromise."

One could of course speculate as to what material the FBI might have. It would inevitably include intercepts: electronic communications and emails sucked up by the NSA, GCHQ, and other agencies from Russian targets. As Simpson put it to me, the US was a "big ears" country. It collected "all kinds of stuff," some of which underpinned Mueller's report and some of which didn't. Simpson likened this evidence to an iceberg. It was mostly underwater. Its full size was unknown.

Smolenkov may have fled, but did the FBI have other moles in Moscow? The answer was again opaque. There was nothing from Mueller to suggest that the US had further sources inside Russia supplying interesting material on its leaders. The report's understanding of Russia in Volume One appeared rather basic. "There is no evidence of humint [human intelligence] from Russian counter-intelligence sources," Steele said, speaking to friends.

In his Congress hearing Mueller didn't address the Steele dossier or what he thought of its veracity. It was under investigation "elsewhere in the Justice Department." In 2017 Steele had spent two days briefing the FBI in London about his work and secret sources. Presumably this evidence had gone somewhere. But neither Steele, Simpson, nor Schiff knew for sure.

It seemed unlikely that the FBI counter-intelligence probe had been wound up, since the threat of disruption from Russia was very much alive. As Steele put it, "Russia is as much a menace as it was four years ago." Still, he too wondered, "What happened to the counter-intelligence?" The conflict between Moscow and Washington would go on for another decade or two, Steele felt, and probably longer.

In the meantime, Democrats in the House and Senate said they would investigate what had eluded Mueller. Schiff mentioned several areas. They included Russian money laundering and whether "people still serving within the administration" should be denied clearance because they posed a security risk. "We need to find out," he said. Plus whether Gulf states, the Saudis, the Turks, and maybe other nations too were buying US foreign policy via "financial inducements."

Mueller's testimony had proven less helpful to the Democrats than they might have wished. It left one TV viewer distinctly thrilled, however. "This has been a disaster for the Democrats and a disaster for the reputation of Robert Mueller," Trump tweeted, citing a remark from Fox News host Chris Wallace. It was, as Trump saw it, a triumphant ending, the fizzling out of a shabby and meritless affair and shameless Democratic witch-hunt.

For more than two years Trump's enemies had accused him of the gravest of crimes. The biggest was soliciting the help of a foreign power to discredit a political opponent and then lying about it afterwards. Mueller's investigation had failed to find enough evidence to substantiate this charge, at least to a criminal level. Trump was in the clear! More than that, he was unleashed.

The following day Trump picked up the phone. He made a call to a foreign leader. This time not to his enduring friend Putin. Trump got on the line with Ukraine's new president, a comedian whose career and destiny through life were every bit as improbable and fantastic as Trump's own.

CHAPTER 12

QUID PRO QUO

Kyiv–Washington
2010–2020

You know what Trump is? He's Putin's shithouse cleaner.
He does everything for little Vladi that little Vladi can't
do for himself: pisses on European unity, pisses on human
rights, pisses on NATO. Assures us that Crimea and
Ukraine belong to the Holy Russian Empire.
JOHN LE CARRÉ, *AGENT RUNNING IN THE FIELD*

In 2010, while living in Moscow and working for the *Guardian*, I received an enigmatic summons from London. The message: come back.

My newspaper was sitting on a trove of leaked documents. These were a quarter of a million secret and confidential cables sent by US embassies and missions around the world. A disillusioned twenty-two-year-old army intelligence analyst, Chelsea Manning, had downloaded the files from a defence server in Baghdad and—it was said—given them to WikiLeaks.

My task was to sift through about three thousand telegrams sent from former Soviet Union countries, including Russia. I found myself in an airless fourth-floor room, with a view of a canal basin and houseboats, typing search terms into a secure internal "leak-server." I began with "Litvinenko."

To my disappointment, it seemed the US didn't know who had ordered Litvinenko's murder. But it had suspicions: soon after the killing US assistant secretary of state Daniel Fried said it was unlikely rogue elements could operate in the UK without Putin's knowledge. The Russians were "increasingly self-confident, to the point of arrogance," Fried remarked.

The cables were a revelation. The Obama administration, I learned, had reached a similar pessimistic conclusion to my own about the nature of the Moscow regime. Under Putin, Russia had become a virtual Mafia state in which the government, its spy agencies, and organized crime had merged into a single entity. The thesis was Litvinenko's. He had shared it in summer 2006 with Spanish prosecutors investigating the Russian Mafia, shortly before the two Kremlin assassins killed him. The cables spoke of Putin's alleged "illicit" fortune, hidden abroad.

After a few days I turned my attention to Ukraine. I visited the country often from Moscow. There was much to like: a capital city built among steep hills, with Orthodox churches and monasteries, the Dnipro River, and fading art deco buildings. The same Soviet political traits of corruption and misrule were visible. But Ukraine felt freer and more plural than Russia; you breathed a little easier.

Putin's contempt for Russia's smaller neighbour was evident. He viewed it as sub-sovereign—a "cobbled together" state with six million Russians in it, according to Polish foreign minister Radosław Sikorski. There were dispatches chronicling the ups and downs of Ukrainian politics, a bewilderingly complex subject shot through with feuding and prolonged strife. Its protagonists were at semi-war with each other. There was the president, Viktor Yushchenko. Yushchenko was at odds with Tymoshenko, a one-time ally. Then there was Yanukovych, leader of the clan tied to Russia.

One cable stood out. It was marked "secret." (This was the second-highest level of classification among the leaked documents, just

below "secret/noforn"—that is, not to be read by non-Americans.)
It described a meeting late in 2008 in Kyiv, inside the US embassy
building, a 1950s mansion with classical columns previously owned
by the Communist Party. The dispatch's author was the US ambassador at the time, William Taylor.

The cable said:

> Controversial Ukrainian oligarch Dmytro Firtash, best known
> as co-owner of gas intermediary RosUkrEnergo (RUE), called
> upon the ambassador on December 8. Firtash did not explicitly
> state why he requested the meeting, nor did he ask the USG
> [US government] for anything, but he spoke at length about his
> business and politics in a visible effort to improve his image
> with the USG. The soft-spoken billionaire, arguably one of
> Ukraine's most powerful people, expressed strong support for
> President Yushchenko and equally strong contempt for Prime
> Minister Tymoshenko.

Firtash's hatred of Tymoshenko was coolly pragmatic, Taylor
intimated. She was determined to abolish Firtash's gas company
RosUkrEnergo, half of which belonged to Gazprom and Russians.
"He [Firtash] sees Tymoshenko as a clear threat to his business,"
Taylor commented, estimating Firtash's wealth as "tens of billions"
of dollars.

The meeting lasted two and a half hours, I read. Firtash told the
ambassador he was not a "public person" but had been sucked into
Ukrainian politics. The oligarch said he was an "unofficial adviser"
to Yushchenko—during political crises and "tense gas negotiations"
with Moscow. Firtash was close to Yanukovych too. He told the
ambassador he had "torpedoed" an alliance between Yanukovych
and Tymoshenko, persuading Yanukovych to repudiate a deal on
Firtash's television station.

The cable included fascinating biographical details. Firtash described himself as a simple person who grew up in the village of Synkiv in Ternopil Oblast, in western Ukraine. His mother worked in a sugar factory; his father was a driving instructor. Firtash said he was unable to get into a university because his parents "hated communism." He did military service and studied to be a fireman.

The USSR's collapse radically changed his life prospects, as it did for many. Firtash's parents thought it the "end of the world." Firtash said that he too felt caught between two countries, the old one and the new one, his future uncertain. But as a "natural businessman" with a nose for opportunity, he said he was well placed to "make the best of uncertainty." Not least because in the new Ukraine there were—as he frankly set out—"no laws and no taxes."

His rise was extremely rapid. First he started a food and commodities business in western Ukraine with his then wife, Mariya. Then he became friendly with a Ukrainian who was selling cars in Turkmenistan. Firtash began trading with another Ukrainian tycoon who sold Turkmen gas to ex-Soviet republics. In 2001 Firtash ousted the businessman, according to the cable, and set up his own concern, EuroTransGas. His gas trading operation grew into an empire, with Firtash owning majority shares in companies in Russia, Germany, Austria, Italy, and Estonia.

How had he prospered so quickly? The US suspicion: he was a front man for "far broader interests."

The dispatch laid out Firtash's alleged connections to Semyon Mogilevich, an organized crime don born in Soviet Ukraine. It became something of a foundational document, albeit one that Firtash strongly disputes. According to Taylor, Firtash said that in January 2002 he met Mogilevich in Kyiv. The ambassador asked Firtash to clarify these alleged ties.

The cable said:

Firtash answered that many Westerners do not understand
what Ukraine was like after the breakup of the Soviet Union,
adding that when a government cannot rule effectively, the
country is ruled by "the laws of the streets." He noted that
it was impossible to approach a government official for any
reason without also meeting with an organized crime member
at the same time. Firtash acknowledged that he needed, and
received, permission from Mogilevich when he established
various businesses, but he denied any close relationship to
him.

The alleged "bottom line": Firtash was forced into dealing with
Mogilevich and organized crime associates. Without them "he
would never have been able to build a business."

(Firtash says Taylor's account of their meeting is untrue. In a
statement the oligarch denies that Mogilevich ever had any part-
nership or holding or other direct or indirect commercial associa-
tions or business interests with him.)

Nonetheless, the cable offers a persuasive explanation of how
these shadow arrangements could have worked: if Firtash needed
a permit from the government, he first had to get permission from
the "appropriate 'businessman' who worked with the government
official," it said. Firtash denied any link with Moscow's notorious
Mafia group the Solntsevo Brotherhood and said the "law of the
street" had "passed." "Businesses could now be run legitimately in
Ukraine," he told Taylor.

A few months later Firtash went to see the ambassador again.
His attempts to improve his image with the Obama administration came at an interesting moment. The oligarch was one of
several powerful figures who bankrolled the Party of Regions.
Together they persuaded Yanukovych to hire Manafort. Firtash
and Manafort even went into business together, in 2008 drawing

up a plan to develop the site of the Drake Hotel in Manhattan and replace it with a luxury building, at a cost of $850 million.

The cable was explosive stuff. By the time it leaked, Firtash's protégé Yanukovych was president and Tymoshenko, the woman who tried to destroy Firtash's gas monopoly, in jail.

Sitting in my fourth-floor bunker, I typed a story, published in December 2010. There was a blurry photo of Mogilevich, a bald, overweight figure in late middle age, with a triple chin and wearing a jacket and tie and a fawn-coloured flat cap. It said, "Allegations have long swirled that the Russian crime don Semyon Mogilevich had covert interests in Swiss-registered RUE, which distributes gas from central Asia." The article said Firtash "nominally owns nearly half of the company and the Russian state firm Gazprom the other half."

The Mogilevich photo came from the FBI. It had been searching for Mogilevich; he was wanted for stock fraud, money laundering, and racketeering, among other felonies. One of those tracking him was Steele, working in conjunction with Michael Gaeta, the FBI agent whom Steele would contact in 2016 over Trump and Russia. Orbis found Mogilevich living in a small village north of Moscow under Russian government protection.

The *Guardian* ran a series of articles on the leaked US files. Firtash's meeting with Taylor appeared under the headline "WikiLeaks Cables Link Russian Mafia Boss to EU Gas Supplies." Another article—on the State Department's bleak assessment that Putin presided over a mature kleptocracy—was titled "Inside Putin's Mafia State." Six weeks later, arriving back in Moscow, I was detained at the airport. My press visa was cancelled. After forty-five minutes in a holding cell I found myself back on the same plane, tossed out of the country, an enemy of the Kremlin.

Firtash's own woes began three years later. In spring 2014 a Chicago federal court alleged that he had bribed Indian officials over a titanium deal. It sought his extradition. The oligarch denied the "absurd" charge and said it was political—retribution from the Obama White House for his support of Yanukovych and alleged close ties to Kremlin figures.

At the time Firtash was in Vienna, his hub since 2007. The Austrian capital had long been a congenial place for spies. It was right next to the Eastern Bloc. During the Cold War the authorities agreed to ignore the activities of the KGB. In modern times Ukrainians used Vienna for sensitive meetings.

Over the next few years Firtash's legal fight went up and down. There were wins—in 2017 an Austrian judge ruled in his favour and agreed that the US court action was brought to keep him out of Ukrainian politics. And there were setbacks—another accusation of money laundering in Spain, court papers filed by Chicago's acting attorney general describing him as an "upper-echelon associate" of the Moscow underworld.

Firtash lavished millions of dollars on attorneys. A phalanx of bodyguards and flunkies accompanied him, I was told, into case meetings. These took place in Austrian castles and luxury ski resorts. Firtash's tug-of-war with the Justice Department would go on for more than five years. Were he to lose, he faced the prospect of decades behind bars. Russia, too, didn't wish to see him extradited. Firtash knew Gazprom's secrets. These might embarrass Putin insiders, were they to reach the FBI.

As part of this struggle Firtash set about cultivating the Trump administration. He needed a landing strategy—a route out of trouble were his plane to arrive on US soil. The solution to his problems wasn't legal, he may have figured; it was political.

With a mercurial person like Trump in charge, someone not averse to mixing business with politics, perhaps it would be possible to cut a deal? Identify something Trump wanted. And give it to him.

Then maybe the extradition charges would melt away like Moscow snow in May.

SPRING 2019. AFTER five years in power Ukraine's president, Petro Poroshenko, was facing re-election. The polls weren't encouraging. In fact, they presaged a disaster. Barring some last-minute miracle the next president of Ukraine was going to be a popular TV actor known for his role in a comedy show, *Servant of the People*.

The show's plot was endearing, especially to citizens fed up with rampant graft. A thirty-something history teacher rants about corruption. One of his students films this outburst and puts it online. The clip goes viral and the teacher—played by Volodymyr Zelensky—runs for election and sweeps to victory. What better way to chronicle the nation's woes than through satire and fairy tale?!

Not that Poroshenko was amused. In 2018 Zelensky announced that he was going into politics for real. He took over a party with the same name as his show. Zelensky's actual political persona blurred with the fictional image of his onscreen avatar: clean up the country, end impunity, and bring peace to the east, where the war with Russia had turned into a grisly impasse of shelling and sniping across World War I-style trenches.

Zelensky's real-world knowledge of politics was zero. It was therefore easy to write off his candidacy as a joke, another absurd storyline tossed into global politics by the same capricious postmodern gods that gave us Trump and Boris Johnson. Easy, but wrong. Zelensky's lack of experience was a plus. Voters saw him as an outsider, a blank slate, untainted by association with Ukraine's grubby ruling elite, of which the wealthy chocolate magnate Poroshenko was undoubtedly a part.

On March 20, 2019, I flew to Kyiv ahead of the first round of voting. Polls pointed to a Zelensky landslide. A run-off between the two top candidates was due in April. It seemed probable that Poroshenko would face Zelensky. Much was riding on the outcome. Would Poroshenko concede? (Peaceful transfers of power were rare in the post-Soviet world; incumbents invariably "won.") And would Moscow interfere in Ukraine's domestic politics, as it had so many times before?

To answer these questions I set off for Bankova, a pedestrian street blocked by a police booth. This was the centre of Ukrainian power. I showed my passport and walked through. To the left was the presidential administration building, designed in grandiose Soviet style. On the right an art nouveau mansion adorned with beasts and chimeras—giant frogs, hippopotamuses, mermaids—used for meeting visiting heads of state.

The bloody events of 2014 had taken place nearby. Down the hill from Bankova were memorials to the hundred protesters shot dead in the anti-Yanukovych uprising. Kyiv residents had laid candles, carnations, blue and yellow Ukrainian flags, and children's poems. Mostly, young men stared out from photos, but there were some middle-aged faces too. The cobbled street had been named in honour of the "heavenly hundred." It led past the Ukraine Hotel— where bodies were lodged in the lobby during the revolt—to Independence Square, the focal point of the "revolution of dignity."

Five years on the mood inside the presidential office was still embattled, I discovered. Ukraine was at war with a deadly enemy whose leader, Putin, hated Poroshenko personally. As Poroshenko saw it, his re-election would deal a blow to Russian ambitions. Conversely, Putin would be happy if anyone other than Poroshenko won. At stake—in the administration's gloomy view— was Ukraine's survival or capitulation.

Inside I met Kostiantyn Yelisieiev, Poroshenko's foreign policy adviser and deputy head of office. The building's interior was decorated with chandeliers and a gilt-framed nature landscape. On the second floor I found an exhibition of life at the front, featuring Ukrainian servicemen and servicewomen relaxing, smiling, going about their tasks in life-size portraits. Yelisieiev said he kept his military uniform in a small closet in an office. He was ready at any moment to go and fight the invaders.

Ukraine was under Russian bombardment, and not just from artillery, he told me. There were cyber attacks against critical national infrastructure, including the election commission and foreign ministry—four hundred in 2018, hundreds more in 2019. Moscow was spreading fake news via Kremlin federal TV, widely viewed in Ukraine. This propaganda corroded public sentiment. "They [the Russians] use democratic tools against democratic institutions. We can't just switch it off," he explained.

What, I wondered, was Putin's ultimate aim? The adviser's answer: reconstituting a "second" USSR. Ukraine was at the heart of this idea. If the country became a success, pro-Western and democratic, there would be implications for Russia's own authoritarian system. Putin wanted all of Ukraine in his sphere of influence; it was central to Moscow's conception of itself as a great empire, he said.

At this difficult moment, what Kyiv needed from America and Europe was solidarity in the face of Russian aggression. And reinforced sanctions. Yelisieiev was full of martial foreboding. "I think that Putin will not stop," he predicted. "Ukraine is at the centre of a geopolitical battle, unfortunately." This last observation was certainly true.

I had come to Kyiv on a pre-election study tour organized by the German Marshall Fund of the United States and the think tank Chatham House. In 2010 I had been on a similar trip to Crimea—at that point still part of Ukraine—led by David Kramer, the former Bush-era assistant secretary of state who leaked the Steele dossier.

My group was staying at the Hyatt Regency, across the plaza from the Foreign Ministry. Walking into the atrium it was hard not to think of Manafort and Kilimnik. Manafort spent months in the hotel. Now he was far away—behind bars. Kilimnik was in Russia. It was easy to imagine their ghosts inhabiting the place still, flitting over the lobby and the ground-floor coffee bar with its open fire—one tall spirit, the other small and Puck-like, sticking out his tongue.

We were due to have breakfast with three ambassadors. The line-up included Marie Yovanovitch, US ambassador to Ukraine, as well as her UK counterpart, Judith Gough, and Germany's envoy, Ernst Reichel. At the last minute Yovanovitch fell off the schedule. Taking her place was the deputy chief of the US mission to Ukraine, Joseph Pennington—a smart-looking, bespectacled American of middle years, wearing a career Foreign Service uniform of grey jacket and thin tie.

A little odd, I thought.

What had happened to Yovanovitch?

At the time her absence struck me as unremarkable.

Later it would become clear that—as Yovanovitch herself put it—something exceedingly strange was going on just as we flew into town.

The ambassador was the unwitting victim of a shadow foreign policy, it would emerge, enacted by Trump's personal lawyer, Rudy Giuliani, and directed by no less a person than the president himself. Other White House persons included Yovanovitch's boss, US secretary of state Mike Pompeo; acting chief of staff Mick Mulvaney; and Devin Nunes, the ranking Republican member on the House Intelligence Committee who had previously chased after Steele.

This irregular channel took in two criminally indicted individuals living in Florida: Lev Parnas and Igor Fruman. And a trio of Trump appointees: Gordon Sondland, Kurt Volker, and Rick Perry. Other parts were played by crooked Ukrainian prosecutors, American TV lawyers, and the billionaire Firtash, marooned as he was in central Europe.

This plot—when it was discovered six months later—would upend American politics in the same way the Russia scandal had done previously. Indeed, the two were closely connected. The allegation against the president was essentially the same: that he solicited help from a foreign power to smear a political rival at home in America—not Clinton this time but Joe Biden, the challenger whom Trump apparently feared most in 2020.

The new scandal appears to have come about from a desire by Trump to kill off once and for all the notion of collusion with Moscow and to replace it with a counter-idea: "collusion" by Kyiv and the Democrats. A strange compulsion! As the *Washington Post*'s David Ignatius pointed out, it was akin to a murderer trying to cover up his bad deed by going back to the scene of the crime. There was something Greek or Shakespearean about it: an act of hubris born from a deep-seated pathology and a refusal to let things lie.

There would be constitutional consequences. Before the year was out, the House would begin impeachment proceedings, with a trial soon after in the Senate. The charges: abuse of power and obstruction of Congress.

None of this was apparent as we discussed Ukraine's political situation over croissants and coffee at the Hyatt. The ambassadors agreed on Zelensky: a sincere, bright, politically inexperienced guy; young, vague on policy and *pro bono, contra malum*, as the German envoy put it—in favour of good and against evil. Zelensky was the change/protest candidate. Except he didn't protest or make political statements. Mostly he left the talking to his fictitious TV self.

That spring the biggest question wasn't Trump but whether Zelensky was a puppet of powerful external forces. Specifically, of the oligarch Ihor Kolomoisky, owner of the 1+1 TV channel where *Servant of the People* was shown. Kolomoisky was in dispute with Poroshenko's government. Ukraine's troubled banking sector was undercapitalized; in 2016 the state took over Kolomoisky's PrivatBank after $5.6 billion went missing. Kolomoisky wanted his bank back. He said he was owed $2 billion.

If Zelensky was elected, would Kolomoisky become the country's shadow ruler? Ukraine's oligarchs had long enjoyed enormous informal power, owning media channels and influencing executive decisions to favour their financial interests. The judicial system was broken and unfair. It lacked credibility. Publicly, Poroshenko talked anticorruption. Privately, the US embassy critique went, he did little to tackle the problem, especially when it came to friends and political allies.

Ukraine was at a crossroads. It could go forward with reforms or regress, Pennington told us. Yovanovitch's deputy let his colleagues do most of the talking, I noted.

Perhaps Pennington was aware of the great storm that was coming.

The next stop on our fact-finding tour was Zelensky's campaign headquarters, in a modern building in Kyiv's Pechersk diplomatic quarter, not far from the botanical garden. Four aides—all of them male, none previously connected with politics—explained the candidate's modernizing mission. "We want to convert a monster state into a service state," campaign chief Ivan Bakanov said. That meant repatriating offshore wealth and cancelling immunity from prosecution for Duma politicians.

What about relations with Moscow? "Our country was the victim of bullying. We have an existential problem with Russia," Bakanov admitted.

Two days later I saw Serhiy Leshchenko, the famous reporter

turned lawmaker. Leshchenko was already the target of wild Republican allegations: that he had collaborated with Steele and Simpson and was an anti-Trump activist. None of this was true. Leshchenko had publicized the black ledger—first dug up by the *New York Times*—because he wanted to expose corruption in Ukraine. He had been elected as a deputy for Poroshenko's bloc and had subsequently broken with him. Poroshenko, in his view, had continued the corrupt practices of his predecessor.

We met for breakfast in the Honey Café, not far from the city's reconstructed medieval golden gate. I found a basement table. Leshchenko—a fluent English-speaker—arrived wearing a modish T-shirt. We had seen each other a few times in London and Kyiv. Leshchenko was friendly but evidently much in demand, overworked and warmly indignant at the foreign press's patronizing take on the election. Zelensky's candidacy wasn't a joke. He was serious about cleaning up the swamp, Leshchenko said.

We touched on Yovanovitch. Leshchenko told me that Ukraine's prosecutor general, Yuriy Lutsenko—a close ally of Poroshenko's—was seeking "revenge" against the US ambassador.

This was news to me. Lutsenko was apparently unhappy at US embassy criticism over his failure to take action on corruption. The prosecutor and his wife, Iryna, were both members of parliament for Poroshenko's party and closely aligned with him. Recently Lutsenko had been penning pro-Trump tweets.

Yovanovitch's non-appearance at the Hyatt was starting to make sense. Something was afoot, at a time when Poroshenko was staring at defeat and a wipeout. It was beginning to look as if he and the crooked prosecutor Lutsenko had agreed to some sort of backroom deal with the Trump administration and its emissaries. In return for—what, exactly?—Lutsenko was making statements that were helpful to the US president. Why Yovanovitch was in the firing line was unclear.

At this late hour Poroshenko may have been hoping for an April surprise—a *deus ex machina* that would confound his opponents. An invitation from Trump to a meeting in the White House, perhaps? Or an all-smiles photocall with Vice President Pence? An agreement of sorts appeared to have been reached, somewhere out of sight, with vows, whispers, nods.

At this penumbrous moment in his fortunes Poroshenko would have done well to study Trump's record in real estate and politics. One theme stood out: a serial failure to deliver on his promises—as Syria's Kurds were about to discover. This occasion was no different. The moment of rescue never arrived. Poroshenko was swept away.

YOVANOVITCH'S ABSENCE WAS significant.

On the same day I flew into Ukraine the conservative columnist John Solomon published a curious story in *The Hill*. It said:

> After three years and millions of tax dollars, the Trump–Russia collusion probe is about to be resolved. Emerging in its place is newly unearthed evidence suggesting another foreign effort to influence the 2016 election—this time in favor of the Democrats.

Solomon reported that Ukraine's top prosecutor—Lutsenko—had opened an investigation into whether his country's law enforcement apparatus had deliberately leaked the black ledger. He was investigating Ukrainian "collusion." The alleged beneficiary was Clinton. The US embassy in Kyiv had been complicit in this affair, the story said.

Not only that, but Steele had played an ancillary "role." The logic was a little hard to follow. But, according to Solomon, Steele worked as an FBI informant at the same time that the bureau's agents had practically "set up shop" at the US embassy in Kyiv while delving into Manafort's financial affairs.

The article ended with an allegation that—if true—was exceedingly damning. The relationship between Lutsenko and the embassy had grown "dysfunctional," Solomon reported. The "troubling dynamic" came about after Yovanovitch gave Lutsenko a list of defendants whom the US didn't want prosecuted. The ambassador had also spoken "disdainfully" about Trump, Solomon wrote, citing a Republican congressman.

"Unlike the breathless start to the Russia collusion allegations—in which politicians and news media alike declared a Watergate-sized crisis before the evidence was fully investigated—the Ukraine revelations deserve to be investigated before being accepted," Solomon opined.

This column delighted one reader: Trump, who tweeted out its headline, "As Russia Collusion Fades, Ukrainian Plot to Help Clinton Emerges," making sure to copy it to Sean Hannity and Fox News. It appeared that a smear campaign against Yovanovitch—now in plain sight—had support at the highest level. Donald Trump Jr. joined in. He tweeted that the ambassador was one of several diplomat "jokers."

A week later Solomon was back with another hit piece containing allegations that were even more gunpowderish than before. Citing Ukrainian officials, he said that Biden had pressured the government of Ukraine to fire Lutsenko's predecessor, another dubious prosecutor called Viktor Shokin. This had happened in late 2015 and early 2016, when Biden was vice president.

Biden's motive for getting rid of Shokin, according to Solomon, was to end a "wide-ranging corruption probe" into a Ukrainian gas firm. Its name was Burisma Holdings. Biden's son Hunter was a member of Burisma's board. And a handsomely paid one, earning

$50,000 a month for what looked like a sinecure. Solomon's allegation: to protect his greedy son the vice president had improperly used his influence to shut down a corruption probe.

Solomon's claims were untrue. They came from a surreal Alice in Wonderland place, described by Simpson as "upside-down world." In this parallel metaverse Ukraine was guilty and Russia innocent, Clinton the colluder and Trump the wronged victim, Putin the good guy, Poroshenko the villain. Like the best conspiracy theories, these mythical narratives contained a small element of truth, baked in to leaven the lie.

Biden *had* pressured Ukraine to fire Shokin. But this was not because Shokin was investigating corruption but because he wasn't—a complaint made by civil society, EU countries, and leading financial institutions such as the IMF. The idea that Shokin would instigate a "wide-ranging" probe into anything was ridiculous, at least to pro-reform citizens in Kyiv, some of whom protested against Shokin in the cold, calling for his dismissal.

Hunter Biden's decision to join Burisma was a mistake. It certainly looked as if he was cashing in on his father's name. The firm was murky. It had close ties with the old regime. Its founder, Mykola Zlochevsky, was a Yanukovych crony.

By the time Biden Jr. joined the board, however, the corruption investigation against Burisma was already mothballed. This had nothing to do with Biden. It was entirely down to the Kyiv prosecutor's office. The office failed to pursue members of the Yanukovych ex-government. It was generally reputed to be the country's biggest bribe factory and a byword for inefficiency.

Solomon was right about one thing, though: in summer 2016 Poroshenko didn't want Trump to win. This wasn't "collusion": most other Western nations felt the same way. Poroshenko's sceptical stance was understandable. Trump's pro-Moscow sympathies, his shameless flattery of Putin, and his glib assertion that Crimea wanted to "be with Russia" were hardly going to endear him to Ukrainians, especially after two years of war.

What is less understood is how swiftly Poroshenko moved to reverse his mistake once Trump became president. Poroshenko embarked on an operation in Washington to retrieve his position and hired a lobbying group, BGR. For months nothing happened.

Then, in summer 2017 and ahead of a Poroshenko White House visit, Ukraine's own investigation into Manafort was halted. It was transferred from the anti-corruption bureau, known as NABU, to the prosecutor's office—in effect, killing it. The decision was made after Giuliani met with Poroshenko and Lutsenko in Kyiv. A special prosecutor, Serhiy Horbatyuk, had been investigating black-ledger payments to Manafort. Suddenly he wasn't.

Largely unnoticed, the political terrain was shifting. The Poroshenko government shut down cooperation with Mueller. It allowed Kilimnik to escape to Russia before the FBI could reach him. Back in the US, Trump floated the Kilimnik–Manafort conspiracy theory, telling the *Washington Examiner* that Ukraine was behind the DNC hack—an early sign of Trump's bizarre Ukraine fixation. Seemingly, disinformation seeded by Russian spies was reaching the top of the White House.

The smear campaign against Yovanovitch in 2018 and 2019 flowed from earlier attempts to dig up dirt helpful to Trump and his pseudo-theories. The original focus was to find "evidence" that might exonerate Manafort. And to substantiate the idea—which appeared to exist in the president's head, if not in reality—that Ukraine's special services were behind the Steele dossier, something, Steele told me and others, that was emphatically not true. Thus one fantasy project grew into another.

As Ukraine's election neared, Giuliani's contacts with Poroshenko's administration intensified. In January 2019 he met the corrupt prosecutor Lutsenko in New York. They saw each other again in mid-February in Warsaw and for a third time, according to Lutsenko, in an undisclosed "European country." According to the *Wall Street Journal*, in March there was a group meeting in Kyiv featuring Giuliani, Fruman, Parnas, Lutsenko, and Poroshenko. It took place at Lutsenko's office, near the Klovska metro station, the visitors swooping in via an underground entrance.

Unknown to Yovanovitch, a secret mission was under way. It had nothing to do with the US's declared foreign and national security policy in Ukraine, run out of the embassy and the State Department, and everything to do with Trump's re-election.

Trump's purpose was to pressure Ukraine to "investigate"—in other words, to objectify allegations of Biden "corruption" and Ukrainian "collusion." Fruman and Parnas were emissaries, the Rosencrantz and Guildenstern of the piece, acting surreptitiously under orders from a king haunted—you might say—by fears of illegitimacy.

The mission was bound up with Fruman and Parnas's personal moneymaking interests. They intended to sell US natural gas to Ukraine via Poland. They had founded their own company, Global Energy Producers. If the proposed pipeline were to happen, it would need the support of Ukrainian officials and Naftogaz, a state-owned energy company. The country's energy sector was hugely profitable and notoriously corrupt. Fruman and Parnas wanted a slice of it.

Despite their connections to the president, however, the pair faced obstacles. Naftogaz's board deemed the scheme impractical. Yovanovitch had championed its reform-minded boss. Therefore, she was a threat to their ambitions. Fruman and Parnas set about undermining her, while simultaneously seeking to replace the head of Naftogaz with someone more amenable.

The ambassador learned of the moves against her in February 2019, a month before I arrived in Kyiv.

By this point the conspiracy was well developed. It took the form of phone calls and WhatsApp messages, hundreds of them, secretly exchanged by Parnas with Lutsenko, Shokin, and others. Parnas was simultaneously in touch with Giuliani and a pro-Trump ex-marine Robert Hyde. Hyde's texts are distinctly creepy; they suggest that Yovanovitch may have been under surveillance in Kyiv by people in Ukraine reporting back to him.

The messages show that it is Parnas who arranges Lutsenko's interview with Solomon. The prosecutor is sometimes angry, saying that he is doing "everything" and getting nothing back. At one point he writes, "Fuck these adventures!" The exchanges are in Russian, with the ambassador called "*dura*"—a fool. Parnas also contacts the interior minister, Arsen Avakov.

As Yovanovitch told Congress, it was Avakov who warned her that shady forces were seeking her removal. Fruman and Parnas regarded her as inimical to their interests, Avakov said. The ambassador was mystified. She hadn't met either individual. Her job involved promoting legitimate US business. Neither Fruman nor Parnas had been in touch. She was unaware that the pair's activities ran alongside a grander scheme against the Bidens.

By the time Solomon's March article appeared, Yovanovitch could be in no doubt that some powerful people had it in for her. She spoke to her boss—European Bureau acting assistant secretary Phil Reeker—and to Fiona Hill at the National Security Council. Both offered total support, Yovanovitch said. At the request of David Hale, US undersecretary for political affairs, she wrote a classified note, setting down what was going on to the best of her knowledge.

There was a crumb of comfort from the State Department. It described Lutsenko's claim that she had given him a "do not prosecute" list as an "outright fabrication."

But Pompeo failed to issue a broader statement of support. Meanwhile, Sondland, the US ambassador to the EU and a hotelier appointed by Trump following a $1 million campaign donation, advised Yovanovitch to praise the president on Twitter. She declined, seeing it as incompatible with her non-partisan status.

The end came in a late-night phone call that April. The director general of the Foreign Service, Carol Perez, phoned the ambassador, saying that there was "a lot of nervousness on the seventh floor and up the street." That meant Pompeo's office and the White House. Perez called again at 1:00 a.m. local time and told Yovanovitch that she needed to come home on the next available plane. Back in Washington, she was informed that since summer 2018 Trump had wanted to be rid of her. The news, she said, was shocking.

Yovanovitch's removal was a miserable affair. Worse was to come.

ON MAY 1, 2018, Lev Parnas was "feeling fantastic." This is what his Facebook status said. He posted photos from a meeting in Washington. He is doing a thumbs-up—a moon-faced man, considerably older-looking than his forty-six years, smiling, dapper in a suit, and palpably starstruck. Next to him is Trump. The venue is the White House. Parnas gushes, "Thank you, Mr. President!!! Making America great again!!!"

Not bad for a boy from Soviet Ukraine who came to the US at the age of four. And one who, it was alleged, never lost touch with his roots in Odessa or its Mafia-linked overlords.

This wasn't the first time Trump and Parnas met. The previous month Parnas and Fruman—another Jewish émigré, from Belarus—got chatting with the president over dinner. A political action committee allied to Trump organized the event at Trump's Washington hotel. It was a chance for donors to raise private matters and whisper in the ear of America's very own czar.

In Parnas's case that meant taking a few minutes to slime Yovanovitch. According to the *Washington Post*, he told Trump that the ambassador in Ukraine didn't like the president. Trump's predictable reaction: get rid of her. Subsequently Trump said he could scarcely recall the two naturalized Soviet Americans, whom he had also seen at Mar-a-Lago. "Maybe they were clients of Rudy's," he said, referring to Giuliani, whom that month Trump had taken on as his attorney.

Parnas and Fruman had no history of giving to Republican causes. In short order, they became big-league donors. They threw $325,000 at a pro-Trump action committee and made contributions to Texas congressman Peter Sessions and other Republicans. (After meeting Fruman and Parnas in his DC office, Sessions wrote the letter calling for Yovanovitch to be removed.) There was a breakfast with Donald Trump Jr. in Beverly Hills.

Money opened doors. But where was it from? The official answer was Global Energy Producers, Parnas and Fruman's firm. The company existed only on paper. The actual answer, according to US prosecutors, was an unnamed wealthy Russian known as "Foreigner-1," who wired them $1.26 million. Parnas and Fruman hid this fact. It was a crime that would see them indicted for electoral fraud and detained at the airport while on a one-way trip to Vienna.

Before this reckoning, Parnas and Fruman energetically advanced their own interests—in tandem with Trump's. They introduced Giuliani to people in Ukraine. In December 2018 they facilitated a Skype call between Giuliani and the crooked prosecutor Shokin. Shokin would become an essential player in Giuliani's efforts to fabricate dirt against the Bidens. The same month, Giuliani, Fruman, and Parnas went to the White House's Hanukkah party and held a private meeting with the president.

By spring 2019 Giuliani had assembled a shadow foreign policy team. He recruited two lawyers—Victoria Toensing and Joe diGenova—to go after potential anti-Biden witnesses. The husband and wife were fanatical Republicans and long-time colleagues of

Giuliani's from the Justice Department. Other members included Solomon, whom the couple represented, and Derek Harvey, aide to Nunes. It came about "organically," Solomon said.

This small, conspiratorial group met on the second floor of Trump's Washington hotel, according to Solomon. In the best traditions of Leninist cell-making its members had different skills. Parnas and Fruman were fixers and interpreters; Toensing and diGenova attorneys; Solomon a writer and co-publicist; Giuliani the front man. All appeared regularly on Fox; they commentated on the news without revealing their own attempts behind the scenes to shape it.

One person Parnas and Fruman put the group in touch with was Firtash.

In June 2019 they flew to Vienna to meet with the oligarch. As ever, their own business interests were to the fore: they tried to enlist Firtash's support for their liquefied natural gas project. And then they made an offer. The pair said they could put Firtash in touch with lawyers in DC—Toensing and diGenova—who might be in a position to resolve his extradition situation. The couple could "deliver a message" to the Justice Department on Firtash's behalf—and maybe to Trump himself.

There was, of course, an ask. In return might Firtash use his connections and abundant resources to . . . turn up incriminating matter on Burisma?

Firtash had previously used Lanny Davis as his US representative. At Giuliani's initiative, Firtash swapped Davis for Toensing and diGenova. The oligarch hired them on a four-month contract. Parnas was retained to translate for Firtash, who didn't speak English. Parnas and Fruman made multiple trips to Vienna, shuttling between America and Austria on Firtash's dime. Their financial prospects looked considerably brighter; they travelled on private jets and in SUVs.

This was a grubby affair—and one that would soon burst into the public domain. As Firtash told it, he was a reluctant participant in Giuliani's shabby schemes—a victim, almost. "Without my will and desire I was sucked into this internal US fight," he told the *New York Times,* shaking his head practically in lamentation.

Sucked in or not, Firtash was apparently ready to pony up large sums—$1.2 million to his new, Trump-connected lawyers, with $200,000 of this cash given to Parnas as a referral fee. These dollars secured a meeting between diGenova and Toensing and Attorney General Barr. Barr saw the pair in August, despite being warned about Firtash by others inside the Justice Department, per the *New York Times.*

Firtash's lawyers met with Shokin in Vienna. In September 2019 they draw up a document that—on the face of it—should have sunk Biden's 2020 prospects. It was titled "Witness Statement of Viktor Shokin."

The affidavit lays out a doleful tale. Shokin alleges that in 2015 Biden stopped Firtash from returning to Ukraine. The sacked prosecutor then relates a further example of US meddling in Ukrainian affairs, even more blatant. Shokin says that Poroshenko forced his resignation because of pressure from Biden:

> The official reason for my dismissal was that I had allegedly failed to secure the public's trust. . . . The truth is I was forced out because I was leading a wide-ranging probe into Burisma Holdings.

This, at last, was what Giuliani had been seeking! Proof of Biden's criminality! Evidence that would crush the Democrats in 2020!

Shokin's statement, though, was at odds with the known facts. Everyone in Ukraine was aware that Shokin was a creature of the old system. He was one of many venal prosecutors who failed to reform the courts. He lost his job because he didn't bring anyone to trial, especially the country's pre-2014 villains. The witness statement was dodgy. It was made before lawyers acting for a billionaire with an agenda. It was helpful to Trump. It had no bearing on Firtash's own case.

Giuliani waved it around in a series of prime-time interviews. But his triumph was short-lived.

POROSHENKO'S ELECTION defeat meant that Giuliani had a problem. In February 2019 the Ukrainian president had agreed to reinvestigate Burisma. Two months after that, he was gone. It was necessary to strike the same arrangement with the new guy in Bankova.

Days after Zelensky's victory Giuliani spoke to Bakanov, the Servant of the People Party chairman, whom I had met in Kyiv. Bakanov was Zelensky's new intelligence chief and the former head of the president's television production company, Kvartal 95. The same day Trump told Fox News that Ukraine interfered in 2016—basing his claim on his favourite source, "people."

Meanwhile, Parnas and Fruman travelled to Israel to talk to Kolomoisky, the tycoon widely seen as Zelensky's godfather. The encounter was comically disastrous. After pitching their pipeline idea, the pair asked the oligarch if he could arrange a meeting with the new president. The answer: no, fuck off. "I told them I'm not going to be a middleman in anybody's meetings with Zelensky," Kolomoisky said, adding that their dropping of Trump's name left him unmoved.

Undeterred, in May the duo set up camp at the Hilton Hotel in Kyiv, across the square from the Hyatt—Fruman a chunky figure wearing a dark baseball cap. He and Parnas met with Zelensky's aides. At about the same period the crooked prosecutor Lutsenko had an uncomfortable two hours with the new president, pleading unsuccessfully to keep his job.

With Lutsenko out, Giuliani's scheme was in trouble. Frustrated, Trump decided to get tough. He initiated a series of aggressive moves against the Ukrainian administration. Kyiv's war with Russia and its weak economy meant it needed US support, diplomatic and military, to push back against Putin.

Trump instructed his national security adviser, John Bolton, to ring Zelensky. The president wanted to make sure Zelensky would meet with Giuliani, who was planning to travel to Ukraine. Bolton said he ignored Trump's directive. The conversation took place in the Oval Office, Bolton wrote in his memoir, *The Room Where It Happened*.

Trump also told Vice President Pence to skip Zelensky's inauguration. A scaled-down delegation led by Secretary of Energy Rick Perry went to Kyiv instead.

By early summer Zelensky found himself in a tricky situation. He wanted good relations with Washington and an early meeting with Trump at the White House. Without US backing he looked weak—to Ukrainians and to the Kremlin. And yet if he acceded to Trump's demands, he risked being dragged into domestic US politics.

In July Trump took several fateful steps. All were coordinated with a group that styled itself the "three amigos": special envoy to Ukraine Volker, EU ambassador Sondland, and Perry. Trump put a hold on $391 million in military aid promised to Ukraine. Zelensky was simultaneously informed via aides that he had to resume "investigations." That is, if he ever wanted to make it to the Oval Office.

It was against this backdrop that Trump and Zelensky spoke on July 25, 2019.

Declassified by the White House in September, the partial call readout doesn't exonerate Trump. Rather, it reveals a crime in progress, another one: a pretty blatant extortion attempt by Trump to get Zelensky to produce "proof" of Biden's guilt. It reveals the inchoate workings of Trump's mind, a place where conspiracy theory and alternative "facts" had congealed to form a strange and shallow mulch.

And if on the call Zelensky appears too eager to please, a supplicant, this might be put down to inexperience and ill luck. He wasn't expecting his private remarks to be sprayed around the world.

Trump begins in breezy style, telling Zelensky, "Congratulations on your victory!" After complaining about Merkel ("She talks Ukraine, she doesn't do anything"), he asserts that the US has been "very, very good to Ukraine." Zelensky agrees. He says Kyiv is ready to buy more American Javelins—anti-tank missiles that would be used defensively in the event of further Russian attacks.

Trump then says, "I would like you to do us a favour, though, because our country has been through a lot and Ukraine knows a lot about it."

The "though" makes it clear that the president's goodwill is conditional. It's predicated on Zelensky doing something for Trump. There is a shopping list. The first involves "Crowdstrike"— shorthand for the debunked assertion that Ukraine hacked the 2016 election. Trump praises Lutsenko as a "very good" prosecutor and hints it would be wise to reinstate him. The president then turns to his main ask: Burisma.

Trump says, "There's a lot of talk about Biden's son, that Biden stopped the prosecution, and a lot of people want to find out about that, so whatever you can do with the attorney general would be great. Biden went around bragging that he stopped the prosecution, so if you can look into it. . . . It sounds horrible to me."

As for how all this might be achieved, Trump says he will get

Giuliani ("a highly respected man") and Barr to call, acting as his personal envoys. Zelensky responds positively. He promises to get his new prosecutor to "look into the situation." The conversation takes a black turn. In an apparent attempt to win Trump's approval, Zelensky calls Yovanovitch a "bad ambassador" who had supported his rival Poroshenko. Trump concurs and says:

"Well, she's going to go through some things."

It's unclear what these "things" are. Perhaps Trump didn't know. The line sounds like a mobster threat, straight out of an amateur remake of *The Godfather*. When Yovanovitch heard it in September, she had a physical reaction, saying the "colour drained from my face." Trump's comment was astonishing, inappropriate, and laced with the casual misogyny and menace that had come to define the Trump brand.

Zelensky appeared to think the call went well. Later the same day Trump formally implemented the hold on security assistance to Ukraine, a nation at war with Putin.

TRUMP WOULD DEFEND his Zelensky conversation as "perfect." By this point his staff had grown used to his erratic chats with world leaders—his obsequious behaviour towards Russia's president, his habit of dialling Emmanuel Macron or Justin Trudeau on a whim, his perverse dismissal of Theresa May when she told him Moscow had poisoned Skripal. And a rambling discussion with China's Xi about chocolate cake.

Still, aides had expected the 9:00 a.m. call with Zelensky to be routine. A mix of policy officials and duty officers in the White House situation room were listening in. Several of them were disturbed by what they'd heard. It sounded as if the president were abusing his office for personal gain. Or, put another way, pressuring a foreign state to interfere in the 2020 election on his behalf.

Trump's offer of a bribe—give us this, you get that—was certainly unethical and possibly illegal. And maybe impeachable as well.

Moreover, the call's timing was dumbfounding, coming the day after Mueller's testimony before Congress on Kremlin interference. It looked like a replay of 2016, season two to Moscow's season one, with a new Ukrainian storyline.

In the aftermath of the call senior White House officials took pre-emptive steps to hush up Trump's quid pro quo. According to a CIA whistle-blower—whose complaint would lift the lid on the scandal—they "locked down" all records of the call. The word-for-word transcript was taken from the computer system where it would normally sit, ahead of distribution to cabinet-level officials. It was placed in the equivalent of a strongbox—a separate electronic system used to store "classified material of an especially sensitive nature," such as clandestine CIA programmes.

This was a serious abuse of procedure. And, apparently, a regular one. This was "not the first time" transcripts had been inappropriately locked away in the stand-alone code-word-level system, the complaint said, citing multiple White House officials. Other incriminating transcripts had been buried for political reasons rather than on national security grounds.

The system, it seemed, would contain the darkest secrets of Trump's presidency: his conversations with Putin. The contents of these calls—at least sixteen of them by 2020—were unknown. White House readouts were so brief as to be meaningless. Face-to-face chats, in Hamburg and Helsinki, went unrecorded, at least from the American side, with Trump even confiscating his interpreter's notes in Germany.

As Simpson put it to me, there was likely to be at least "one black swan in the pond." Almost certainly Putin had used the calls to push the line that Ukraine had "colluded."

In August the whistle-blower typed the complaint. The author was clearly an intelligence professional, plugged into the White House and an expert on Ukrainian affairs. He or she had come forward not because of a political grudge but out of genuine public concern.

The complaint was sent to Richard Burr, chair of the Senate Intelligence Committee, and to his House counterpart, Adam Schiff. The document must have struck both men as cogent, thorough, and calmly devastating. Writing it was brave. The whistle-blower must have envisaged an enraged push-back from the White House.

The document offered a full and credible timeline of Trump's high crimes and misdemeanours. And of what looked like a White House cover-up. Democrats used it and the Zelensky transcript as a route map. In September House Speaker Nancy Pelosi announced a formal impeachment inquiry against the forty-fifth president. There would be closed-door and public sessions. The evidence piled up. Shortly Parnas would break with Trump, saying the president was fully aware of his efforts.

THE HEARINGS TOOK place that autumn in a cavernous, ornate committee room on Capitol Hill. They were gripping drama. There was the sheer politics of it all: Trump was only the third US president to be impeached, after Clinton and Andrew Johnson.

The choreography inside the Longworth Building was quite particular. Committee members would arrive from the back of room 1100, Democrats through one door, Republicans through another, and arrive at their chairs simultaneously. They rarely exchanged a word, certainly not Chairman Schiff or his opposite number, Devin Nunes. The mutual contempt was palpable and continuous.

It seemed certain that the Democrat-controlled House would vote to put Trump on trial in the Senate. And equally sure that the Republican majority there would acquit him and keep him in office until the 2020 election. Before each session Republican members set up placards behind their seats, deriding Schiff and the whole process.

The political calculus was only part of the story. The witnesses who turned up, defying White House instructions, were an impressive bunch. They were Foreign Service officers: Yovanovitch and Taylor, the author of the Firtash memo; and Hill, the former national security director for Russian and Eurasian affairs; plus one of the "three amigos"—Sondland, who would crater Trump's defence of ignorance by cheerfully testifying, "We were following the president's orders."

Collectively they offered a calm and sober rebuke to a debased White House. As Yovanovitch put it, under Trump "shady interests" around the world had learned how little it took to get rid of an ambassador they didn't want. The *New York Times* noted that Trump was both perpetrator and mark. He ran his own anti-Biden op in Ukraine. At the same time, sinister forces found it easy to target the president and manipulate him for their own get-rich schemes.

The most anticipated moment of the inquiry came when Hill walked into the room, a cool and indomitable figure. Her answers were sharp and lucid. And a reassertion of reality against what she—addressing Republican members directly—called "fictional narratives" on Ukraine, contrived by Russia's spies. Putin had done everything Mueller laid out "and then some." On the dossier, Hill said Steele had gone down a "rabbit hole." Oh, and Moscow would be back at the next election.

This last remark was certainly true. As the hearings got under way, GRU hackers broke into Burisma's servers. They used the method deployed against the Democrats in 2016: phishing emails sent to Burisma's unsuspecting staff. Some logged on to fake GRU websites.

At the same time, Russian spies tried to find information in the analogue world that might embarrass the Bidens. The stage was set for the Kremlin to interfere again in US politics, just like the last time. Anything dug up from Burisma might be leaked and spun by Russian trolls. The goal: to provide Trump with ammunition in his battle for re-election.

Under Trump's watch the US had become uniquely vulnerable to Russian disinformation games of this kind. It had acquired some distinctly Putin-like tendencies. It was a place where personal vendettas and moneymaking deals were conducted under the cloak of executive power, just like in Russia. And where a couple of scheming opportunists from Florida could end up mightier than the entire State Department. The White House and Russian organized crime appeared to have a thing going. From Mogilevich to Trump was a couple of hops.

In Moscow a group of KGB officers led by Putin had taken over the government machine. For two decades, they had used it for self-enrichment. Their stealing was done stealthily, under the din of state propaganda. Increasingly, Trump's America seemed to be going in the same corrupt direction. As the *Kyiv Post* pointed out, by following his natural instincts the president was creating a political system that eerily resembled Russia's. Putin's son-in-law, Kirill Shamalov, became a billionaire, while Jared Kushner was rescued from insolvency when his father-in-law took over the White House. There was the distinct possibility of a Trump political dynasty.

In the meantime, the effectiveness of Russian active measures was worrying. Lies dreamed up in Moscow were reaching US public life, thanks to Trump and his Republican associates, who repeated them. The same post-truth politics was visible in other Western democracies, including Boris Johnson's Britain and a growing number of nations across Europe.

As Trump geared up for the 2020 election, his relationship with Putin was still not fully explained. Russia didn't invent Trump or the isolationist forces he represented, but it certainly encouraged him. That Putin had leverage of some kind over Trump seemed indisputable. There was no alternative explanation for Helsinki. Putin was a wilier and more experienced operator than Trump, as their one-sided encounters illustrated. In international affairs, the US had embraced the Russian agenda. Global enforcement and alliances were a thing of the past; the US's new creed was nationalism and unilateralism.

The two leaders had some shared personal impulses—negative ones. They included insecurity, a quickness to take offence, and vengefulness, demonstrated in Putin's case by a series of ruthless hits against "traitors." Trump and Putin shared a paranoid view of the world grounded in conspiracy. The informal rules of Trump- and Putin-land were not so very different. Personal loyalty was everything; the law, something for your enemies. Friendships were stronger than institutions. Human rights and values were a joke, climate change a con.

America's twenty-first-century wounds were largely self-inflicted. But at the dawn of a new decade, the twenties, it was possible to conclude that Russia had done more than game politics and democracy. It had succeeded, to some degree, in remaking the United States in its own shadow image.

EPILOGUE

The figure was immediately recognizable. Unruly blond hair, broad grin, out of shape, accompanied by a much younger woman . . . it was Boris Johnson, stepping out in December 2019, just hours after his victory in the UK general election.

Johnson and his girlfriend Carrie Symonds were in celebratory mood. The prime minister had defeated Jeremy Corbyn's Labour and won a handsome eighty-seat majority. Pro-Europeans inside Johnson's Conservative Party were out. He could anticipate five years in power, and probably much longer. Brexit was a reality.

In Washington, Trump praised Johnson as a "friend of mine," and said his success was a "harbinger of things to come." The runes were favourable! The president said he anticipated re-election and a similar landslide victory. In the view of conservatives such as Steve Bannon, Brexit and Trump were conjoined events; the same anti-elite movement in America would propel Trump to a second term.

That there were parallels between the US and the UK was undeniable. The progressive vote was split, its candidate weak. Johnson persuaded working-class voters in the north of England and Midlands to switch allegiance from Labour to Conservative. Blue-collar Democrats in rust-belt states had made a similar journey over to Trump. Nationalism worked. So did populist slogans—"Get Brexit Done," "America First."

Unmentioned, of course, was the role Russia had played in helping Trump and Johnson along.

The day after his victory the prime minister dropped in on a Christmas party. The venue was a £6 million stuccoed property overlooking Regent's Park in central London. The hosts were Alexander and Evgeny Lebedev. Alexander—the one-time KGB agent turned media tycoon—had flown in from Moscow. He was celebrating his sixtieth birthday with a few friends.

There were rock stars (Mick Jagger, Bob Geldof) and royals (the Queen's grand-daughter Princess Eugenie), as well as models and A-list actors. And British politicians: the former prime minister David Cameron and his wife Samantha; plus George Osborne, the former chancellor turned editor of the Lebedevs' *Evening Standard* newspaper.

Johnson's decision to pay homage to the Lebedevs was an "up yours" to his critics. During the campaign, the prime minister had refused to publish a report by Parliament's Intelligence and Security Committee that had been two years in the making. The report wasn't as elaborate or detailed as Mueller's. Its subject was similar: Kremlin influence on the UK and its allies, especially in the field of politics.

Witnesses gave evidence. One of them was Christopher Steele. Security agencies approved the final document. And yet ahead of the poll Johnson sat on it. Why? Some of the material submitted was embarrassing, I was told. It included claims that Prime Minister May and then Foreign Secretary Johnson had deliberately ignored warnings that the Russians had likely compromised Trump. And that there were "indications" Moscow may have covertly funded Brexit.

In late 2016 Steele had briefed intelligence professionals in London about his dossier. A summary was given to the cabinet. Instead of taking steps to find out if it was true, the British government ignored it, I discovered. No inquiries were made. No action was taken. Then, and now, Johnson appeared terrified of offending Trump. Any mention of Moscow's contribution to the president's 2016 victory was, it seemed, taboo.

The implication was explosive: that the Conservatives had put party political considerations above potential national security concerns. A post-Brexit trade deal with the US was evidently important. But so was the question of whether Trump was under obligation to Moscow or being blackmailed in some way—a strategic threat to the UK, if correct. Four years on, this question remained unwanted and unasked.

This denial and cover-up augured badly for the integrity of future elections. By 2020 the prospect of Russian meddling in the US, UK and elsewhere hadn't receded. It was a sure bet that Putin would carry on using the same methods—hacking and dumping, support for far-right political actors, and KGB-style disinformation campaigns—which were already visible in a slew of European countries, including Hungary, the Czech Republic, and Slovakia, as well as Austria and even Italy.

Certain, too, that RT, Sputnik, and other Russian state channels would back Trump's re-election bid, using false news and inflammatory stories to sway the vote. The US media environment felt increasingly Moscow-like. Fox News behaved in an analogous way to Russia's Channel One or NTV. The common aims: to glorify the president, to smear critics and to repeat false narratives and lies.

Inside Russia, it was clear Putin was going nowhere. In January 2020 he announced radical constitutional changes—a coup of sorts. These were widely seen as ensuring he remained in power once his fourth presidential term ended in 2024. He got rid of Russia's prime minister—Medvedev, described in US diplomatic cables as "Robin" to Putin's "Batman." Medvedev's replacement was a little-known tax official.

With no successor on the horizon, Putin was apparently planning to govern well into his seventies. His future role was undefined. It appeared he might become chairman of Russia's State Council, a previously unimportant body, with the presidency in the meantime downgraded. Quite possibly, Putin would eclipse Stalin's thirty-odd years inside the Kremlin. There seemed only one way he might exit: horizontally, in a coffin.

The same authoritarian traits were visible in the US. Trump probably envied Putin's ability to get round term limits and repeatedly mused about staying on after a second term. A joke, Trump said. Or was it? Meanwhile, his administration seemed hell-bent on hollowing out government departments. State, the FBI, the National Security Council . . . all were stripped of influence, personnel, prestige. Critics talked of totalitarian creep.

As John Le Carré noted, writing in the *Guardian*, Johnson had taken his place beside two other accomplished liars of the age: Putin and Trump. Globally, it was hard to avoid the conclusion that liberal democracy was in retreat, and populism entrenched.

At the same moment Britain left the EU—at 11 p.m. on January 31, 2020—Republican senators voted on whether to allow witnesses to testify in Trump's impeachment trial. The result: 51 votes against, 49 in favour. The Republican Party's refusal to allow evidence—from John Bolton and from others who had first-hand knowledge of the president's role in the campaign to pressure Kyiv—was predictable and depressing.

And redolent of Russian and Soviet practice. Not a show trial as such, but a bad day for the rule of law and for the future of the American republic. It appeared to mark the end of constitutionalism and the beginning of something darker: one-man rule by a president above the law. A president whose personal interests were now being defined as synonymous with the state's. There was, Trump's defenders said, no limit to his executive authority.

The president's attorney, Alan Dershowitz, argued as much from the Senate floor, during dispiriting hearings. Trump could do anything he wanted to secure his re-election since he believed this was in the public interest. Therefore, there couldn't be a quid pro quo that led to impeachment, Dershowitz said. Trump was the state! A tsar, practically. And—like the Kremlin leader—not subject to account-ability or co-scrutiny, by Congress, the judiciary, or any other branch.

In February Trump was acquitted, after a trial scarcely worthy of the name. The result was a win for Putin and for despots every-where. It confirmed that you could engage in corrupt and criminal practices without serious consequences. And that for Republicans the pursuit of power and tribal loyalty were more important than democracy or conscience. It normalized wrongdoing. It was an invitation to any foreign power to meddle in US politics—this was OK, the message said, provided it benefited Trump.

The geopolitical situation was now very much to Putin's advan-tage. Over two decades, he had provoked and tested the West with one outrageous deed after another. There was the nuclear murder of Litvinenko; the 2016 pro-Trump espionage operation; the chemical hit in Salisbury; an assassination in a Berlin park. Not to mention invasions of neighbours and annexations. A Trump second term would guarantee more of the same. And leave Russia emboldened on the global scene.

It was Lenin who best described Moscow's enduring strategy vis-à-vis the West as "a state of partial war." This not-quite war involved the elastic and opportunistic use of a wide variety of tac-tics. They included deception, concealed penetration, and subver-sion and psychological warfare. And—as George Kennan, the US ambassador in Moscow, noted back in the fifties—the adroit exploitation of every conceivable form of division in Western societies. This was true internationally and within the domestic framework of "enemy" states.

This unofficial war was set to continue. Russia's spies had suf-fered recent stumbles. GRU chiefs had a remarkable habit of drop-ping dead. But Moscow's secret services were formidable—a deadly shadow monster, on the rampage still.

ACKNOWLEDGEMENTS

The author would like to thank:

Chris Barter, Julian Borger, Roman Borisovich, Irina Borogan, Jonathan Burnham, Carole Cadwalladr, Roman Dobrokhotov, Yuri Felshtinsky, Peter Fritsch, Owen Gibson, David Godwin, Cristo Grozev, Laura Hassan, Sarah Haugen, Elliot Higgins, Nick Hopkins, Scott Horton, Jonathan Jao, Peter Jukes, Sergei Kanev, Mikhail Khodorkovsky, Alex Kovzhun, Susanna Lea, David Leigh, Paul Lewis, Marina Litvinenko, Sean McTernan, Mark Medish, Huib Modderkolk, Dina Nagapetyants, Stephen Page, Noa Rosen, Robert Service, Iida Simes, Glenn Simpson, David Smith, Andrei Soldatov, Phoebe Taplin, Katharine Viner, Andrew Wilson, Jamie Wilson.

A NOTE ON SOURCES

Robert Mueller's report is an invaluable source of information on Donald Trump and Russia. It gives us witness statements, private emails, and the president's own grudging replies to FBI investigators. There are startling new details. Who knew that Joseph Mifsud—the mysterious London-based professor—was friends with an executive from Russia's notorious troll factory? Or that the Trump aide George Papadopoulos sent a LinkedIn request to a Moscow diplomat who was believed to be a top-ranking spy?

The FBI's probe gives us a comprehensive portrait of the interactions between the Trump campaign and Russians. There are plenty of them. We learn of Michael Cohen's furtive dealings with Vladimir Putin's press secretary. And that after Trump's 2016 victory a senior Russian texted: "Putin has won." Some facts are hidden. The name of the jubilant texter is blacked out, beneath the words "investigative technique." There are other redactions. The FBI knows more about the Kremlin's elaborate social media operation in support of Trump than it's prepared—at least for now—to reveal.

The Mueller report allows us to reconstruct much of what happened in 2016. It offers lessons for 2020 and beyond. But it leans heavily towards the American side and the electronic record. Mueller has less to say about Russians and the Kremlin's secret leadership processes. Important Russian witnesses—Konstantin Kilimnik, Sergei Millian—go AWOL. On the question of whether Putin holds *kompromat* on the US president, Mueller is silent. Nor does he follow Trump's money or examine murder by the Russian state in the UK and elsewhere.

In writing this book, I turned to other sources to fill in some of these gaps. My goal was to tell the lesser-known story of the GRU spies and SVR operatives whose job it is to subvert the West. During four years in Moscow as the *Guardian*'s correspondent, I gained first-hand experience of clandestine Russian methods. They were crude. The FSB spy agency broke into our apartment and bugged the bedroom. There was physical surveillance too, carried out by unpromising young men wearing cheap leather jackets.

The inner workings of the Kremlin are exceedingly hard to fathom. Unlike in Washington, there are few leaks. Nor is there a mainstream free press to expose abuse. Nevertheless, some information seeps out. I developed a range of useful contacts in Moscow: journalists, academics, and members of the Russian opposition. Brave reporters exist in Russia. They dig up uncomfortable facts and shine light on high-level corruption, at the risk of arrest or worse.

In London I got to know Russian émigrés who had fallen out with the Putin regime. They included Boris Berezovsky and Nikolai Glushkov. Both are dead—Glushkov strangled by an unknown intruder, Berezovsky found hanged in his ex-wife's bathroom. I became friends with Alexander Litvinenko's widow Marina. And I met Viktor Suvorov, whose insights underpin much of this book. Suvorov is—so far as I'm aware—the only former GRU insider to talk publicly about his organization.

In the US I spoke to a wide range of expert sources. Some had served in government, others worked in politics or law. A few were directly involved in the Trump–Russia saga. I met George Papadopolous in Chicago (he was spectacularly late, with our scheduled breakfast meeting turning into an early lunch). Other conversations took place in Washington, New York, and Philadelphia. I travelled to Ukraine. My arrival in spring 2019 coincided with events that would lead directly to Trump's impeachment.

Over the last decade there have been two major developments in investigative journalism. We live in an era of large data leaks: State Department cables; secret logs from the US's wars in Iraq and Afghanistan; Edward Snowden; the banking secrets of the rich and powerful. The Panama Papers include 11.5 million offshore documents. It's an unprecedented trove. And a useful one. There are emails, passport scans, company records. In the archive I found Russian oligarchs and other colourful individuals who appear in this book.

The other development is collaboration. At a time of shrinking newspaper budgets, journalists have joined forces to pursue complex stories which span multiple countries. I'm grateful to the investigative website Bellingcat, which identified Skripal's poisoners and other GRU staff. And to the Dossier Centre, which provided leads and photographs. The *Guardian* has worked closely with the International Consortium of Investigative Journalists in Washington DC, the *New York Times*, *Süddeutsche Zeitung*, and many other publications.

This solidarity will stand us—the fourth estate—in good stead, at a time when lying and cover-ups have become the political norm. I'm grateful to my colleagues at the *Guardian*—Kath Viner, Owen Gibson, Nick Hopkins—for allowing me to combine book writing with international reporting. And to my wonderful publishers Harper Collins and Guardian Faber, and agents Susanna Lea and David Godwin.

This book is dedicated to my parents, John and Felicity Harding. Thanks also to my wife Phoebe Taplin, my reader and co-traveller.

INDEX